Astronomical!

44 ACTIVITIES, EXPERIMENTS, AND PROJECTS

Ormiston H. Walker
illustrated by Lloyd Birmingham

J. WESTON WALCH
PUBLISHER

PORTLAND, MAINE

User's Guide to *Walch Reproducible Books*

As part of our general effort to provide educational materials which are as practical and economical as possible, we have designated this publication a "reproducible book." The designation means that purchase of the book includes purchase of the right to limited reproduction of all pages on which this symbol appears:

Here is the basic Walch policy: We grant to individual purchasers of this book the right to make sufficient copies of reproducible pages for use by all students of a single teacher. This permission is limited to a single teacher, and does not apply to entire schools or school systems, so institutions purchasing the book should pass the permission on to a single teacher. Copying of the book or its parts for resale is prohibited.

Any questions regarding this policy or requests to purchase further reproduction rights should be addressed to:

Permissions Editor
J. Weston Walch, Publisher
321 Valley Street • P. O. Box 658
Portland, Maine 04104-0658

1 2 3 4 5 6 7 8 9 10

ISBN 0-8251-2744-0

Copyright © 1995
J. Weston Walch, Publisher
P. O. Box 658 • Portland, Maine 04104-0658

Printed in the United States of America

*To my dearly loved grandchildren—
Clemency, Amelia, Samuel,
Charlotte, and Thomas*

Contents

Introduction vii

Chapter 1. Astronomy 1

1. Refracting Telescope 1
2. Reflecting Telescope 4
3. Star Finder 6
4. Circumpolar Constellations 12
5. Hunter in the Sky 16
6. Our Nearest Star 17
7. Solar Eclipses and Coronas 25
8. Solar Paradox 31
9. Sun, Earth, and Moon 33
10. Moon Craters 35
11. Finding the Size of the Moon 38
12. Earth-Moon Rotation 41
13. The Spin of the Earth 45
14. Space and Matter 47
15. The Twinkling of Stars 51
16. Dust Clouds in Space 53
17. Why Is the Sky Dark at Night? 56
18. Algol—the Demon Star 59
19. Space Navigation 61
20. Finding Direction by the Stars 63
21. Comets 65
22. Night and Day 74

Chapter 2. A Star's Life 77

23. Star Birth 77
24. The Sun as a Star 80
25. Hot Breath of a Red Giant 84
26. White Dwarfs 87
27. Supernovae—Stars That End with a Bang 90
28. The Pulsar Puzzle 95
29. Black Holes 100

Chapter 3. The Planets 105

30. Mercury 105
31. Venus 107
32. Earth: Rotate and Revolve 109
33. Mars: Making the Red Planet Green 111
34. Jupiter: The Giant Planet 114
35. Io: Jupiter's Incredible Moon 117
36. Saturn: The Ringed Planet 121
37. Uranus 123
38. Neptune and Pluto 126
39. The Solar System 128

Chapter 4. Atmosphere 131

40. Atmospheric Gas Content and Pressure 131
41. Space Environment 133
42. Inflatable Spacecraft 134
43. The Tyndall Effect 135
44. Shock Waves 137
45. Molecules in Motion 138

Index *141*

INTRODUCTION

> *Though my soul may set in darkness, it will rise in perfect light,*
> *I have loved the stars too fondly to be fearful of the night.*
>
> —Unknown—an old astronomer to his pupil (Galileo)

Astronomical! 44 Activities, Experiments, and Projects is a resource book for four major areas of study:

    basic astronomy
    a star's life
    the planets
    the atmosphere

The activities and demonstrations in this book can be done in a classroom setting during the day by using readily available materials.

This classroom resource also features five activities with reproducible pages:

- Make a Star Finder (planisphere): pages 9–11

- Learn the circumpolar constellations: pages 14, 15

- Learn the winter constellations: pages 18, 19

- The orbit of Halley's Comet: page 74

- Sun vocabulary and poetry: page 83

Just turn the page to embark on an exploration of the grandeur and mystery of the cosmos. With this book in hand, the universe will be your home!

Chapter One

Astronomy

1. Refracting Telescope

> *In Nature's infinite book of secrecy*
> *A little I can read.*
>
> —Shakespeare, *Antony and Cleopatra*

A refracting telescope depends on the principle of refraction, the bending of light rays by lenses to magnify a distant object. The first refractor was made about 1610 by the Italian astronomer Galileo. With this telescope, named the Galilean telescope in his honor, Galileo observed sunspots, craters on the moon, and four of the satellite moons of Jupiter.

In the refracting telescope, there is a long focus (objective) lens; this bends the light rays from the distant object until they come to a point called the focal point. Light rays brought to a focus at the focal point carry the image with them and pass on through an eyepiece lens. This enlarges or magnifies the image so that the distant object seems much nearer.

The world's largest refracting telescope, with an objective lens 100 cm in diameter, is at the Yerkes Observatory, Williams Bay, Wisconsin. With the modern solar refractor used there, it is possible to examine, analyze, and map the sun's complex surface.

Make a Refracting Telescope

What you need: reading glass magnifier for objective lens; small nature study magnifier for eyepiece lens; two pieces of cardboard mailing tube, one to take objective lens and one to take eyepiece lens; modeling clay or foam plastic; adhesive; ruler; paper; scissors; tape

1. Hold the hand magnifier in front of the paper and move it back and forth until you get a sharp image of a distant tree on the paper screen (Figure 1). Measure the distance between the lens and the screen and record this as the focal length of the objective lens. (It should be 30 cm or more.) Repeat for the eyepiece lens. Write down the values you get for the focal lengths. What is the sum of the two focal lengths?

Figure 1. Finding the focal length

2. Fix the two lenses to the two cardboard mailing tubes, making the distance between them the sum of the focal lengths. Use modeling clay or foam plastic to hold one tube inside the other (Figure 2), or simply mount the lenses on a meter rule or stick with modeling clay (Figure 3). Make sure the centers of the lenses are in line.

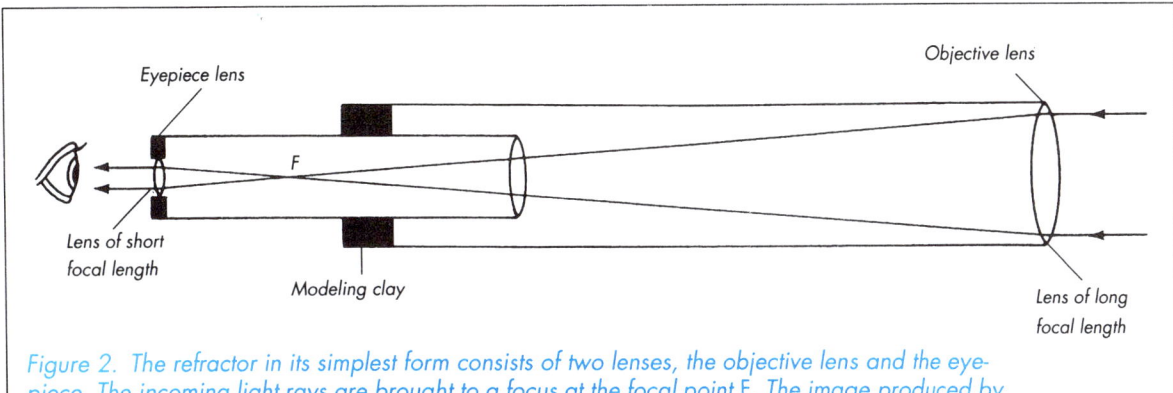

Figure 2. The refractor in its simplest form consists of two lenses, the objective lens and the eyepiece. The incoming light rays are brought to a focus at the focal point F. The image produced by the objective lens is further magnified by the eyepiece.

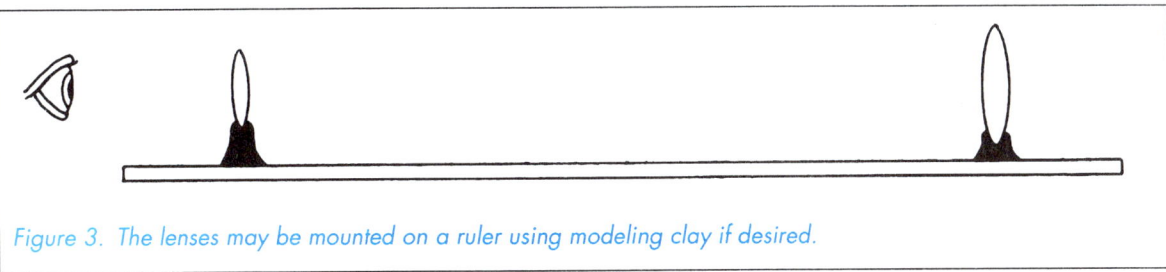

Figure 3. The lenses may be mounted on a ruler using modeling clay if desired.

3. Look through the eyepiece lens at a distant object such as a tree or chimney; you may need to adjust the distance between the lenses slightly to make the image sharper. Do this by sliding the tubes or moving the modeling clay. You can also try making the image sharper by taping a stop, a doughnut-shaped piece of paper, to the eyepiece (Figure 4).

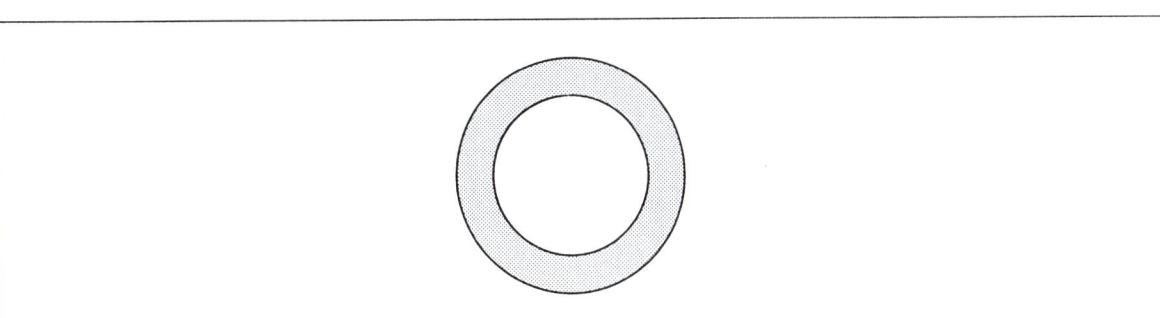

Figure 4. The image may be made sharper by fixing a circular "stop" of paper to the eyepiece with clear plastic tape.

What can you say about the image with regard to:
> closeness?
> size?
> orientation?

2. Reflecting Telescope

The reflecting telescope has a curved mirror at the lower end of a long tube. Light rays are reflected from this—first to a small, flat mirror, then to the eyepiece lens. By using a small, flat mirror, the reflected light is turned at right angles and enters an eyepiece placed in an opening in the side of the tube (Figure 5). Many people make their own telescopes; they grind the lenses and mirrors and design the mounts for them. Special knowledge and skill are needed, but there are hundreds of homemade instruments that perform wonderfully well. A good homemade 15-cm reflector will show some features of Jupiter and Saturn more clearly than photos at an observatory.

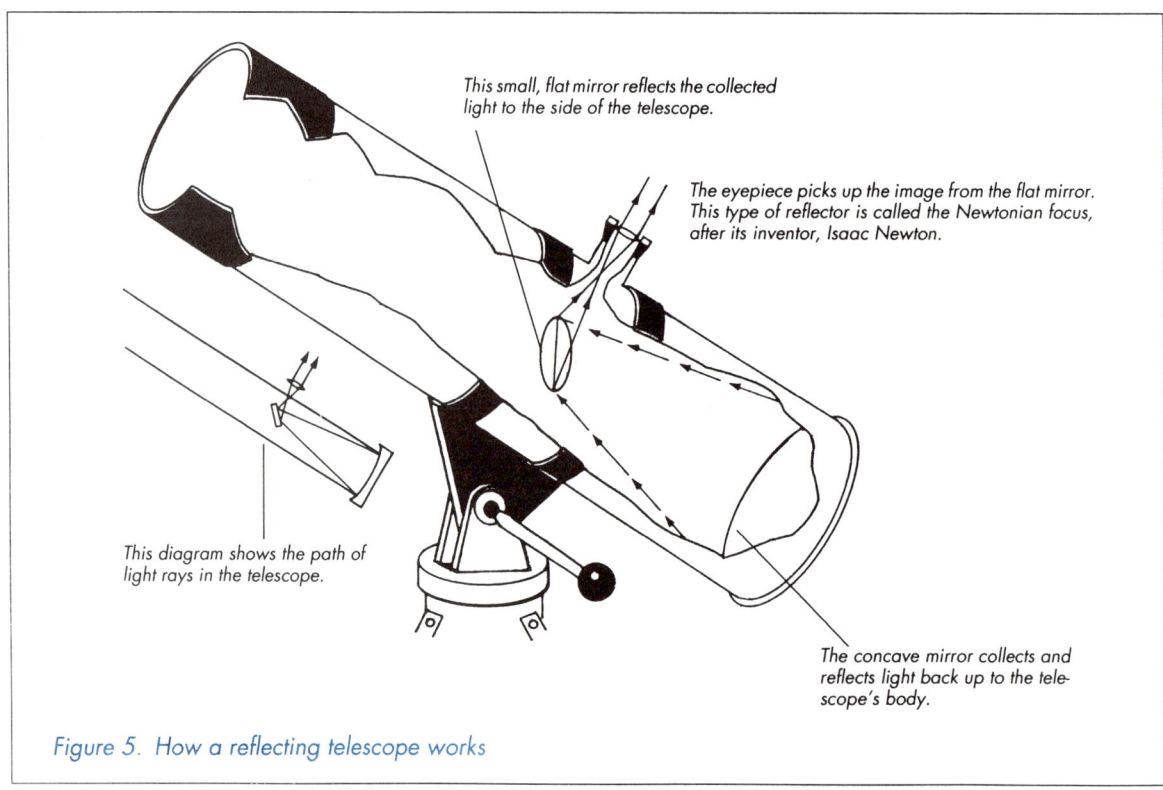

Figure 5. How a reflecting telescope works

Astronomers see out into the universe only through the restless, hazy atmosphere that surrounds our planet. But this ocean of air absorbs, dilutes, and scatters many of the rays the astronomer needs to advance our knowledge of the universe. By placing telescopes in space, astronomers will obtain clearer images of galaxies, star systems, quasars, and exploding galaxies. The distortion problems of earthbound instruments will be avoided; the pictures will be sent to Earth by electronic means.

A Model Reflecting Telescope

What you need: concave mirror—a shaving mirror with a focal length of about 70 cm; small, flat mirror; short-focus magnifier (nature study magnifier) to act as an eyepiece lens; modeling clay; 1-meter piece of wood with back support for shaving mirror

1. Arrange the shaving mirror, the small, flat mirror, and the short-focus magnifier (eyepiece) as shown in Figure 6.

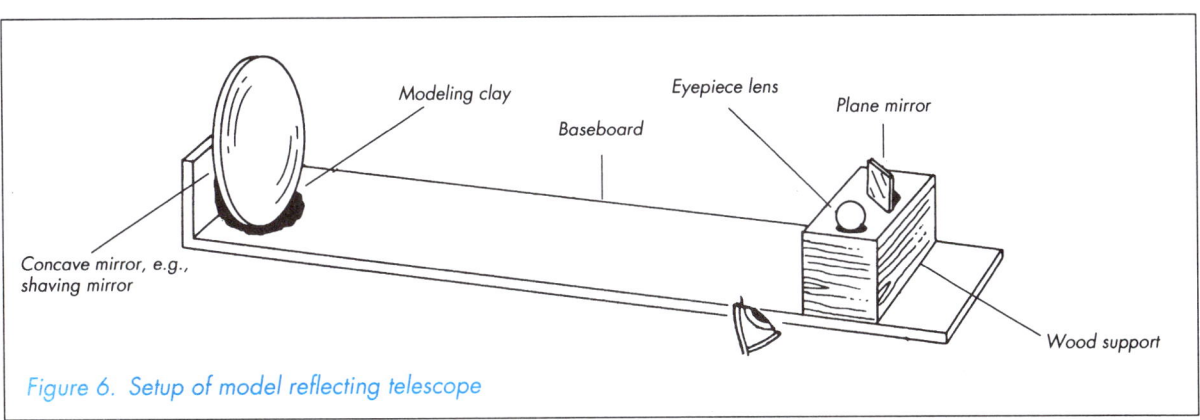

Figure 6. Setup of model reflecting telescope

2. To tell how far apart you should place the concave mirror and the small flat mirror, measure the distance from the center of the concave mirror to where the light rays come to a focus. What is the name for this distance? What is the name for the spot where the light rays come together?

3. Use modeling clay to fix the mirrors and the lens in place. Look through the eyepiece lens as you hold the concave mirror so that light rays from a distant object fall on it. Do you see the object clearly, or is it distorted (Figure 7)?

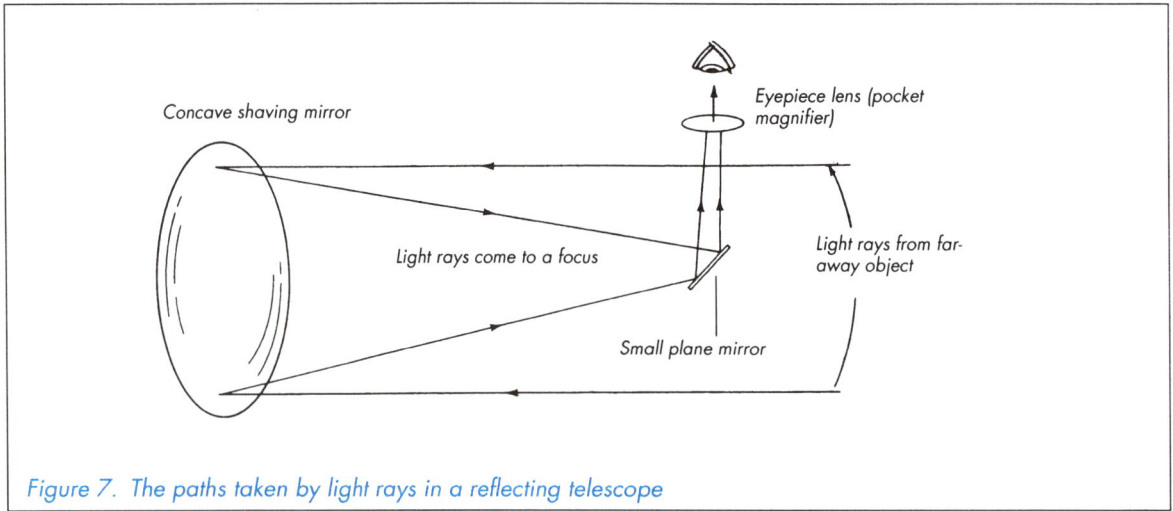

Figure 7. The paths taken by light rays in a reflecting telescope

4. Adjust the positions of the small mirror and the eyepiece lens as necessary to sharpen the image. What does the small, flat mirror do? What is the purpose of the eyepiece?

3. Star Finder

The constellations—groups of bright stars that seem to make a picture—are among the most interesting objects in the sky. Many take their names from myths and legends. Orion was a great hunter, carrying a club and a lion skin. Three stars form his belt; at his shoulder is the giant red star Betelgeuse; at his left foot is the bluish-white star Rigel. Gemini has two bright stars, Castor and Pollux. Taurus the Bull with the red star Aldebaran lies along the ecliptic (the path defined by the sun in its journey across the sky). Nearby are two beautiful star clusters, the Pleiades and the Hyades. Auriga the Charioteer, close to Taurus, contains the bright star Capella. Leo the Lion, with the bright star Regulus, also lies along the ecliptic. Boötes, with the bright star Arcturus, is a herdsman; Arcturus means "bear-keeper," because it follows the Great Bear, Ursa Major, around the North Star.

Cassiopeia and Andromeda are two other famous constellations. Perseus, on his winged horse Pegasus, rescued Andromeda from the sea-monster Cetus. Lyra, the Lyre, contains the brilliant white star Vega, which with two other bright stars—Deneb and Altair—form the Triangle of Vega near Hercules. Deneb is the bright star at the head of the Northern Cross, also called Cygnus the Swan. Aquila the Eagle, a constellation about as bright as Lyra, has the bright star Altair.

Make a Star Finder

You can use the Star Finder to find the stars and constellations.

What you need: heavy card; adhesive; scissors; Star Map (Figure 8); Star Finder frame (Figure 9).

1. This Star Finder is suitable for use in the middle latitudes of the northern hemisphere. Glue the Star Map to a piece of heavy card; cut out when dry. Use the Star Finder frame as a pattern to cut two frame shapes from heavy card. Glue the Star Finder to one frame shape; glue the list of stars and constellations (Figure 10) to the other. Cut out the oval window on the frame, and the circles in the four directional pointers. Cut four triangles from heavier weight card, or use two layers of card glued together; the triangles must be thicker than the Star Map so that the Star Finder can rotate freely. Glue one triangle to each corner of the Star Finder frame, making sure the curve of each triangle matches the curved line of the frame. Place the Star Map in position in the frame, with the stars facing out. Then place the backing piece behind the Star Map so that the list of stars and constellations faces out; glue the two parts of the frame together at the triangles on the directional pointers, making sure that the Star Map rotates freely between them (Figure 11). Finally, glue the charts of stars and constellations from page 11 onto the back of your Star Finder. Follow the instructions on the front of the Star Finder to locate stars and constellations.

2. Turn the star map to the present date and hour. If it is dark and the viewing is good, you should see in the sky the stars in the oval window. First find Polaris, the North or Pole Star, so named because it stands almost directly above the North Pole. It is almost at the center of the star map. To find the North Star you have to know the constellation Ursa Major, the Great Bear. Look close to the center of the star map and pick out the part called the Big Dipper. Two stars in the bowl of the Dipper are called the Pointers because they point to the North Star.

    Can you now locate the Great Bear, the Big Dipper, and the North Star in the sky?

    Note: When looking at the sky at night, a red light is used for reading charts, etc.; this is because the less bright the light, the better the eyes adapt to the dark, and you see more easily. You can attach a piece of red plastic to a flashlight with a rubber band to make your own red light.

3. What other constellations are there in the sky? Use your Star Finder to help you find them in the sky. Do the constellations seem to rotate around the Pole Star?

4. While rotating your Star Finder, you will see that the star picture changes with the seasons. Can you explain why?

5. What is meant by the terms "fixed stars" and "circumpolar stars"? The ancient peoples observed "stars" that seemed to move through the fixed stars; they called them "wanderers." What were these wanderers? What do we call them today?

Star Map

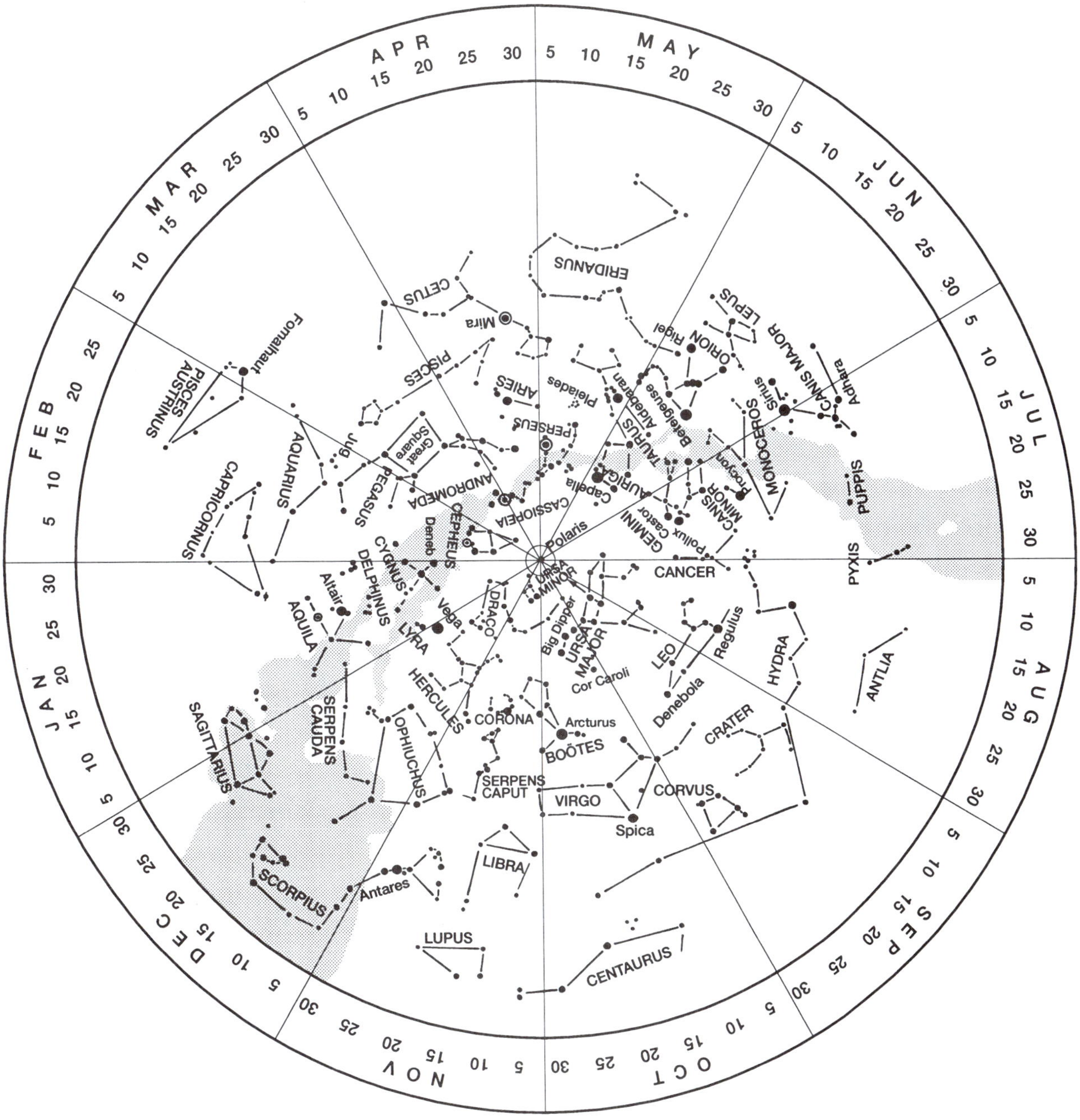

Figure 8

Star Finder Frame

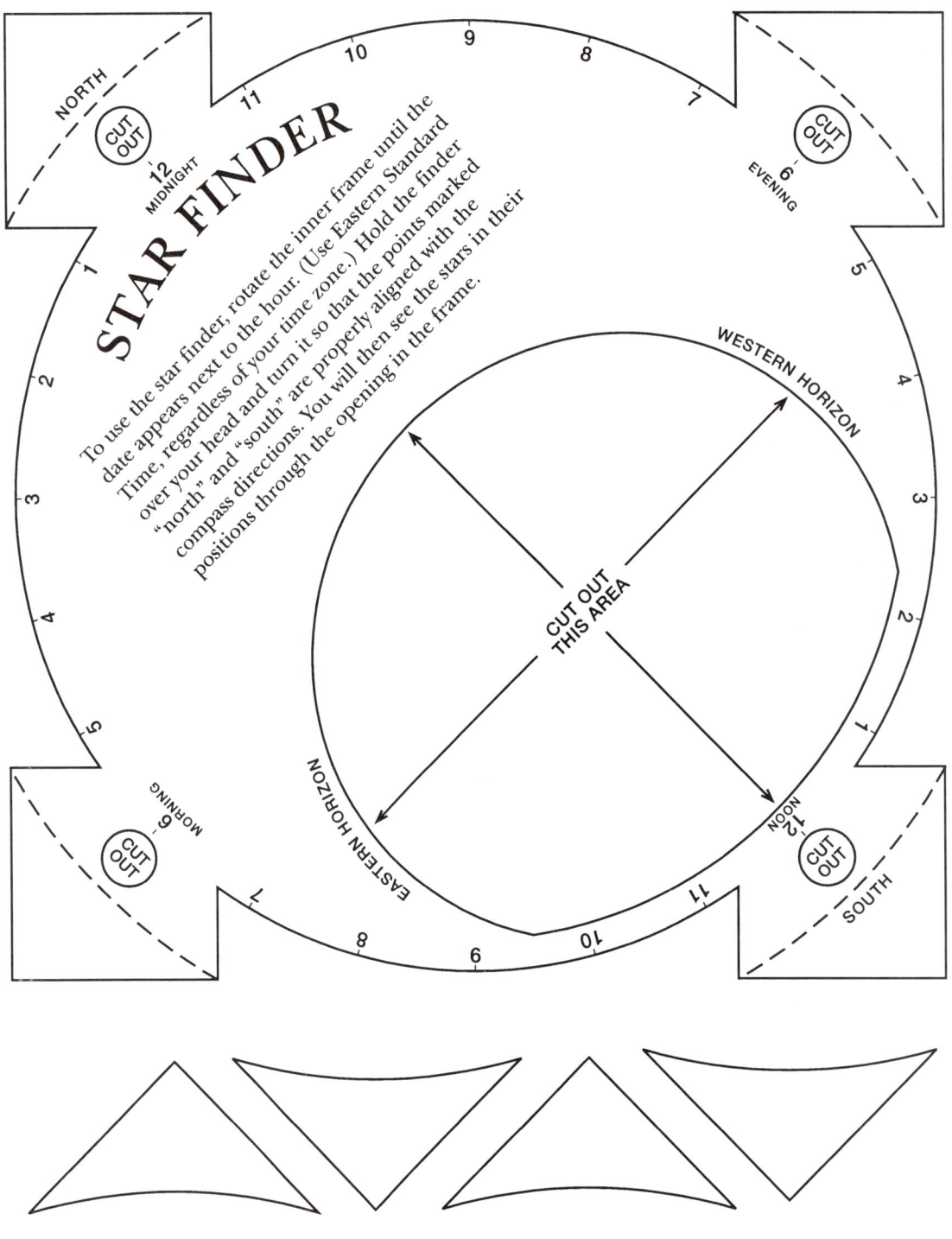

Figure 9

List of Stars and Constellations

Bright Stars Visible at 40° Latitude

Star Name	Constellation	Star Name	Constellation
A. Si´ ri us	Ca´ nis Ma´ jor	J. Al deb´ a ran	Tau´ rus
B. Ve´ ga	Ly´ ra	K. Pol´ lux	Gem´ in i
C. Ca pell´ a	Au ri´ gà	L. Spi´ ca	Vir´ go
D. Arc tu´ rus	Bo o´ tes	M. An ta´ res	Scorp´ i us
E. Ri´ gel	O ri´ on	N. Fo´ mal haut	Pis´ ces Aus tri´ nus
F. Pro´ cy on	Ca´ nis Mi´ nor	P. Den´ eb	Cyg´ nus
G. Al tair´	A´ quil a	Q. Reg´ u lus	Le´ o
H. Bet´ el geuse	O ri´ on	R. Cast´ or	Gem´ in i

The Zodiac

1. Aries, The Ram
2. Taurus, The Bull
3. Gemini, The Twins
4. Cancer, The Crab
5. Leo, The Lion
6. Virgo, The Virgin
7. Libra, The Scales
8. Scorpius, The Scorpion
9. Sagittarius, The Archer
10. Capricornus, The Sea Goat
11. Aquarius, The Water-Bearer
12. Pisces, The Fishes

Meteors or Shooting Stars

These can be seen with the unaided eye. Look in these constellations on the dates given:

The Lyre/Lyriads: April 20–21
Aquarius/Aquarids: May 3–6
July 25–29

Perseus/Perseids: August 11
Orion/Orionids: October 19–22
Leo/Leonids: November 15

Figure 10. Paste the above information on the back of your Star Finder.

The Complete Star Finder

Figure 11

4. Circumpolar Constellations

> *Last night the stars were magnificent. Pegasus and Andromeda faced me brilliantly when I lifted my shade, so I went down and had a friendly reunion with the constellations . . . I get a wonderful peace and the most exquisite pleasure from my friendship with the stars.*
>
> —Ellen Glasgow, *Letters of Ellen Glasgow*

The Great Bear, the Little Bear, and Cassiopeia are three constellations near the Pole Star. None of these constellations ever set; they seem to move around the Pole and so are called circumpolar constellations. As the Great Bear is so readily recognized, this makes it of great value as a starting point when looking for other constellations. These star groups are among the oldest constellations known, Cassiopeia dating back to 4000 B.C.

The Great Bear (Ursa Major) and the Little Bear (Ursa Minor) have within them the Big Dipper and the Little Dipper, respectively. Three bright stars form the handle of the Big Dipper and four bright stars form the bowl. The two stars in the side of the bowl of the Big Dipper are called the Pointers, because they always point to the North Star or Pole Star.

The Little Dipper is made up of seven stars, the last star in the handle being the Pole Star. As the Earth spins on its axis, the Little Dipper seems to swing around the end of its handle. This is because the Pole Star does not seem to move.

Cassiopeia was the wife of the king of Ethiopia and the constellation was well known to the ancients—Greeks, Romans, and Arabs. A brilliant star called a nova blazed forth in Cassiopeia in November 1572. It was brighter than Venus and clearly visible during the day.

Three Circumpolar Constellations

You can look at circumpolar constellations—groups of stars we see in the sky all the year round. **Note:** The Star Finder (see pages 6–7) is needed for the following reproducible activity. Here the Star Finder is used to locate the circumpolar constellations.

What you need: copy of constellation picture (Figure 12); Star Finder

The constellation picture shows you constellations that can be seen in the night sky at any time of the year. Locate them on your Star Finder; then try locating them in the night sky. The bright stars are the large dots and the dotted outlines are the constellation pictures. Use the constellation picture to do the following exercises.

1. Use a colored pen to connect the small dots and complete each star picture.

2. Find two bright stars in the bowl of the Big Dipper and draw a line between them. Print *Pointers* beside them.

3. Find the Pole Star (North Star) and neatly print its name beside it.

4. Print the name below each constellation.

5. With your felt-tip pen, draw straight lines between the stars.

6. Find the stars Alcor and Mizar and print their names beside them.

7. Write two or three sentences of your own on the beauty of the skies.

Circumpolar Constellations

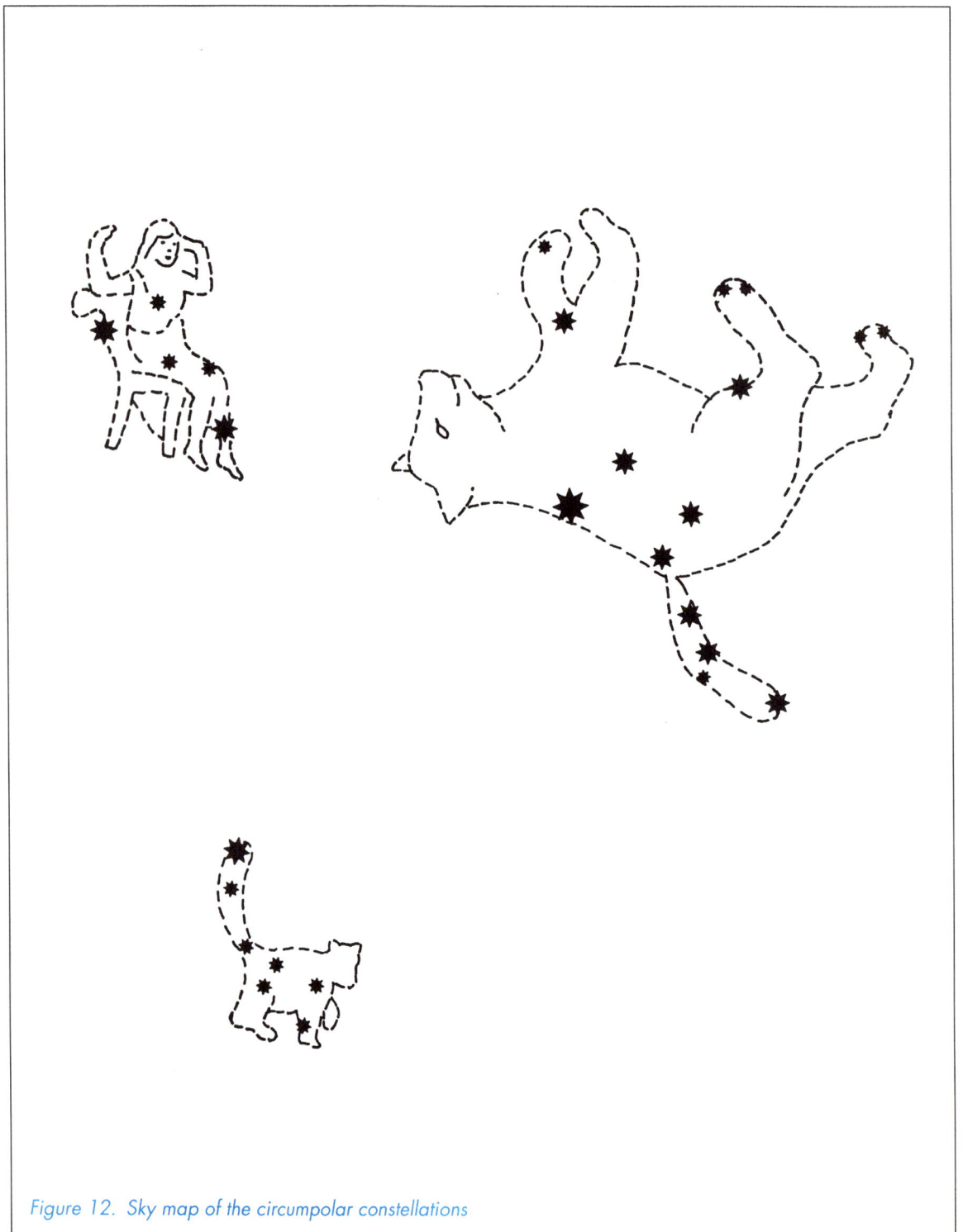

Figure 12. Sky map of the circumpolar constellations

Circumpolar Constellations Key

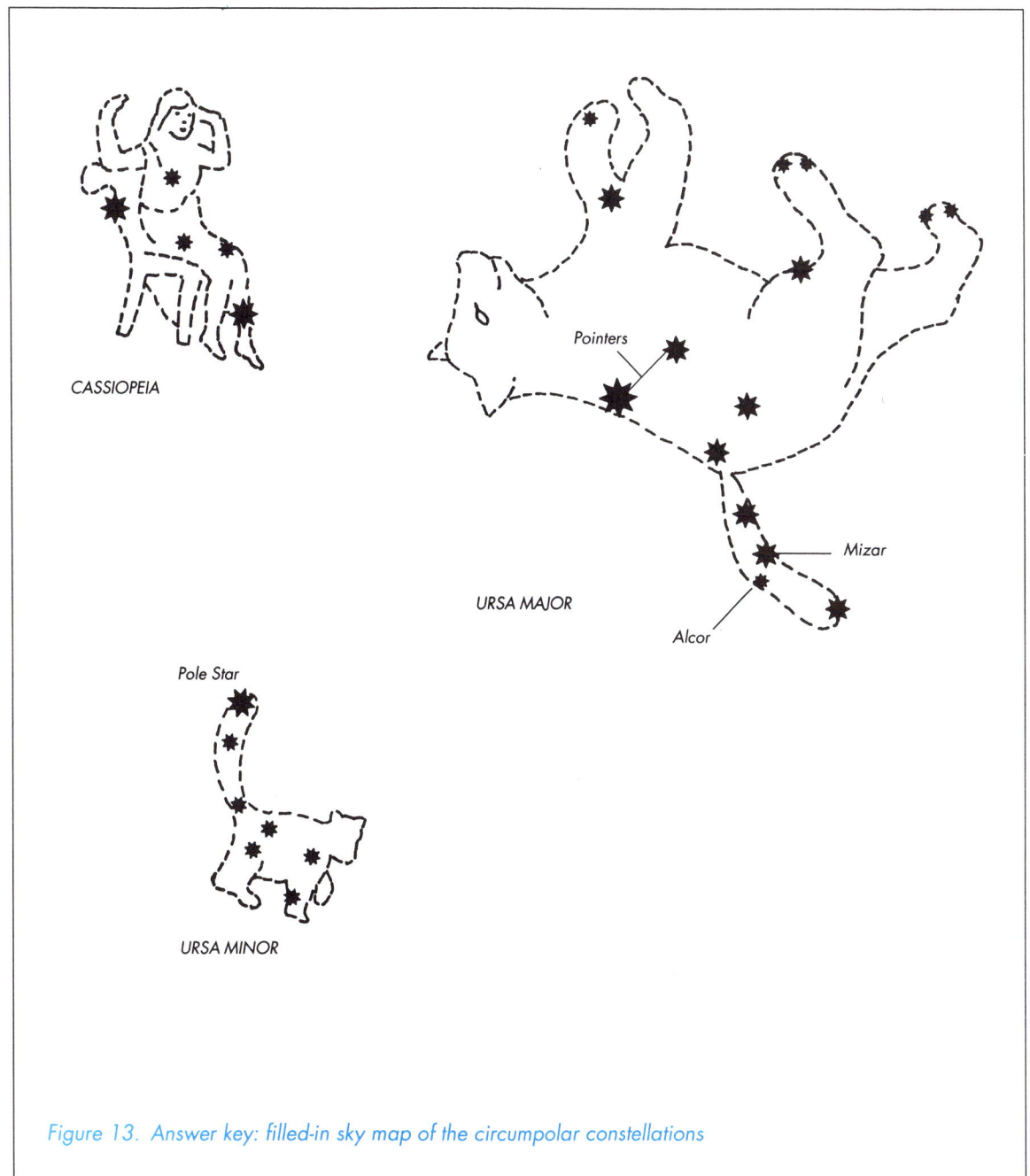

Figure 13. Answer key: filled-in sky map of the circumpolar constellations

5. Hunter in the Sky

In the glittering skies of the northern winter, the constellation of Orion the Hunter reigns supreme. Three bright stars in a slanting line form what is called Orion's Belt. Two stars below the belt are his feet, two above are his hands, and three small stars above these are his head. Three faint stars dangling from his belt form Orion's sword. The star at Orion's left foot is Rigel, a very hot bluish-white star, and at his right shoulder is the red supergiant star, Betelgeuse. One of the most wonderful sights in the sky revealed by the telescope is the great nebula lying just below Orion's belt. Even with the naked eye, one of these stars has a fuzzy, misty look. That star, Theta Orionis, is made up of four components called the Trapezium. This small group makes up the center of the Great Orion Nebula, a cloud of dust and gas some 15 light years across. The brightest star in the Trapezium makes the nebula glow.

Star formation is still taking place in the Great Orion Nebula, and many young stars are found in this area. All are unstable, with the result that their light varies rapidly in an irregular manner.

The ancients regarded Orion as a giant and great hunter. Just as a hunter on Earth is accompanied by dogs, the ancients gave Orion two dogs in the sky. A line through Orion's belt reaching to the left points to Sirius, the brightest star in the constellation of Canis Major, the Great Dog. Sirius is also the brightest fixed star in the heavens. The Arabs called this star Al Shira, the shining one. Astronomers have found that Sirius is a splendid white sun far surpassing our own sun in size and brilliance, but at such a distance that the light rays entering your eye as you look at it have taken more than eight years to reach you.

Three bright stars—Betelgeuse, Pollux, and Procyon—make up a large triangle in the sky. Procyon with its smaller companion makes up the constellation of Canis Minor, the Little Dog. As Orion rises and sets, the two dogs follow their master across the sky.

A line upward from Orion's belt brings you to another star, Aldebaran, which forms the eye of Taurus the Bull. The small stars around it form a cluster called the Hyades; a little further off is the beautiful cluster of the Seven Sisters, or Pleiades, one of the most-photographed groups of stars in the sky.

Legend tells us that Castor and Pollux were twin sons of the king and queen of Sparta. They were famous warriors, and Jupiter rewarded their great love for each other by placing them up among the stars. You can see the Twins in the sky on a winter night behind Orion and a little higher in the sky. The Twins belong to the constellation Gemini, which gave its name to the American space program, Gemini, in which two astronauts were involved.

Note: You will need the Star Finder made earlier to locate stars and constellations.

Looking at Winter Constellations

What you need: copy of constellation picture (Figure 14); color pens; Star Finder

Do these things to the pictures in Figure 14:

1. Draw in the bright stars seen in each of these constellations, and print the name beside the star. Color the star in Orion's knee blue. The blue-white star is Rigel. Color the star in Orion's shoulder red. The red star is Betelgeuse.

2. Find the stars Sirius, Procyon, Aldebaran, Castor, and Pollux and print their names beside them.

3. Print the name of each constellation below it.

4. Use your Star Finder to pick out each of these constellations, then try to locate them in the sky.

6. Our Nearest Star

The sun is the earth's powerhouse: It is a great, hot, glowing ball of gases at very high temperatures. Radiant energy from the sun warms the earth and the air around it. This heated air rising at the equator is replaced by air from the colder poles, thereby creating the winds of the world. The sun's warmth also evaporates millions of gallons of seawater each day; transported by wind, this moisture from the ocean falls as rain on the continents. Energy from the sun is stored by the ocean with its great capacity for absorbing heat, and is spread widely by ocean currents. These processes greatly affect our weather, our way of living, the crops we grow, our trade and commerce. Even the fuels we burn, such as coal, represent the stored energy of sunlight that shone on the earth millions of years ago.

The sun is the hub around which the planets of our solar system turn. Its great mass gives it a very strong force of gravity. This force acts on all the bodies in the solar system, keeping the planets in their orbits.

Heat from the sun comes from hydrogen bomb activity in which hydrogen atoms fuse together to form helium. Energy from this fusion radiates out into space and is received on earth as heat and light. In this furious process, the sun loses mass at the rate of over four million tons per second. Yet it is likely to keep its temperature for another 35 billion years without noticeable loss.

Winter Constellations

Figure 14. Four winter constellations

Winter Constellations Key

Figure 15. Answer key: four winter constellations

The Sun's Energy

You can find out how the sun's energy is absorbed, make experimental thermometers, use a burning glass, and make a model showing forces at work in a star like our sun.

What you need: pieces of card or wood painted various colors; glass bottles; thermometers; small bottles with corks and tubes; food coloring; white chalk dust or milk; hair dryer; bits of black and white paper or cloth.

1. Find out how different colors react to the sun's rays by taking some 15-cm squares of card or wood of various colors and placing them in full sunlight. Examine after 10 minutes to see how each color feels to the touch (Figure 16). Record your results.

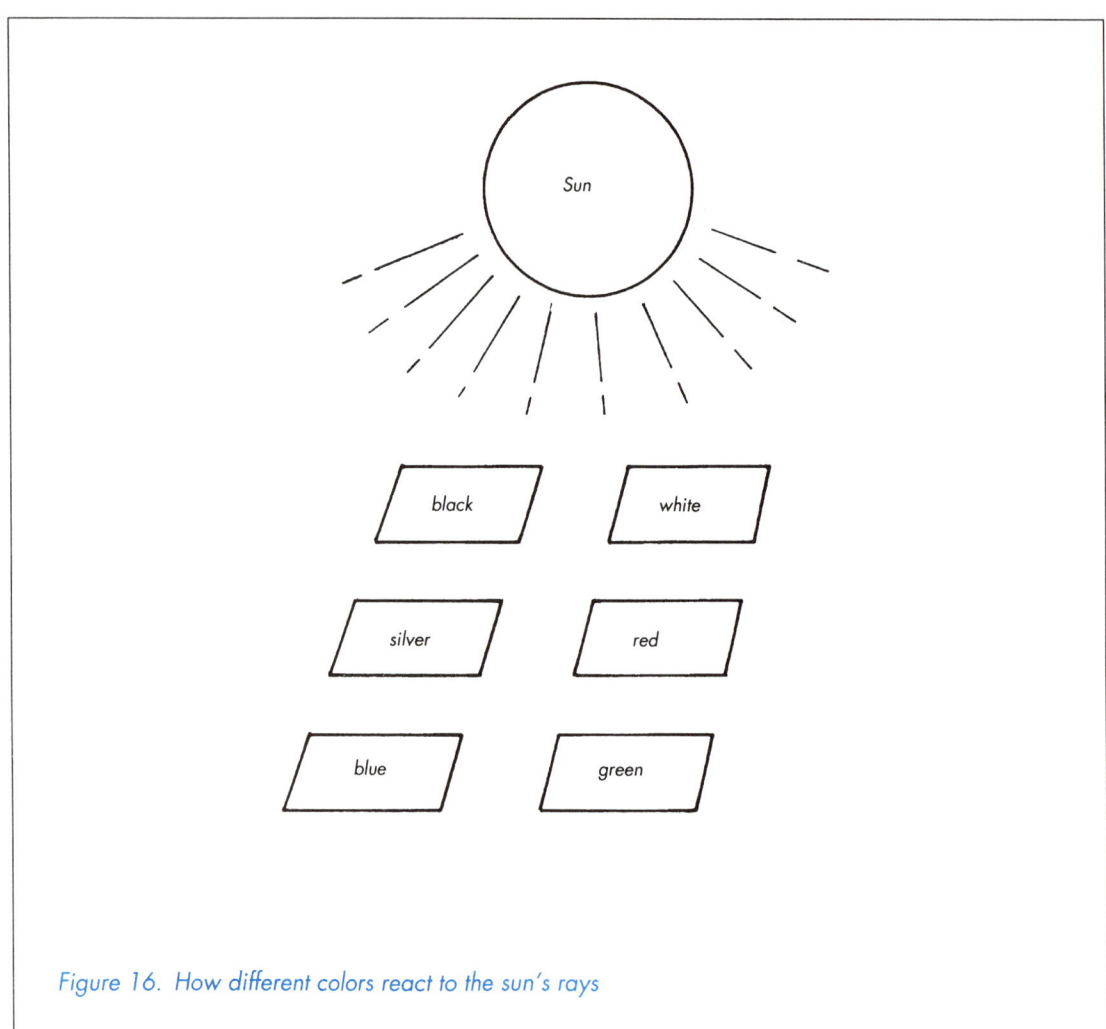

Figure 16. How different colors react to the sun's rays

2. Find out about absorption of the sun's heat by taking two glass bottles and filling them nearly to the top with water (Figure 17). To one, add a mixture of food coloring to create black water; to the other, add some white chalk dust or milk. Shake both bottles. Place a thermometer in each bottle and stand them by a window in the sun. Take the temperatures at intervals. Which bottle warms up more quickly? Which is the better absorber of the sun's heat? If temperatures are taken every five minutes, a temperature/time graph can be drawn for each bottle. (If thermometers are not available, touch the bottles to see which is heating up more quickly.)

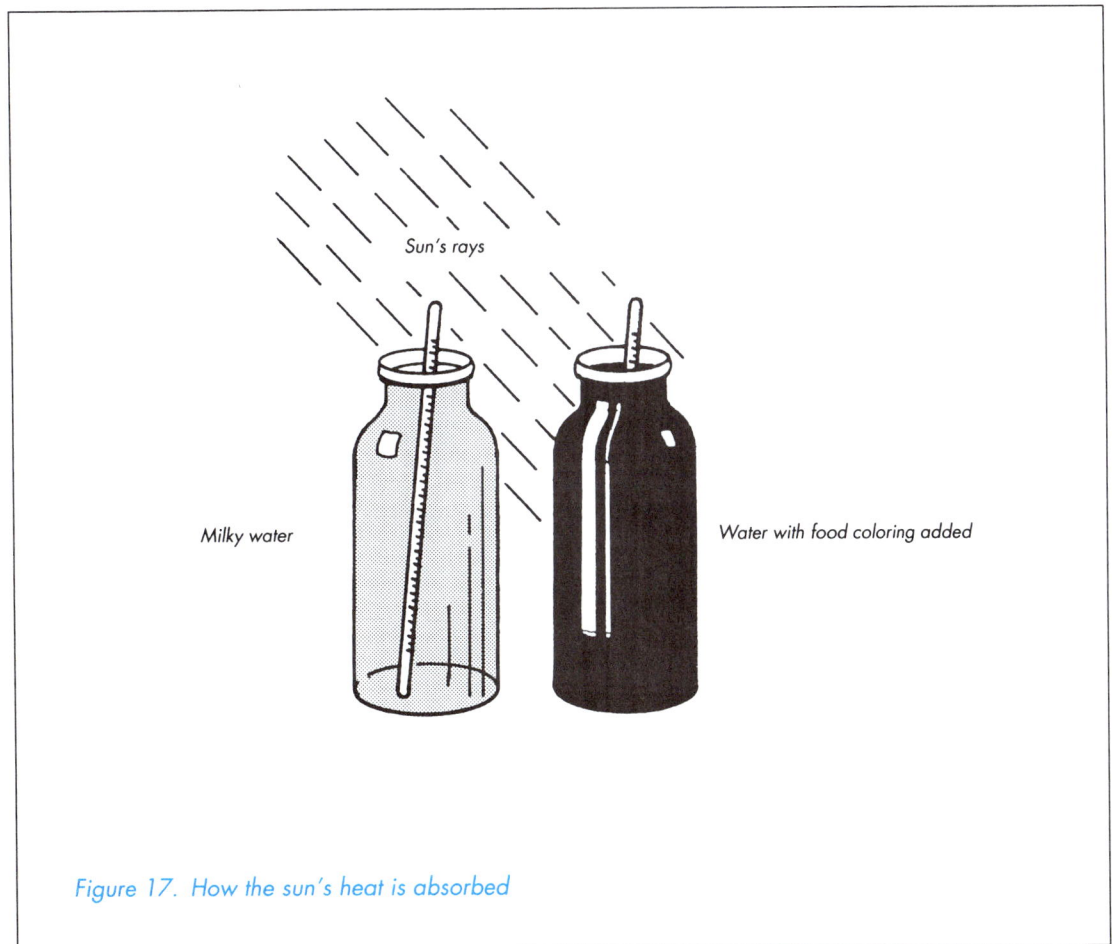

Figure 17. How the sun's heat is absorbed

3. Make experimental thermometers as shown. Set them up in your classroom.

Air thermometer

Set up a small bottle and glass tube as shown in Figure 18. Support the bottle with a clamp stand. The end of the tube should dip into a small jar or beaker of colored water.

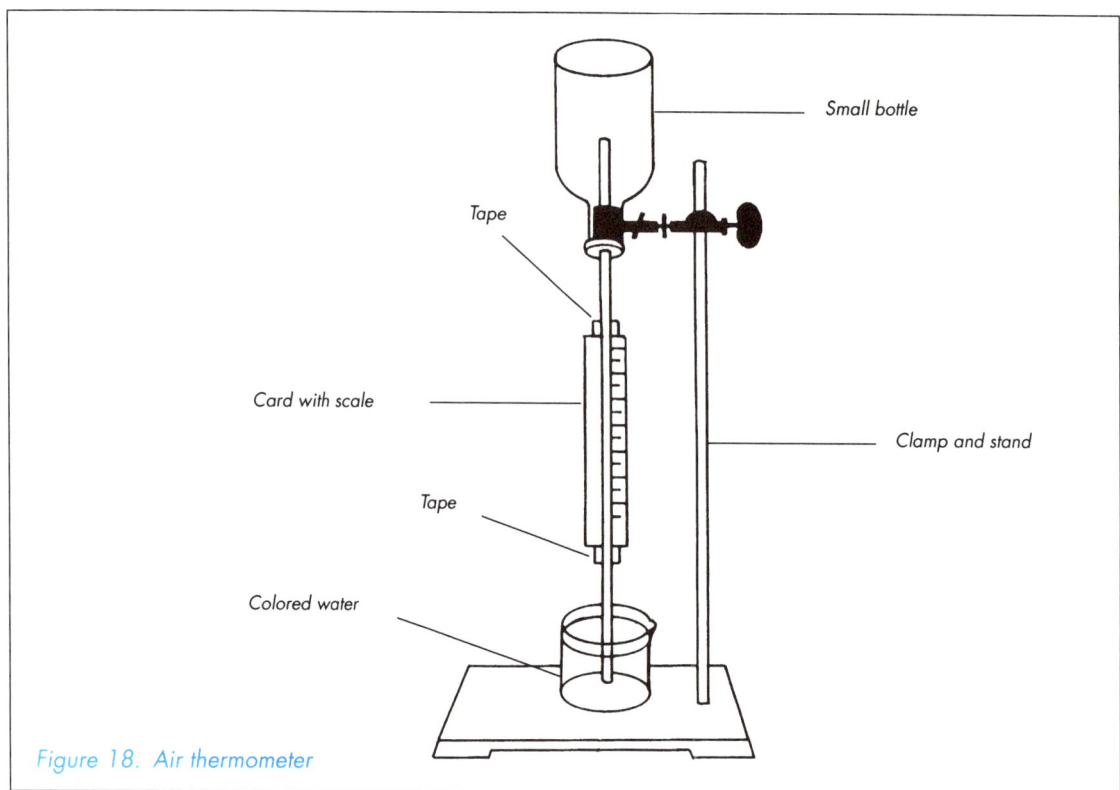

Figure 18. Air thermometer

To get the water about halfway up the tube, warm the bottle to drive out some of the air. Heat the bottle by wrapping it in a cloth that has been dipped in hot water. Repeat this procedure until, when the bottle cools to room temperature, the colored water rises about halfway up the tube. What happens? Explain why.

Tape a strip of light card behind the tube and make a scale for your thermometer by comparing the level of the water in the tube with the reading on a wall thermometer at various times during the day.

Water thermometer

Fit a stopper with a glass or plastic tube into a small flask or bottle. Add colored water to fill the bottle, then insert the stopper so that the water runs about halfway up the tube (Figure 19). Stand the thermometer on a bench near an ordinary wall thermometer. Tape a strip of light card behind the tube and make a scale for your thermometer by reading the wall thermometer at different times during the day.

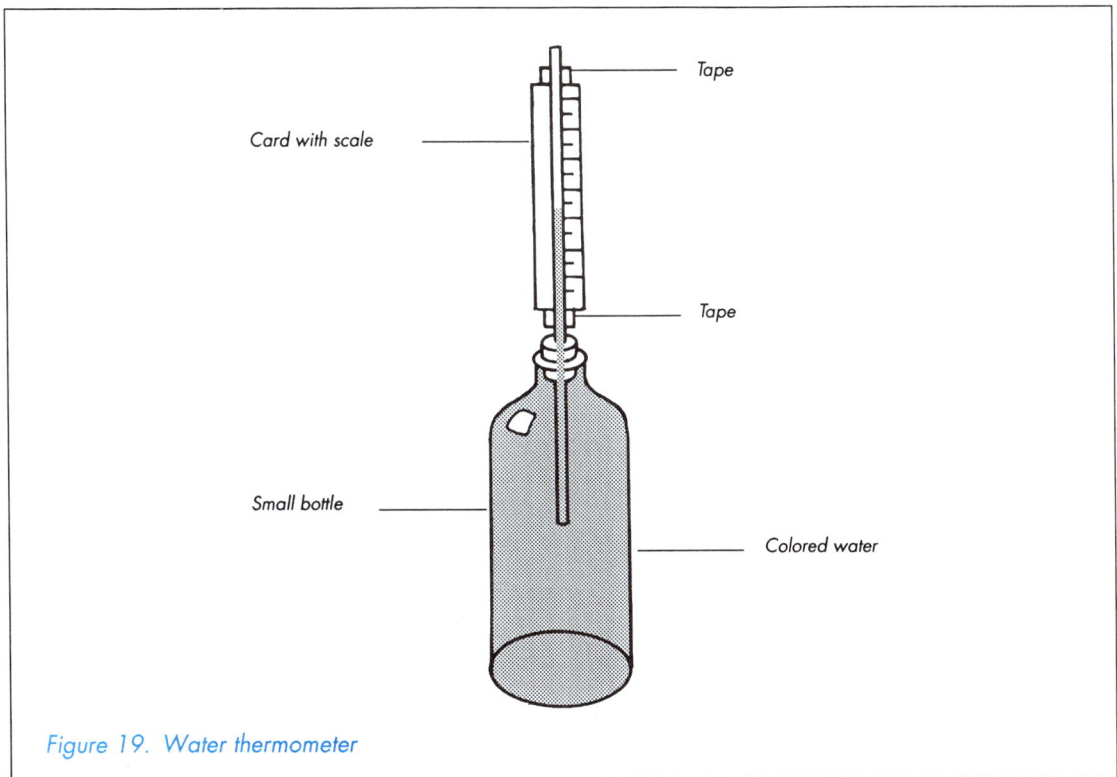

Figure 19. Water thermometer

Devise some experiments for your water thermometer. Try standing it in a dish of hot water and note what happens. Let it cool; what happens? Now try placing it in an ice-water mix and note what happens.

4. Use the magnifying glass to focus the sun's rays on different colored pieces of paper or cloth (Figure 20). What differences in effect do you notice?

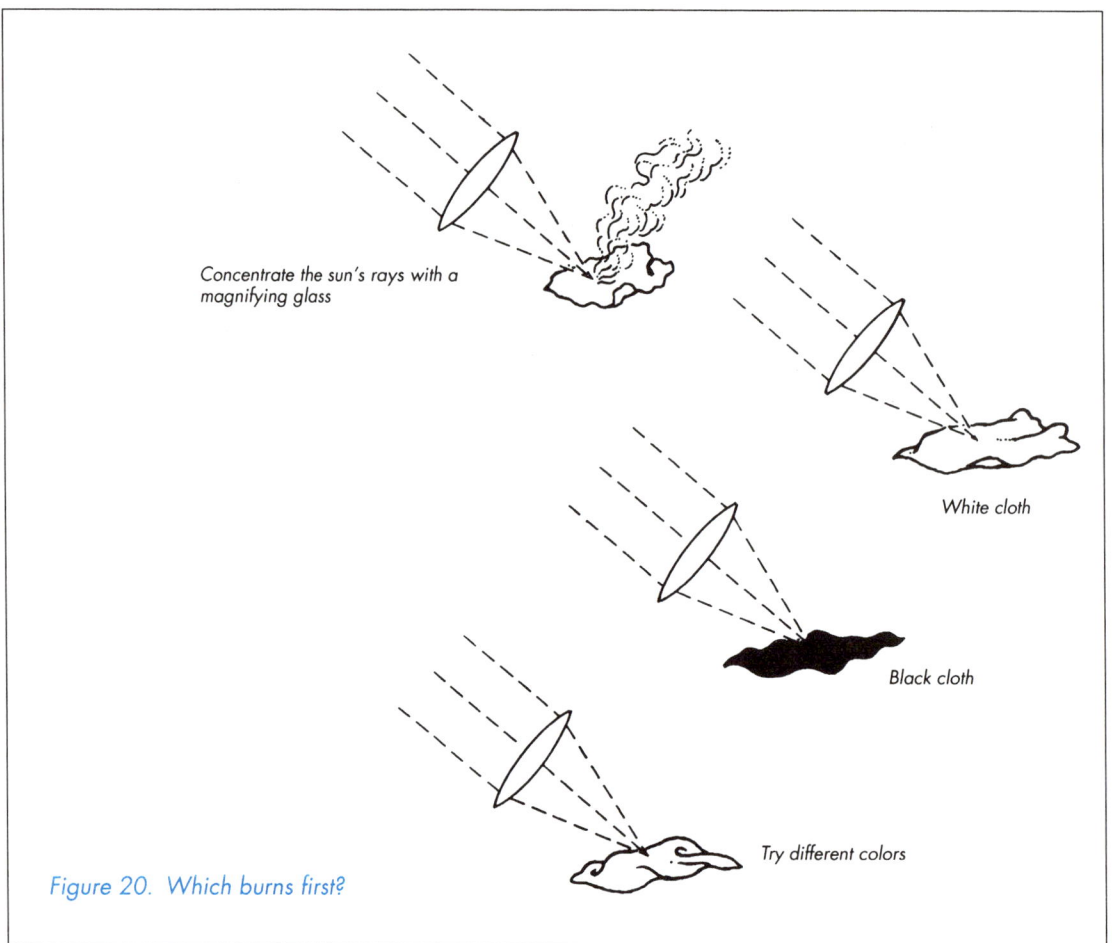

Figure 20. Which burns first?

5. Make a model showing the forces at work in a star such as the sun (Figure 21). Switch on the hair dryer and place the ping-pong ball in the airstream so that it appears to hang in the air. What forces are at work on the ball? In a star like our sun, hydrogen bomb activity at the sun's core creates a radiation pressure trying to blast the sun outward (air pushing on the ball in the model). But the sun's mighty gravity is pulling the stuff of the sun inward (gravity also pulls on the ball). In the sun, the two forces balance to make the sun a stable star. The prodigious energy of the hydrogen bomb exploding outward is balanced by the sun's enormous gravity pulling inward. Explain how your model shows this balance of forces. Is there another effect at work?

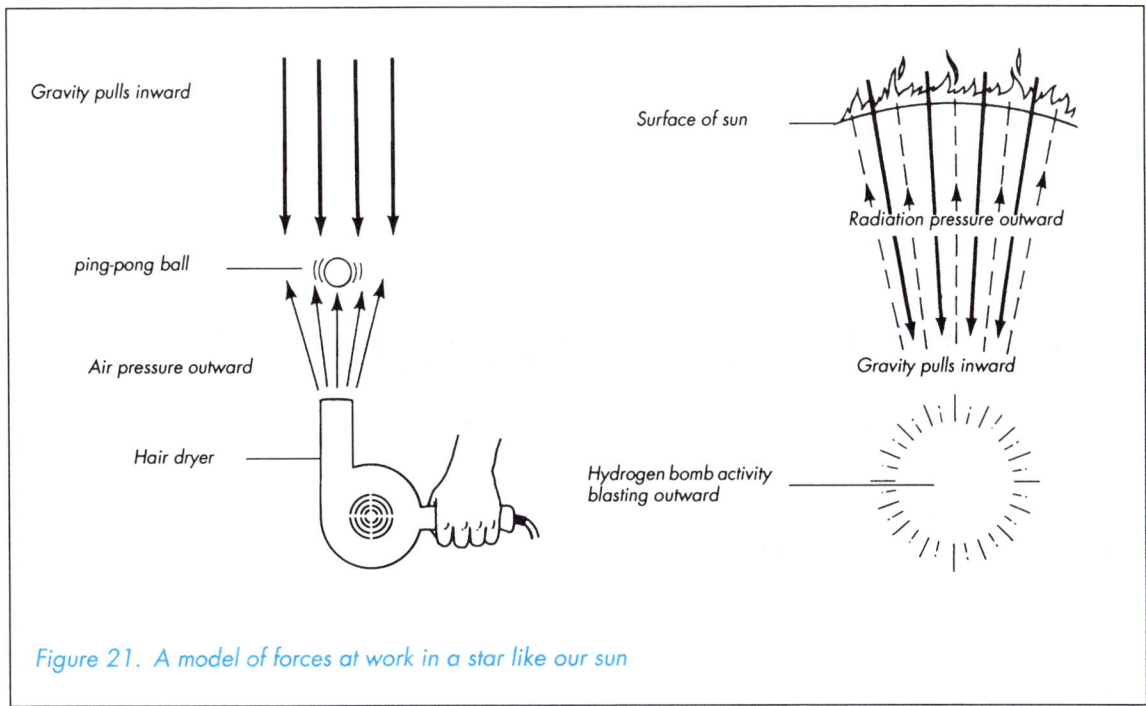

Figure 21. A model of forces at work in a star like our sun

7. Solar Eclipses and Coronas

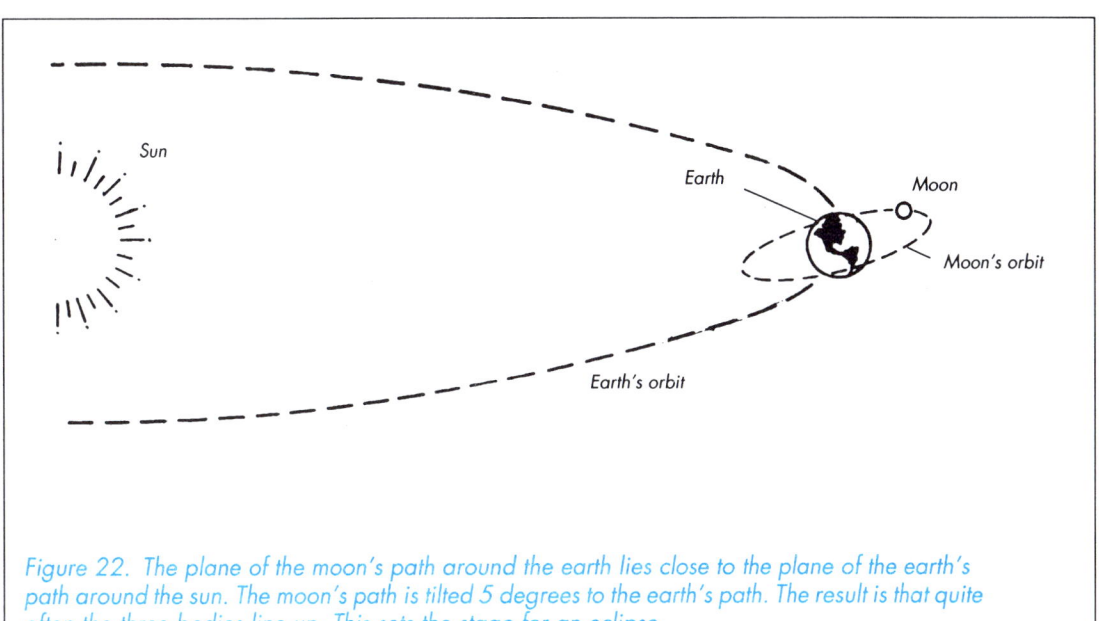

Figure 22. The plane of the moon's path around the earth lies close to the plane of the earth's path around the sun. The moon's path is tilted 5 degrees to the earth's path. The result is that quite often the three bodies line up. This sets the stage for an eclipse.

Solar eclipses (Figure 22) give scientists a unique opportunity to study different wavelengths of solar radiation associated with specific portions of the sun's disc and corona (Figure 23 and 24). The effects of specific wavelengths on the ionosphere can then be studied. Of course, there are only two to five eclipses each year. However, by using a device called a coronagraph, which creates an artificial eclipse (at any time), astronomers are able to make useful studies.

Figure 23. Total eclipse showing the corona of the sun, July 11, 1991

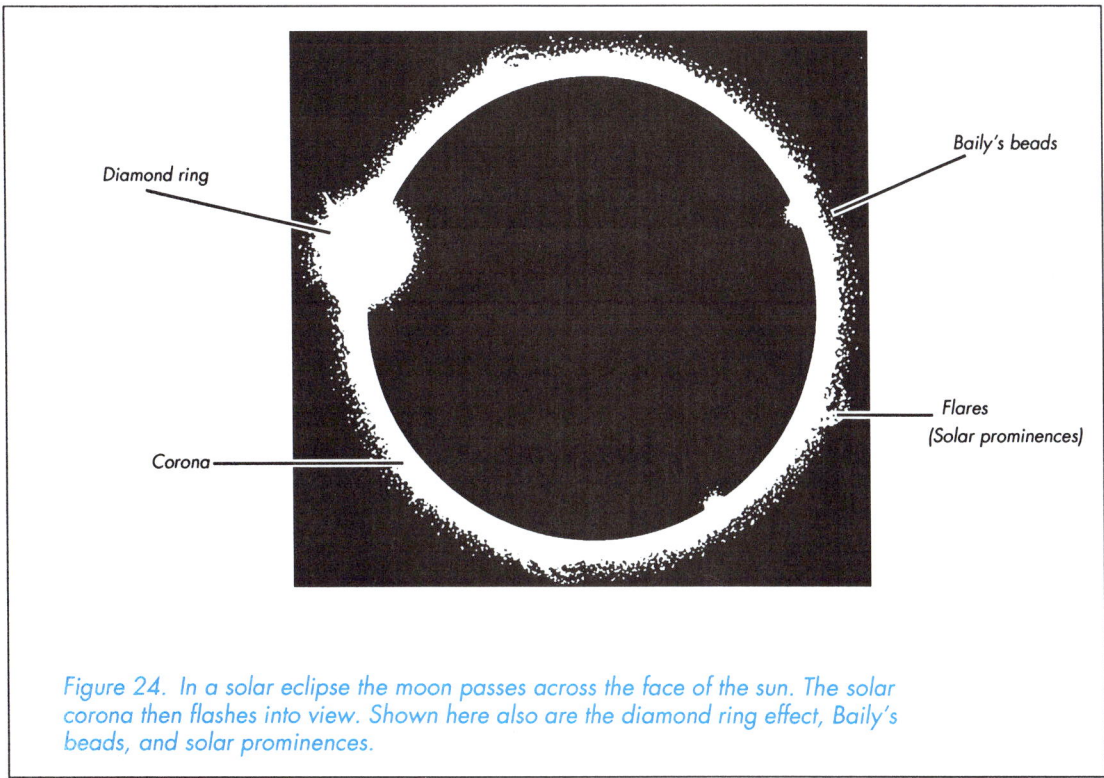

Figure 24. In a solar eclipse the moon passes across the face of the sun. The solar corona then flashes into view. Shown here also are the diamond ring effect, Baily's beads, and solar prominences.

The corona is the outermost layer of the sun's atmosphere and reaches out millions of kilometers into interplanetary space. It consists of clouds of electrons, hot electron gas, and interplanetary "dust"; it reflects the sun's rays and gives out as much light as a half-moon. Seen during an eclipse, the corona take the form of a pearly halo around the sun. Its greatest temperatures are on the order of 2,000,000°K, among the hottest observable temperatures in the universe.

Make an "Eclipsograph"

You can use the eclipsograph to demonstrate what happens during an eclipse of the sun and to show a solar corona.

What you need: cardboard box about 30 × 20 × 15 cm; scissors; drawing compass; pencil; strong lamp—projector or flashlight; crumpled aluminum or tin foil; adhesive; brass paper fasteners; strong cardboard; clear plastic; transparent tape; tissue paper; black felt-tip pen; water; shallow dish; filter paper; stapler; cotton wool

1. Set up your eclipsograph as in Figure 25. Cut a 5-cm hole S to represent the sun in the mid-upper front of the box. Tape the clear plastic and 2–3 thicknesses of tissue paper to the back of S.

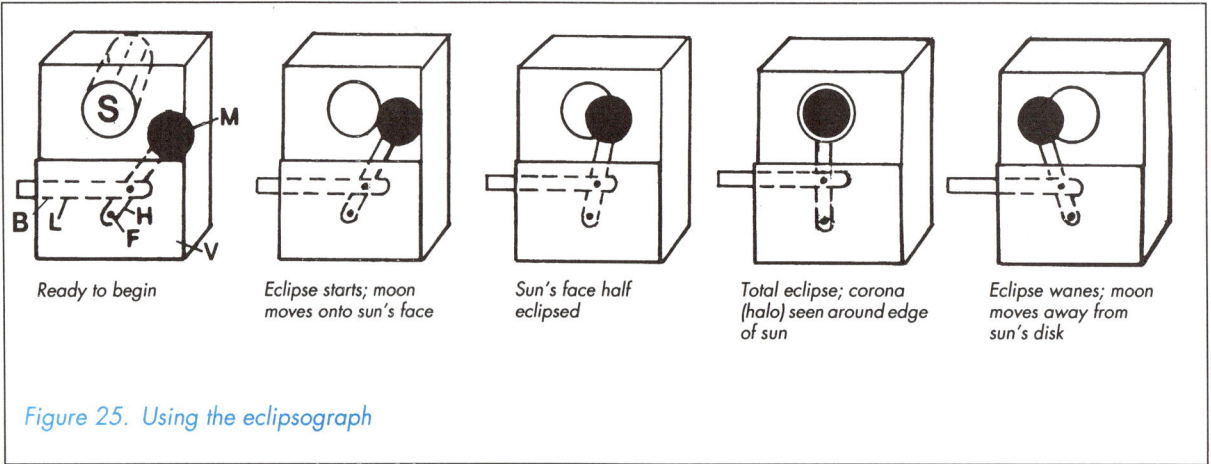

Figure 25. Using the eclipsograph

2. Cut two strips of strong cardboard and stick together to form support holder **H**. Cut a cardboard circle **M** to represent the moon; make this not quite 5 cm across. Blacken the face of this circle with the felt-tip pen and cover the other side with a circle of crumpled foil. Attach to one end of **H**.

3. Fix **H** to the box with a paper fastener at **F** making sure the two circles are exactly centered. Use a paper fastener to attach lever **L** to **H**. A cardboard bracket at **B** holds **L** in place.

4. Cut a card cover **V** and glue or staple in place to shield strip **H** and lever **L**.

5. To show a total eclipse of the sun, start with disc **M** (moon) at the right-hand edge of the box. The room should be darkened. Switch on the strong light (projector) behind the box so that **S** (sun) glows brightly. Now move lever **L** slowly to the left. The black disc **M** of the moon will begin to cut off part of the sun, starting the eclipse. Continue moving **L** to the left until the moon's disc fully covers the face of the sun and the total eclipse is seen. At this point the corona flashes into view. How does the metal foil affect the corona? Continue moving the moon until the eclipse wanes (partial eclipse) and the sun is whole again.

6. Cut small notches (to represent solar prominences—bursts of flame from the sun's disc) at **X** and **Y**, and a few tiny nicks plus a larger nick at **Z** (Figure 26).

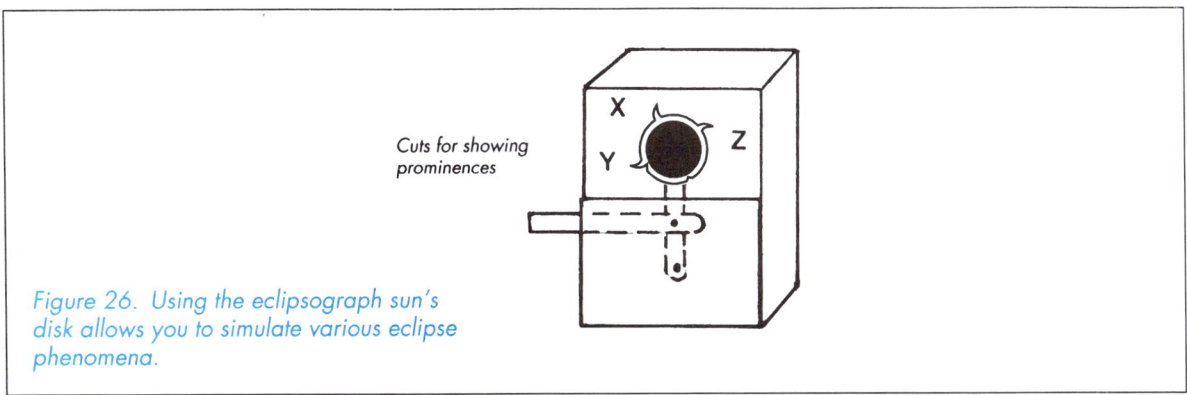

Figure 26. Using the eclipsograph sun's disk allows you to simulate various eclipse phenomena.

7. Repeat the eclipse. Note at total eclipse that the notches look like prominences; at the nicks you see the sparkles called Baily's beads; at the larger nick you get a glow or flash called the diamond ring effect (Figure 27).

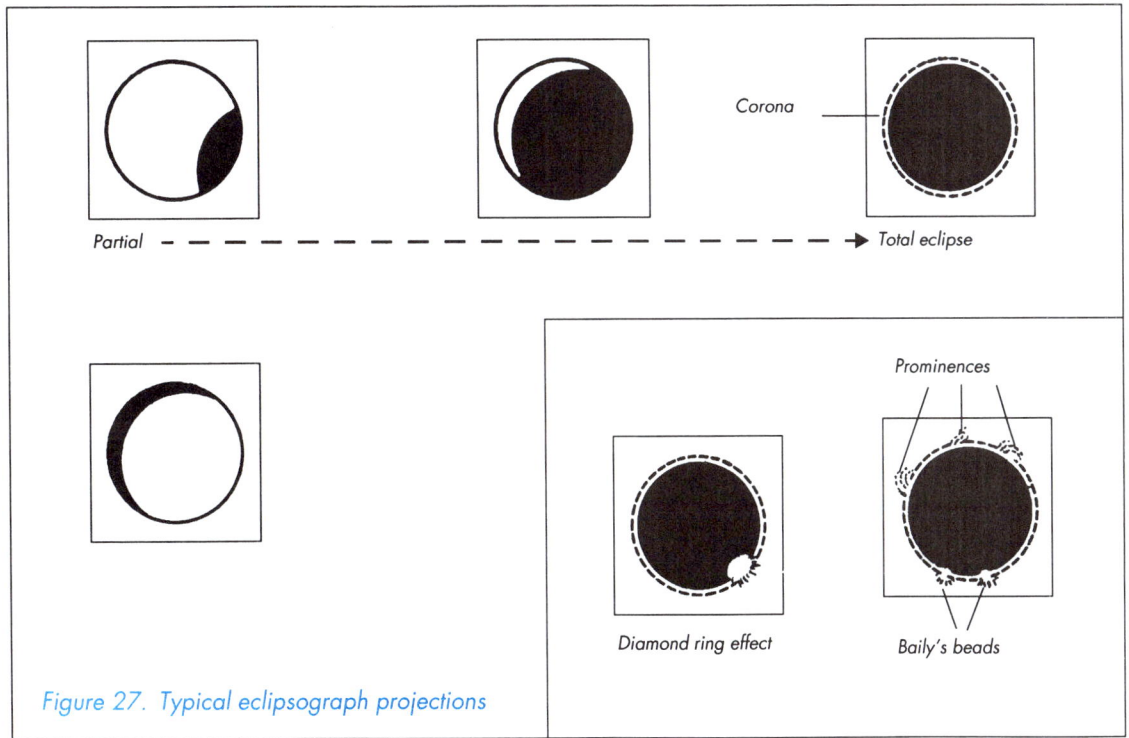

Figure 27. Typical eclipsograph projections

8. Compare the result of your eclipse demonstration with photographs of total and partial eclipses, prominences, Baily's beads, the diamond ring effect, and solar coronas. Write a note on each of these.

9. You can also show a corona another way. Use a coin as a template to make a black circle on a piece of filter paper. This circle represents the sun. Make some large and small dots around the circumference of this circle with a water-soluble, black felt-tip pen (Figure 28). Make a small hole at the center of the circle and thread a cotton-wool wick through it. Then place the filter paper over a shallow dish of water and leave for 20–30 minutes (Figure 29). What do you see when you reexamine the circle? Does there seem to be a streaming effect? How does your filter-paper corona compare with actual pictures in books? What causes the streaming seen in the sun's corona?

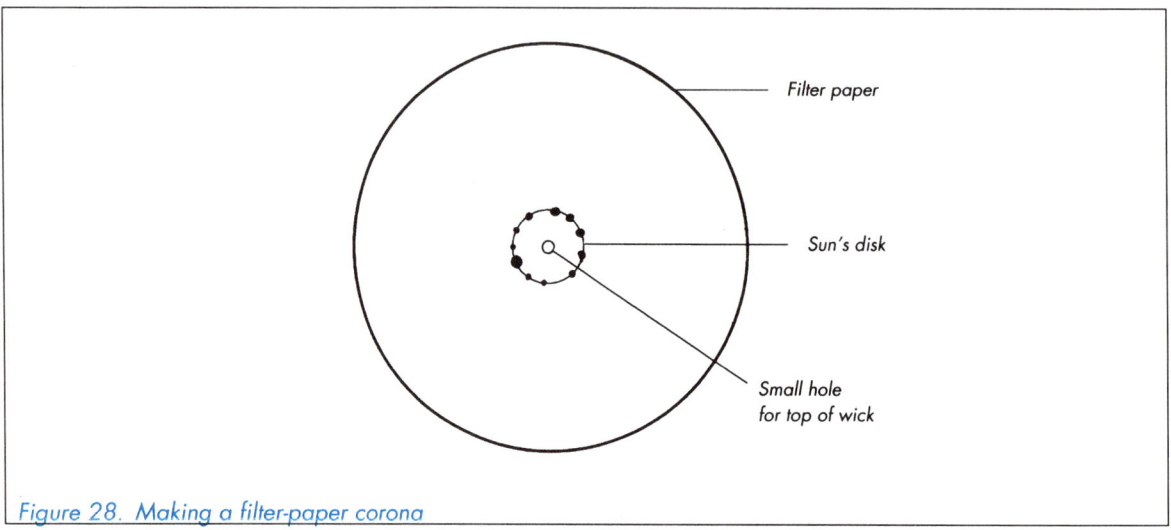

Figure 28. Making a filter-paper corona

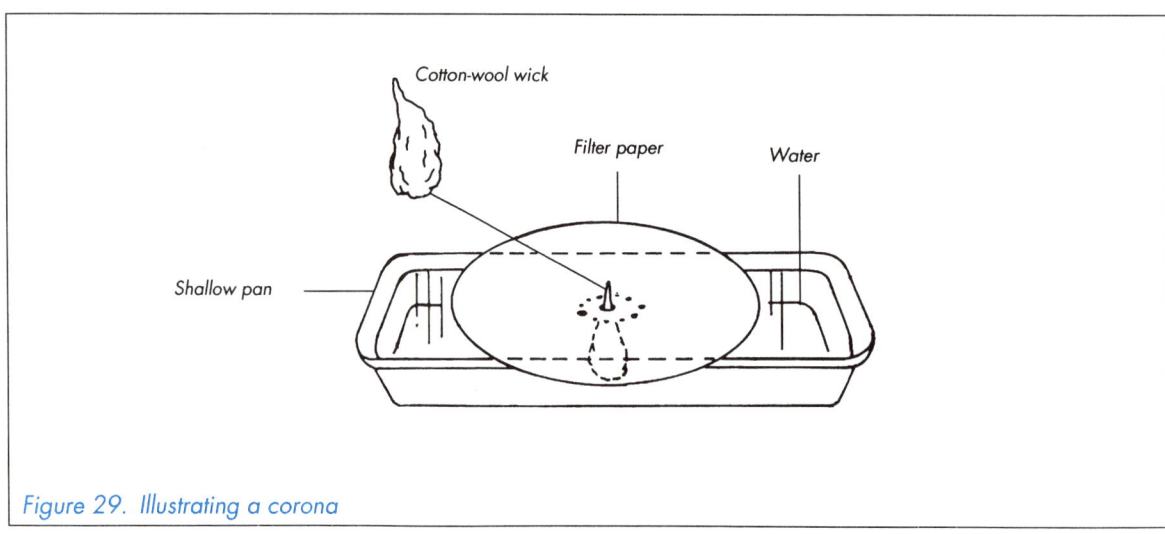

Figure 29. Illustrating a corona

8. Solar Paradox

The law of refraction states that a ray of light that passes in a slanting direction from a dense medium to a less dense medium bends away from the normal. The angle of refraction in such cases is greater than the angle of incidence.

Above the earth, the atmosphere thins out. Light from a star is therefore traveling from less dense to more dense air, and this produces a refraction effect. Due to refraction by the atmosphere, we see the sun above the horizon for some time after it has actually set in the evening, and before it has actually risen in the morning. The refraction effect is responsible for lengthening the day by a period of up to eight minutes. Figure 30 shows the effect of Earth's atmosphere in bending the rays of the sun.

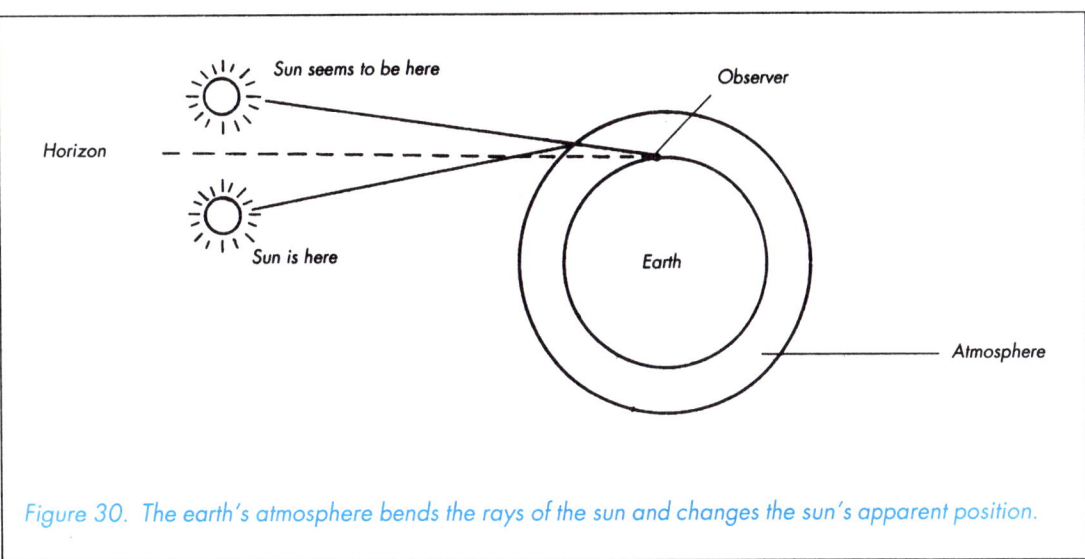

Figure 30. The earth's atmosphere bends the rays of the sun and changes the sun's apparent position.

Atmospheric Refraction

You can show by experiment that the rising or setting sun is actually below the horizon.

What you need: basin; water; drinking straw; milk; flashlight; black paper with a 2- to 3-mm hole at center; coin; glass with parallel sides; rubber band

1. To show refraction or bending of light rays, put the straw into the glass of water at an angle. Then look at the straw through the side of the glass at a point just below the surface of the water. Describe how it looks (Figure 31a).

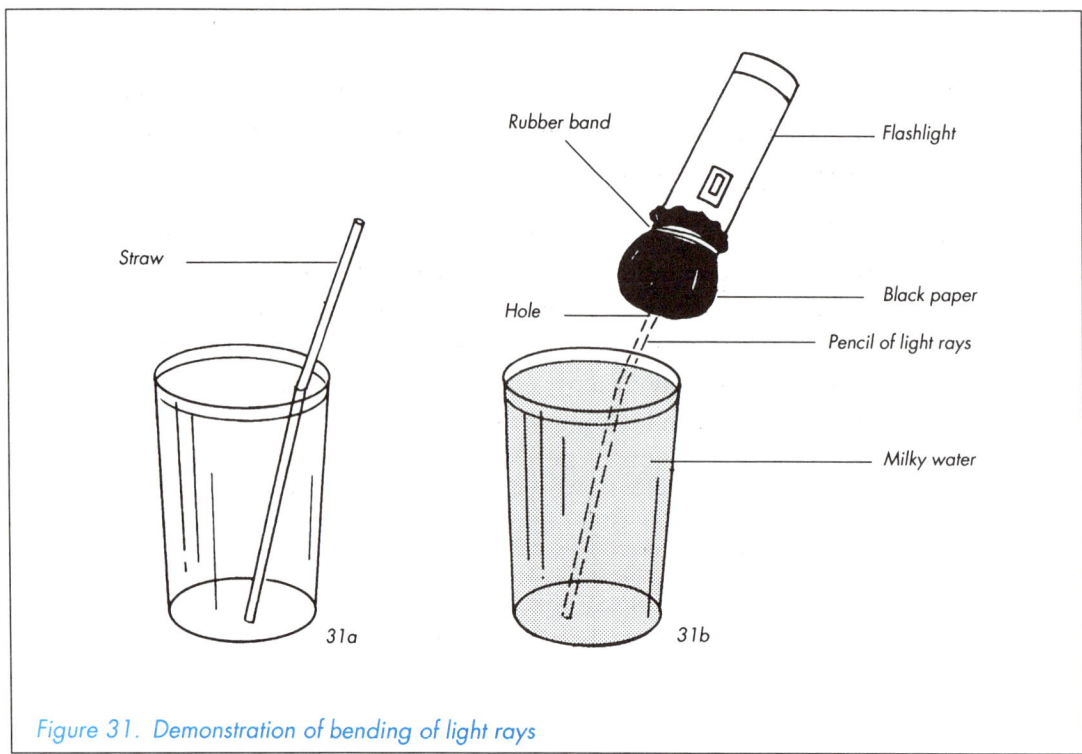

Figure 31. Demonstration of bending of light rays

Now stir a few drops of milk into the water, just enough to make it cloudy. The milk particles reflect the light so that you can see it as it passes through the water. Fix the black paper over the flashlight with a rubber band to give a pencil of light rays. In a darkened room, shine this light at an angle through the cloudy water. Can you see the bending or refraction of the light rays (Figure 31b)?

2. To show that refraction causes us to see the rising or setting sun when it is actually below the horizon, place the coin inside the empty basin, then position yourself so that the edge of the basin just blocks your view of the coin. Stay in the same position and have a partner carefully fill the basin to the brim with water, being sure not to disturb the position of the coin. What do you notice? Explain what the light rays do as they pass from the coin into the water, then into the air and to your eye. How does this help you to understand that the rising or setting sun is actually below the horizon (Figure 32)?

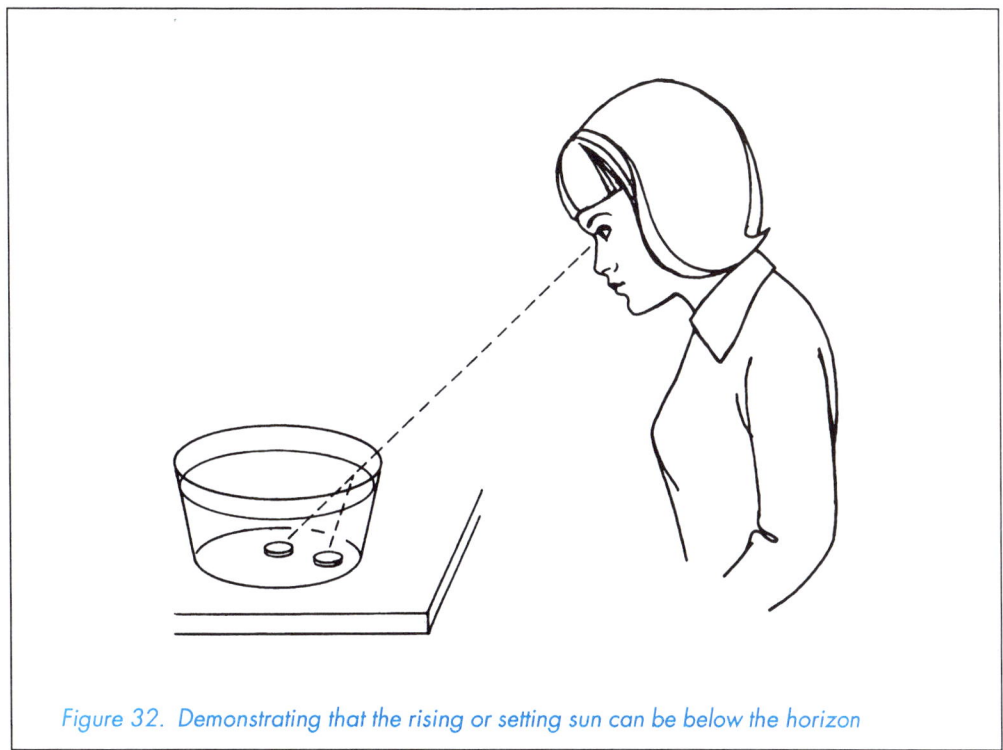

Figure 32. Demonstrating that the rising or setting sun can be below the horizon

While watching the coin, walk backward away from it. Keep watching the coin and walk toward it again. What do you notice? Explain why. Now explain why we can still see the sun after it has set.

Do we ever see the stars and planets in their true positions? If so, when?

9. Sun, Earth, and Moon

The sun is a ball of hot glowing gases, 150 million kilometers distant from Earth and more than 100 times greater in width. The sun is the star nearest to planet Earth and is our greatest source of energy. Without its light and heat, our earth would be a cold, dark world; all life would probably perish. Heat warms the earth's surface and warmth is necessary for living things to carry on their life's activities. Light is also important for life, as we rely on green plants for our food.

Green plants use light energy for photosynthesis, the process by which they manufacture food—the direct and indirect source of energy for nearly all living things. The sun's heat also causes the winds of the world, which give us our weather and climate.

The moon also affects the earth. Its gravity pull causes the high and low tides each day. The moon has no natural light but reflects the sun's light onto the earth. In contrast to Earth, the moon has no atmosphere or water and supports no life on its rough and rocky surface. Earth is about 3.5 times greater in diameter than the moon.

Sun, Earth, Moon Model

You can make a sun-earth-moon model to show their relationship to one another.

What you need: large orange balloon (sun); papier-mâché globe built around a smaller balloon (earth); ball of modeling clay (moon); wire; drinking straw; string to tie balloon; soda bottle

1. Put the materials together as shown. Try to maintain some proportion in size and distance. Bend the main supporting wire and slip the U-bend into the neck of the bottle (Figure 33).

Figure 33. The sun-earth-moon model

2. Use the model to show the changing positions in space of the earth and the moon in relation to the sun.

What makes day and night?

Use the model to show that the earth is a sphere bathed in sunlight. How much is illuminated at any time? What movement of the earth gives us our 24-hour day? What is the turning of the earth on its axis called?

What is a year?

Show the movement of the earth in its 365¼ day's track around the sun. How does a "leap year" come about? Note also that the earth's axis always points to Polaris, the Pole Star. How can we use this to tell direction?

How does the moon move in space?

Use the model to show that the moon moves around the earth as the earth circles the sun. Why do we see only one side of the moon? Show that as the moon moves around the earth, it turns on its axis so only one side faces the earth.

Why does the moon change shape?

Show that the moon, because of its position with respect to us, does not always reveal all of that half. When the earth is between the sun and the moon and the three bodies are in a straight line, the earth blocks the light from the sun and so darkens the moon. Use your model to demonstrate this. Look at books in your library for a way to show the phases of the moon with a flashlight and a globe.

What causes eclipses?

Show that when the sun, moon, and earth are lined up in that order, the moon blocks the light from the sun. Why doesn't this happen every month? It is because the moon's orbit is slightly tilted so its shadow just passes out into space. But when sun, moon, and earth are in a straight line we have an eclipse of the sun. The moon's shadow falls on only a small part of the earth, cutting off the sun's light from that part.

10. Moon Craters

It was Galileo in 1629 who first observed the surface of the moon through his telescope and described its mountains and craters (see moon map Figure 34).

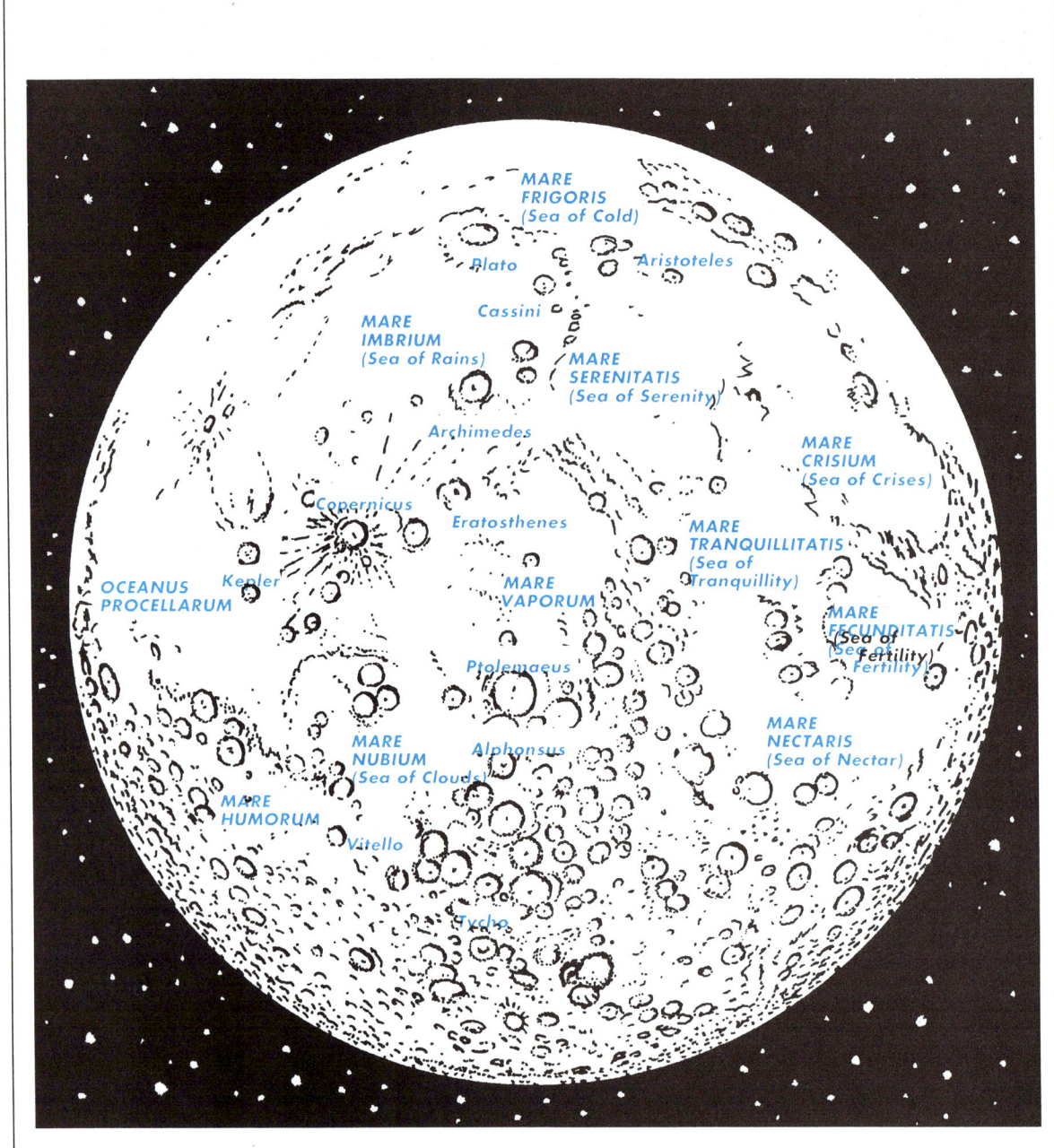

Figure 34. Moon map showing important craters

Figure 35. This NASA photograph shows craters on the far side of the moon.

The moon's craters (Figure 35) are round, saucer-shaped hollows with a surrounding rim or lip. Some scientists think the craters were the result of volcanoes erupting (that is, by a process taking place within the moon); other scientists explain the craters by saying they were caused by pieces of rock called meteorites falling on the moon (that is, by an astronomical process). As the meteorites travel at high speeds—up to 70 km per second—material explodes out of the surface of the moon in the form of dust, sand, and even liquid rock, if the temperatures reached are high enough.

The giant lunar crater Copernicus is 90 km across; its walls tower up to more than 3,600 meters. Some 30,000 lunar craters have so far been identified and named.

Volcanoes and Craters

You can show how craters form and volcanoes erupt.

What you need: large paper plate or shallow container; flour; teaspoon; plaster of paris or spackle (for repairs on plaster walls); water; bead-size balls of modeling clay; fine-toothed saw; apple; plate; apple corer; microwave

1. Fill the paper plate with starch or flour and level it off neatly. This represents the surface of the moon.

2. Stand on a chair or table so that you are about 2 meters from the floor. Drop a teaspoon of flour onto the plate. Repeat this several times using different amounts of flour and dropping from different heights. How would you describe the craters that form—do they have raised lips, are they rounded, saucer-shaped hollows? How do they compare with the craters shown in the illustration? How is this method of crater formation similar to lumps of rock striking the moon from far out in space?

3. Mix the plaster of paris to a creamlike consistency. Then drop the tiny balls (experiment with different sizes) into the plate of plaster, now in the process of hardening. Wait for the plaster to harden, then cut through some of the tiny "meteors" and the craters they have made with a fine-toothed saw. Describe your "crater." Does it look like a moon crater with its surrounding crater-like wall?

4. You can simulate a volcanic eruption with lava flow by trying the following. Core the apple, place it in the plate with about 1 mm of water, and microwave for 3–3½ minutes (depending on the size of the apple). Toward the end of the time, watch the semi-liquid apple—"lava"—bubbling up and over the "crater" top. What is the shape of the "volcanic" crater? How does it compare in shape with the craters you formed earlier? Experiment with the time for improved "lava" and "volcanic crater" formation.

11. Finding the Size of the Moon

Our moon is a natural satellite of the earth and one of the oldest objects in the solar system (Figure 36). Since it is our nearest neighbor in the sky (it is about 380,000 kilometers away), it was the first object to be visited when man became a space traveler. Having no atmosphere, it has no weather patterns, and scientists tell us that it is still in its original state. This makes it an interesting object of study in space research, particularly for studying the problem of its origin.

To primitive humans the moon was a natural calendar: Its phases provided the first means of measuring time, after the pattern of day and night due to the earth's rotation. Every 29 days the moon passes between the sun and the earth and, should the three bodies be in a straight line, an eclipse of the sun takes place. The moon casts a shadow; where this falls on the earth, people are not able to see the sun. The moon's distance from Earth and its size are just right to briefly blot out the entire disc of the sun, causing a total eclipse.

Figure 36. The moon is Earth's nearest neighbor in space, at a mean distance of approximately 380,000 km (240,000 miles).

Many think the rising moon looks larger than when the moon is overhead and that this is a refraction effect. But the effect of refraction is to make the vertical diameter less, giving the moon a flattened appearance when low in the sky. What seems to be an increase in size is an illusion.

The Moon's Diameter

What you need: two pieces of cardboard about 9 × 7 cm; scissors; meter rule or yardstick; drawing pins

1. Cut a pinhole in one card and attach to end of ruler.

2. Cut a 5-mm-diameter hole in the second piece of card. Look at the moon through the pinhole and the slot, keeping your eye close to the pinhole (Figure 37).

Figure 37. Measure the distance between the two cards.

3. Move the card with the 5-mm-diameter hole back and forth until you find a position where the moon just fits in the slot. Take the distance to the moon as 380,000 kilometers.

4. Work out the diameter of the moon from the similar triangles *ABC* and *AXY* (Figure 38).

$$\frac{CB}{d} = \frac{\text{diameter of moon in kilometers}}{380,000}$$

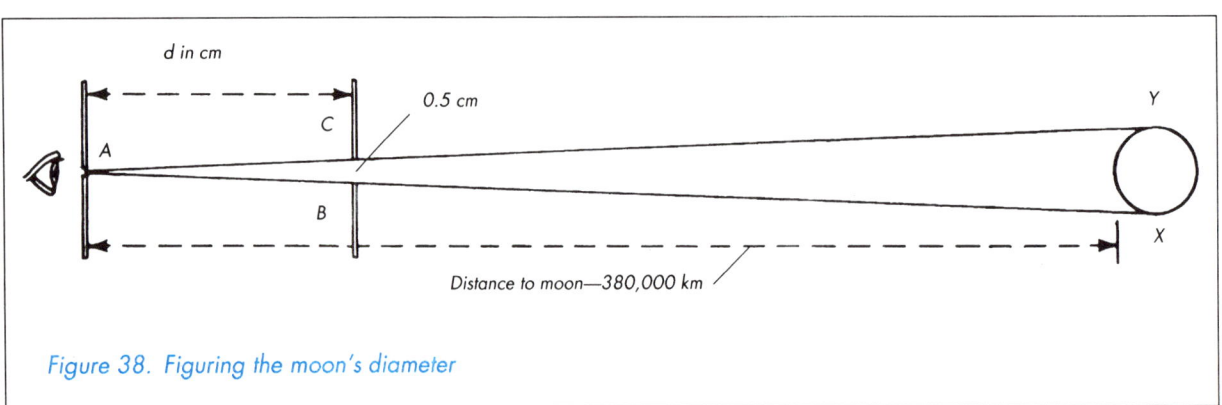

Figure 38. Figuring the moon's diameter

Having made *CB* 5 mm, then the diameter of the moon

$$= \frac{0.5 \times 380,000}{d}$$

What value do you get for the moon's diameter?

5. The moon is approximately one quarter the diameter of the earth, or about 3,000 kilometers. Compare this figure with the value you obtained by experiment. How well did your experiment work?

6. Find out how astronomers explain the seemingly large "harvest moon."

7. Why does the full moon look so big when it has just risen?

8. Look at the newly risen moon through a cardboard tube. Does it look as big? If not, why not?

12. Earth-Moon Rotation

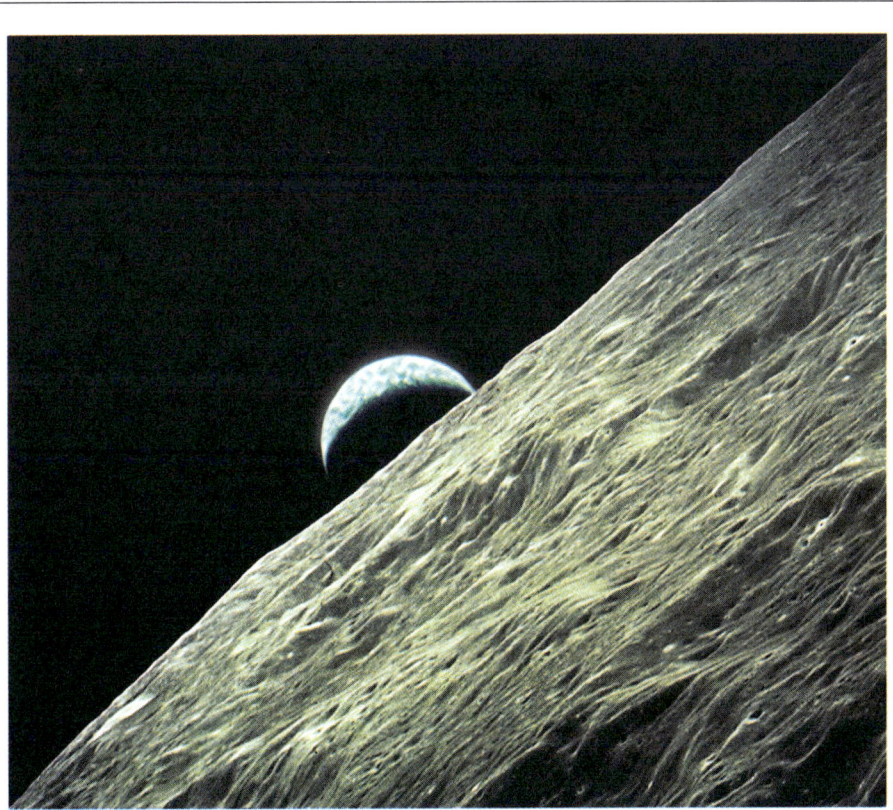

Figure 39. When seen from the moon, Earth appears to rise, just as the moon appears to rise over Earth.

A man whirling a lasso around his head is much like the sun taking its family of planets with it on its journey through space. The earth and the moon travel around the sun, as do other planets and moons within the solar system. The paths they follow, however, are not smooth, even ellipses like a spinning lasso. Instead, Earth's course around the sun is irregular and wobbly, while the moon orbits Earth in the same way at the same time.

Although the moon is only one fourth the diameter of the earth and only about one eightieth the earth's mass, its gravity does have an effect on the earth; the earth has an orbit with respect to the moon just as truly as the moon has an orbit around the earth (Figure 39).

The earth and the moon, acting as a system, actually rotate around a point about 1,500 kilometers under the earth's surface on the side facing the moon (Figure 40). The diagram shows the wavy, wobbly path traced by the earth-moon system as it courses through space on its journey around the sun.

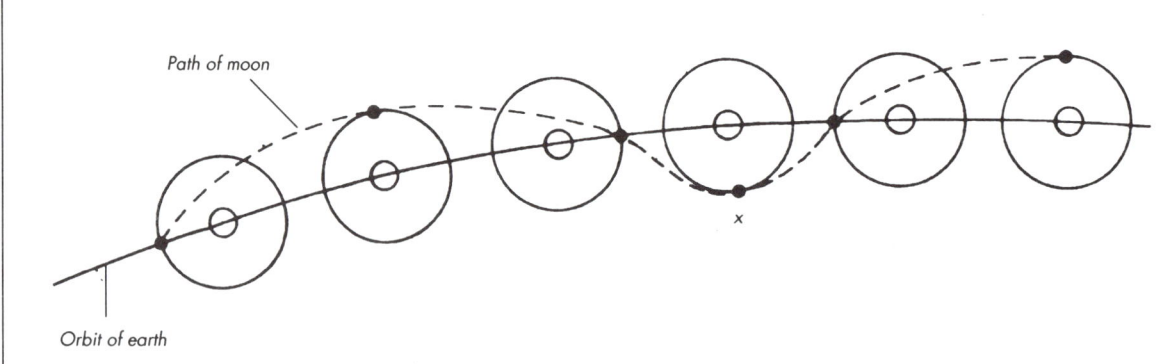

Figure 40. The earth's orbit is the path of the center of mass of the earth-moon system, which revolves around the sun in a wavy, wobbly path. (Note: Since this drawing is not to scale, it gives the misleading impression that the moon's path is convex with respect to the sun at point x.)

Earth-Moon Rotation Model

What you need: light plywood or heavy cardboard; earth-moon diagram (Figure 41); large cardboard box; roundheaded pin; paint; glue; drill or awl; cork; modeling clay

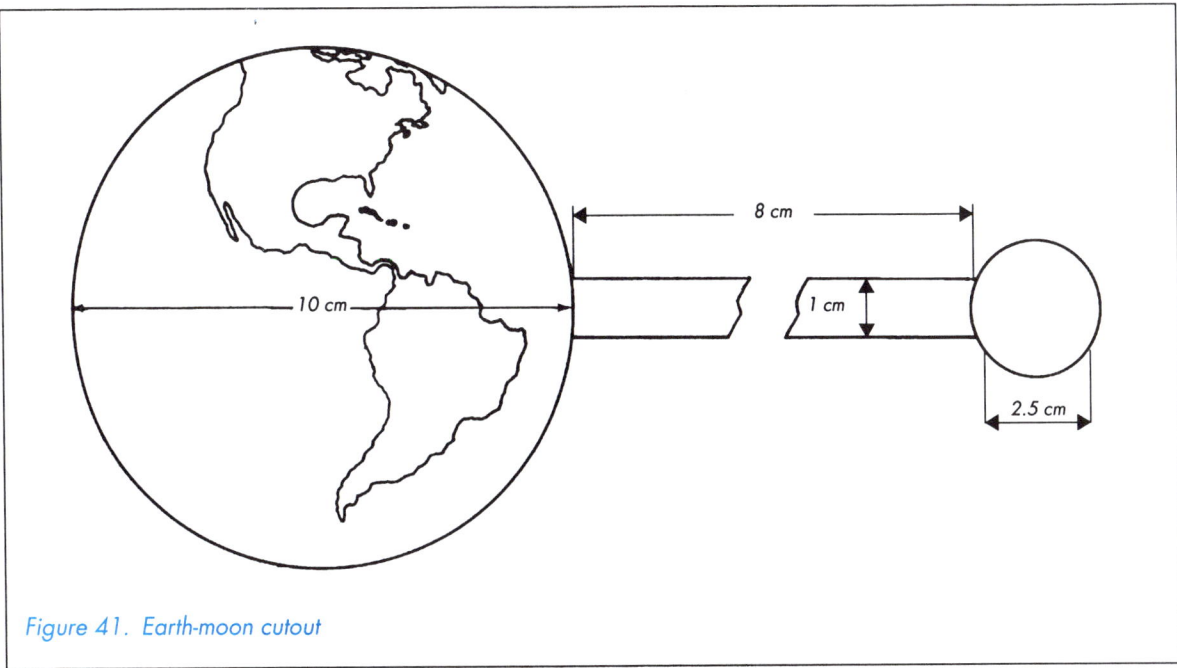

Figure 41. Earth-moon cutout

1. Make a copy of the earth-moon diagram in Figure 41 on the plywood, using the measurements given. (If cardboard is used, use two thicknesses for the connecting strip for strength.) Cut out neatly.

2. Balance the cutout on a finger to get the center of gravity (Figure 42). Place the pin at this point and move it as needed to get the exact balance point (Figure 43). Then make a hole with the drill or awl, pass the pin through, and spin the earth-moon model. How does it rotate—smoothly and evenly, or not? If the spin is uneven, add a little modeling clay to the lighter end to get perfect balance.

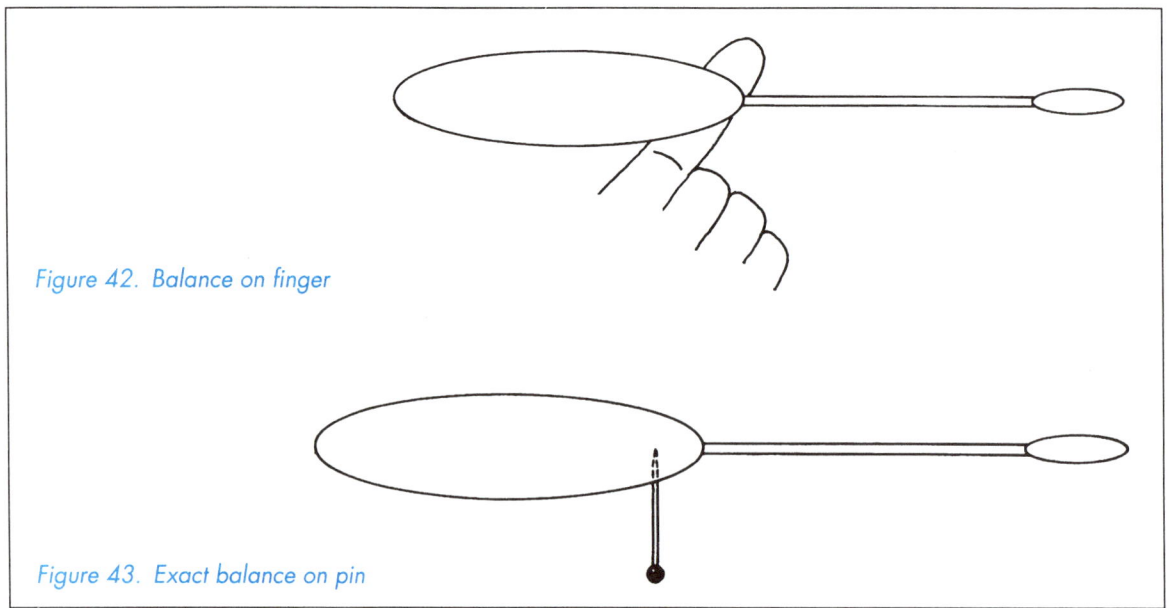

Figure 42. Balance on finger

Figure 43. Exact balance on pin

3. Paint the front of the carton black and paste or paint stars on it for effect. If you wish, you can add comets, shooting stars, etc. (Figure 44). Paint the earth and moon cutout, adding as much detail as you can. Now take the pin with your cutout model on it and push the pin through the side of the carton into a cork on the inside, to fix it there. Be sure to leave enough pin sticking out so that the cutout spins freely. Describe how the earth-moon system rotates.

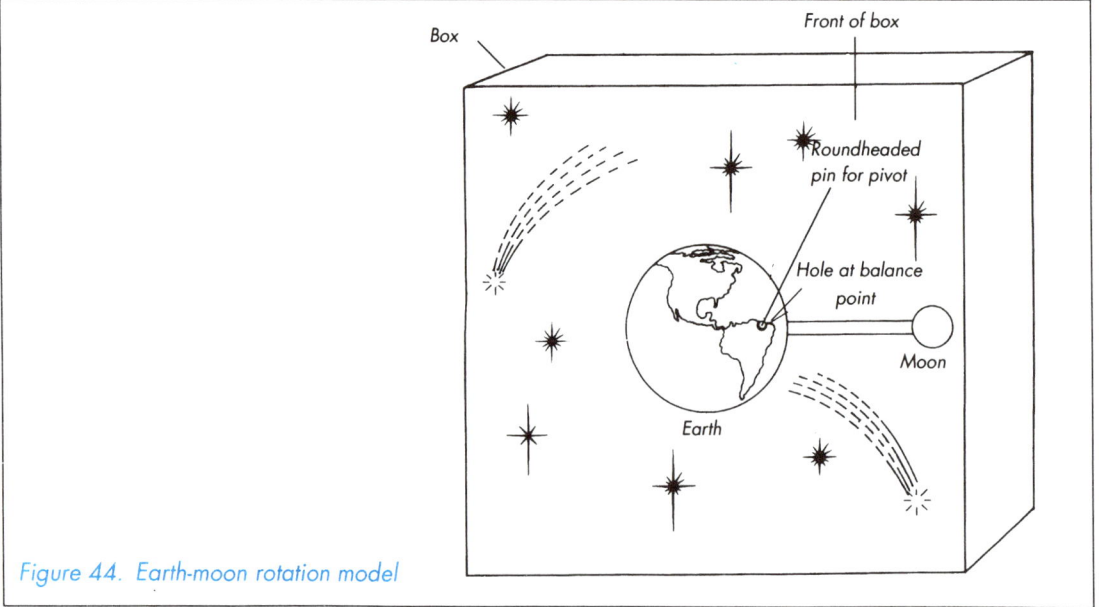

Figure 44. Earth-moon rotation model

13. The Spin of the Earth

A French scientist, Jean-Bernard-Léon Foucault, showed that a pendulum was a simple and direct way to demonstrate the earth's spin on its axis. Foucault hung a pendulum from the dome of the Pantheon in Paris. As the pendulum swung to and fro, the line traced out by the swinging plumb bob rotated about the rest point of the pendulum. So, said Foucault, it was not that the pendulum was rotating, but the rotation of the earth below it was changing the position of the pendulum's swing (Figure 45).

Foucault pendulum in the Pantheon, Paris

Figure 45. In the Foucault pendulum, an iron ball hangs at the end of a 200-foot (61-meter) steel wire. The pendulum is drawn to one side and tied with thread in that position. When the thread is burned through, the pendulum starts swinging slowly. The heavy pendulum keeps to the same direction of swing and the earth rotates below it. In the northern hemisphere it rotates clockwise, in the southern hemisphere counterclockwise.

Due to the spin of the earth, the earth's axis always points in the same direction in space—to the North Star, Polaris, and to the South Celestial Pole. The spinning earth is rather like a spinning top or gyroscope.

In the London Science Museum, the Foucault pendulum is 82 feet (24.98 meters) long and the bob weighs 13.62 kilograms. To make sure the pendulum swings smoothly, the pendulum is not set in motion by hand; a flame is used to burn through a holding thread to start the swing. The plane of the swing of the pendulum turns about 11.75 degrees for each hour.

Foucault Pendulum and the Spin of the Earth

What you need: large bowl; cork powder (rub cork on sandpaper); soot or charcoal dust; for pendulum bob—a lead sinker or a small ball of modeling clay with a sewing needle stuck through it; three knitting needles; plate of water; map of northern hemisphere (photocopy from atlas) to fit over plate; thread; small screw eye; cork

Show the spin of the earth on its axis

1. Fill the bowl with water and place it somewhere it will not be disturbed. Sprinkle the cork dust evenly over the surface of the water. Now make a narrow radial line on it with the soot, continuing the line up the edge of the bowl (Figure 46).

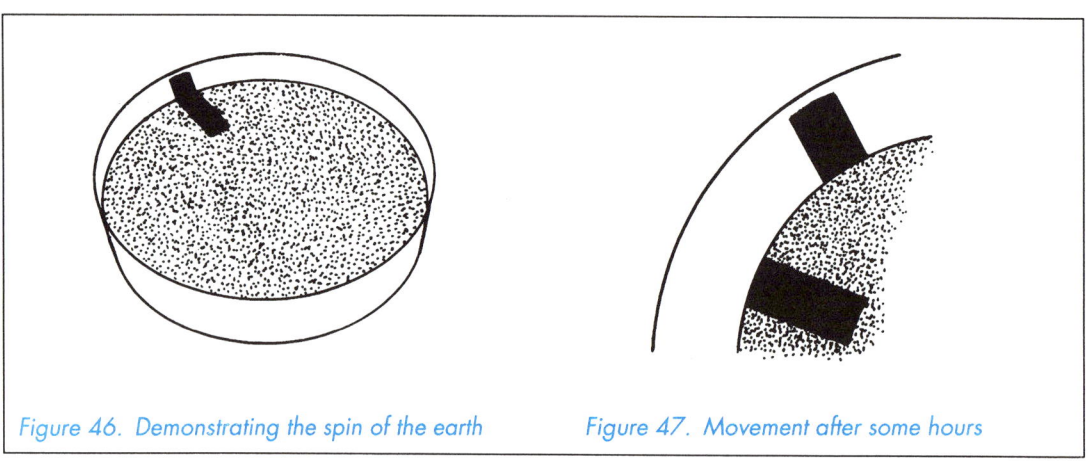

Figure 46. Demonstrating the spin of the earth   Figure 47. Movement after some hours

2. Look at the bowl in a few hours' time. What do you notice about the mark? Which way does the mark seem to have turned? Why has the bowl turned? What is left behind as the bowl turns (Figure 47)?

Make a Foucault pendulum

Screw the screw eye into the center of the base of the cork, making sure it is secure. Then stick the sharp ends of the three knitting needles into the cork to form a tripod on the plate of water. Tie one end of the thread to the loop of the sinker, then pass the free end through the screw eye, adjusting the length so that the pointed end of the sinker almost touches the water surface in the plate. Tie here. Place the map of the northern hemisphere on the water surface (Figure 48). Set your pendulum swinging. Then, evenly and very gently, rotate the plate. This represents the rotation of the earth. What do you notice about the swing of the pendulum? In your small-scale model of Foucault's famous experiment, what does the plate with the map represent? What about the cork?

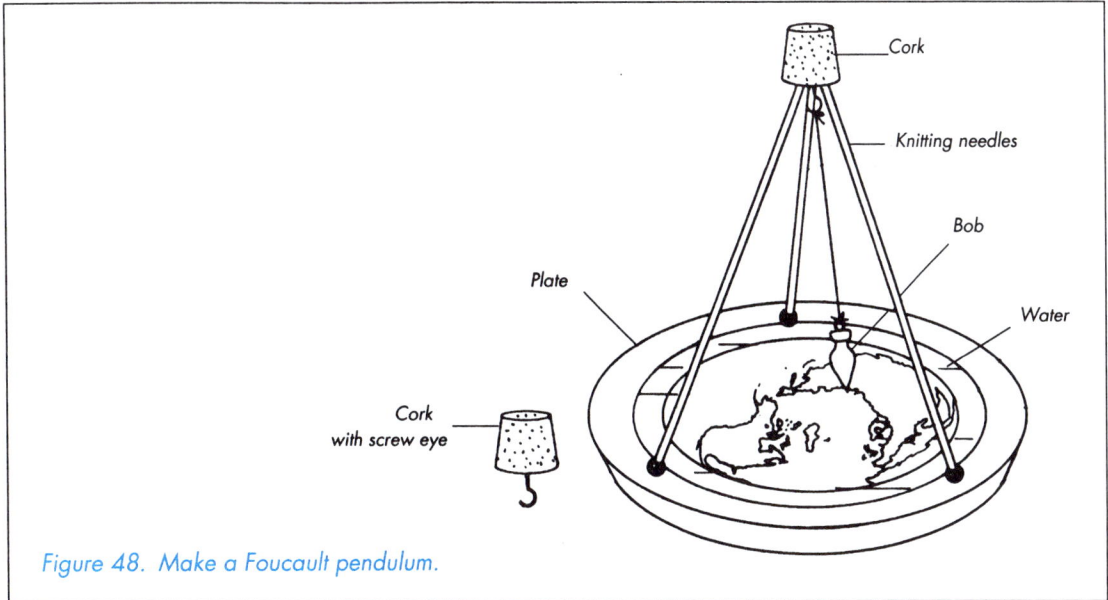

Figure 48. Make a Foucault pendulum.

14. Space and Matter

Galileo said that all objects fall at the same rate. Albert Einstein, in a great flash of imagination, stated that objects get their moving orders from space, not from the distant earth. One of Einstein's happiest thoughts was that when an object is in free fall, as from a roof or aircraft, there is no gravity (see Figure 49).

Figure 49. The boy is weighing himself on the scales. If the earth beneath his feet were whipped away, he would be in the state of free fall. Einstein would say that in such a situation there is no gravity. What would be the reading on the scales?

Suppose you toss a ball to a friend; in flight, it follows an arc. But if the ground beneath you were cut away, leaving you in free fall, the ball would travel in a straight line, free from gravity (Figure 50). In a spacecraft in free fall around the earth, where there is no gravity, the tossed ball would also travel in a straight line. Just as Einstein had predicted, the falling object gets its moving orders from space.

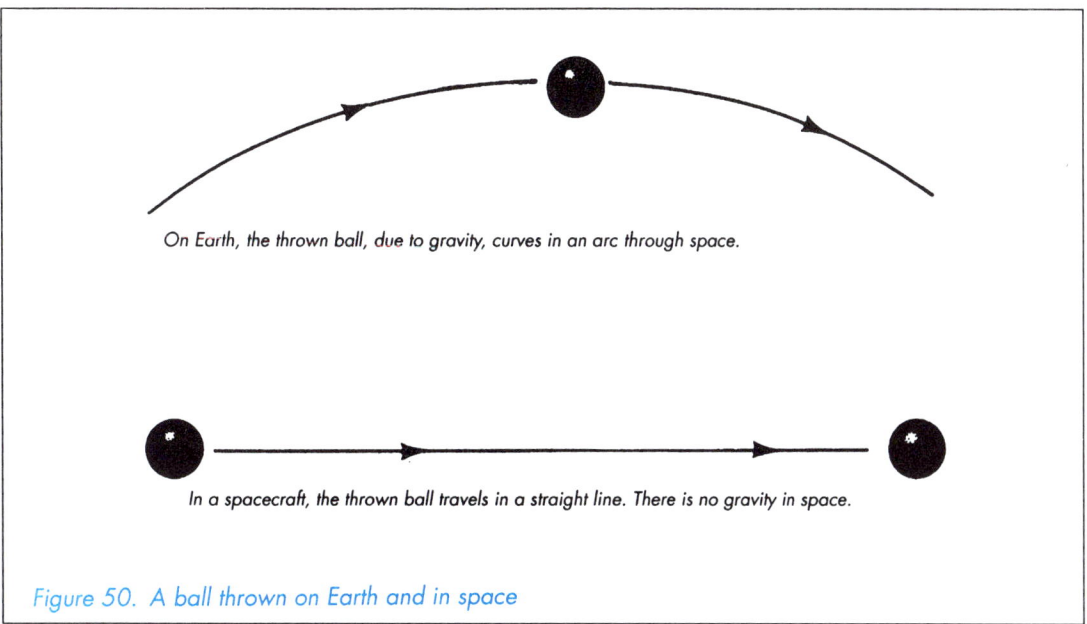

Figure 50. A ball thrown on Earth and in space

When you stand on a trampoline you dent or warp it. In the same way, Einstein said, a massive body like the earth dents or warps the space around it. Warped space was Einstein's way of thinking. So Skylab, instead of traveling in a straight line, went in a circle.

In Einstein's view, space tells matter how to move; matter tells space how to curve. The planet going in its orbit around the sun gets its moving orders not from the sun but from space itself; the same thing holds for the moon going around the earth. Taking away the earth would "unwarp" space and the moon would fly off in a beautiful straight line. What would happen to the earth if the sun were taken away?

But how can nothingness have shape? In Einstein's view, space and what fills space are all one together—there is no such thing as empty space without a gravity field. Einstein's view would be that the properties of space are not independent but are determined by matter.

Einstein's Ideas

You can experiment with some of Einstein's ideas about space and matter.

What you need: plastic mesh (garden windbreak mesh) or sheet about 50 cm square; small balloon filled with water; ball bearing; drawing pins; tape; two desks of the same height

1. Use the drawing pins and tape to fix the plastic mesh between desks. You want to create a level surface without any wrinkles (Figure 51). Place the small balloon of water, representing a massive body such as the earth, at the center of the mesh sheet, which symbolizes space (Figure 52). What do you see happen? What is matter telling space to do? What is warped space? Who gave us this view of space?

2. Roll a ball bearing, representing the moon, toward the warp in the plastic. With practice you should be able to get the "moon" to go into orbit around the "earth" (Figure 53). What gives the moon its moving orders in space? What is space telling matter to do? Take away the balloon representing the earth. What happens to space? What did Einstein mean when he said this would unwarp space? Now roll the ball bearing across the mesh. Make sure the sheet is flat and level. How does the ball bearing travel now? Does this agree with Einstein's ideas?

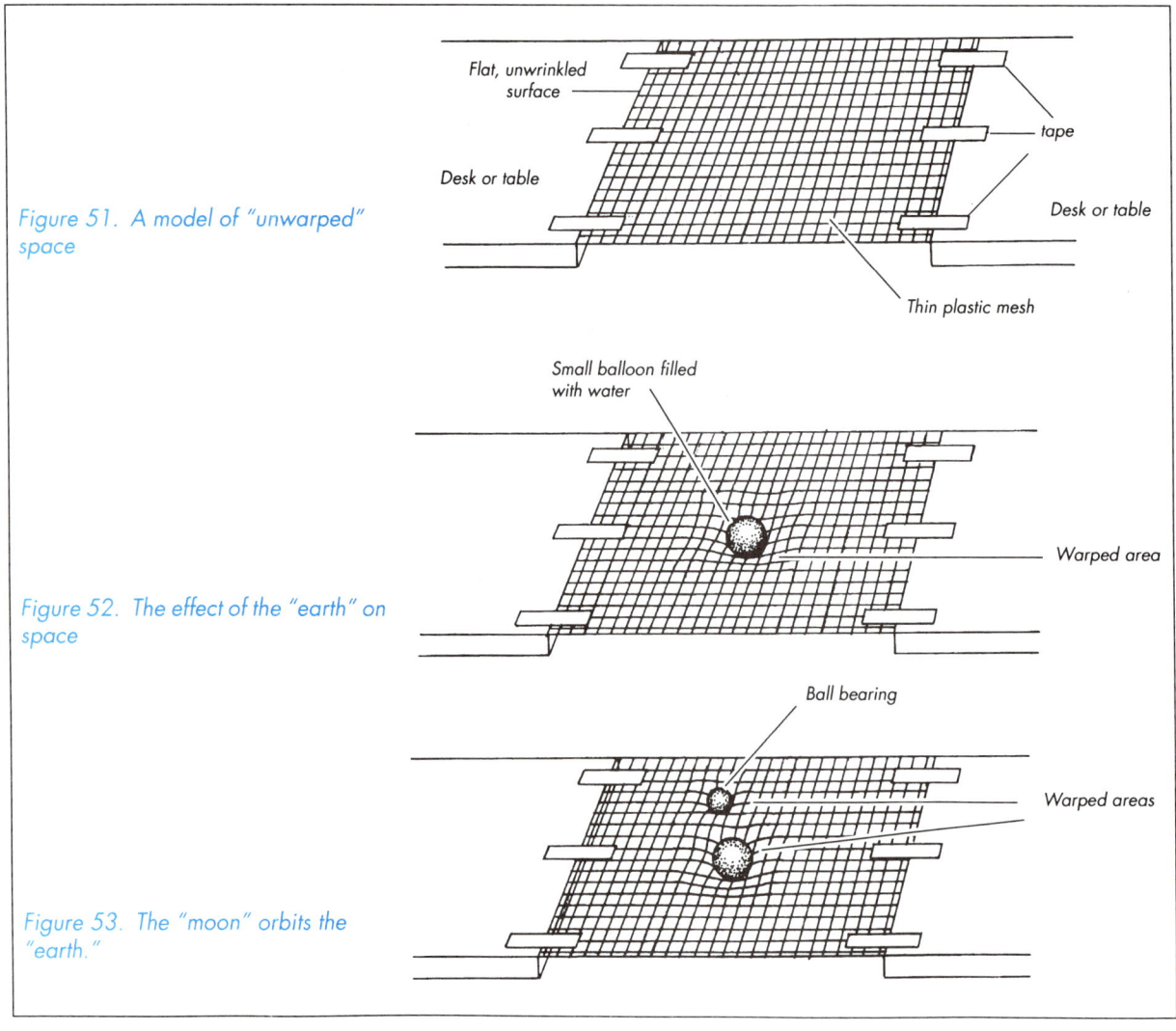

Figure 51. A model of "unwarped" space

Figure 52. The effect of the "earth" on space

Figure 53. The "moon" orbits the "earth."

3. Use a trampoline to demonstrate Einstein's ideas of matter and space. A partner, representing a huge mass such as the sun, stands in the trampoline, representing space. What is matter doing to space? What was the word Einstein used to describe this? Roll in a heavy ball, representing a planet, so that it orbits the "sun." What is space telling matter to do? "Matter tells space how to curve, space tells matter how to move" was Einstein's way of thinking. Discuss this statement. How does your experiment show this? Write a paragraph.

4. Isaac Newton said the orbits of the planets in space always stay the same. But Einstein said the ellipses corresponding to the orbits of the planets swivel around in space. The orbit of Mercury has been studied over a period of years by the radio telescope. Research what has been discovered. Whose ideas give us a truer picture of the universe—Newton's or Einstein's?

15. The Twinkling of Stars

Twinkling—changes in the brightness, color, and position of a star—is a trembling motion of light from the stars. When we look up at the stars they often seem to change in brightness and color. Stars near the horizon show the twinkling best (Figure 54).

Figure 54. What causes the twinkling of stars? As light from a star enters the earth's atmosphere it seems to wobble or dance about. Magnification by telescope can make matters worse.

This effect is caused by the earth's atmosphere and has nothing to do with the stars themselves. The twinkling is caused by small pockets of hot and cold air moving through the atmosphere between the star and our eyes. This produces uneven bending or refraction of the light from the stars so that the starlight entering our eyes shows trembles and changes in color (Figure 55).

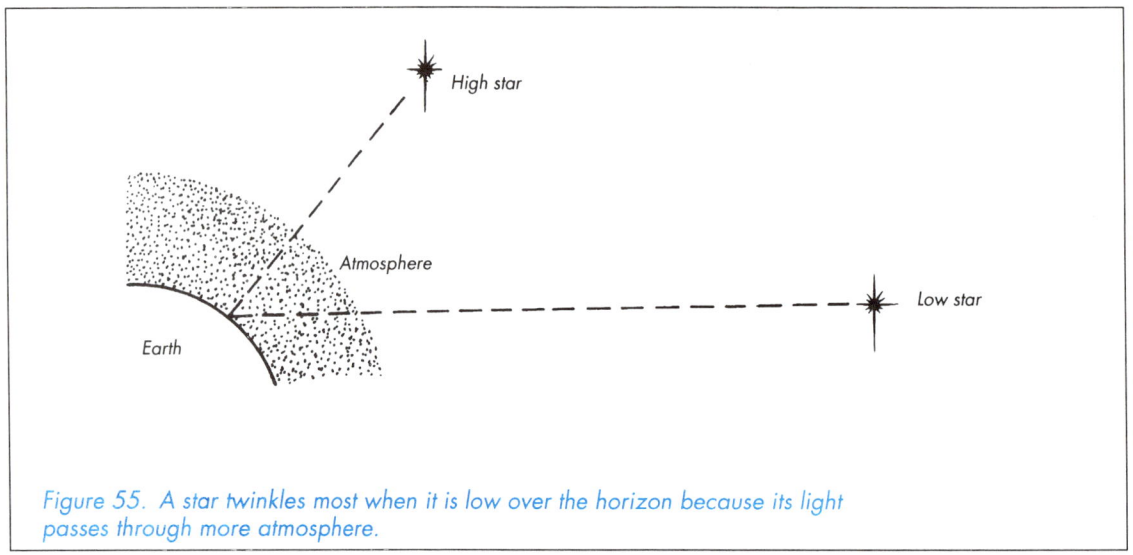

Figure 55. A star twinkles most when it is low over the horizon because its light passes through more atmosphere.

Twinkling is a nuisance to an astronomer; in order to reduce it, observatories are built high up mountains. By placing telescopes in satellites, which orbit the earth high above the atmosphere, twinkling is avoided. Since planets are closer to us than stars, they show as small discs rather than as points of light and so do not twinkle. But Mercury and Mars, when close to the horizon, may be seen to twinkle a little.

How Stars Twinkle

What you need: flashlight; electric toaster or heater; screen or wall

1. Place the toaster or heater between yourself and a window. Switch on the toaster and look over the hot glowing elements at objects outside. What do you notice about the objects—do they seem to shimmer? What is causing uneven bending or refraction of the light? How is this similar to what happens with starlight?

2. Try this experiment in a darkened room if possible. Arrange the flashlight beam to shine on the wall or screen. Place the heater or toaster between the light and the wall (Figure 56). What do you notice about the light on the wall?

Does it seem to flicker or shimmer? Explain why. How is this like looking at stars on nights of "bad seeing"?

3. Next time you have a barbecue, look over the glowing coals to objects beyond. What do you notice? Are the objects uneven? Flickering? How do your experiments help you to understand why stars twinkle?

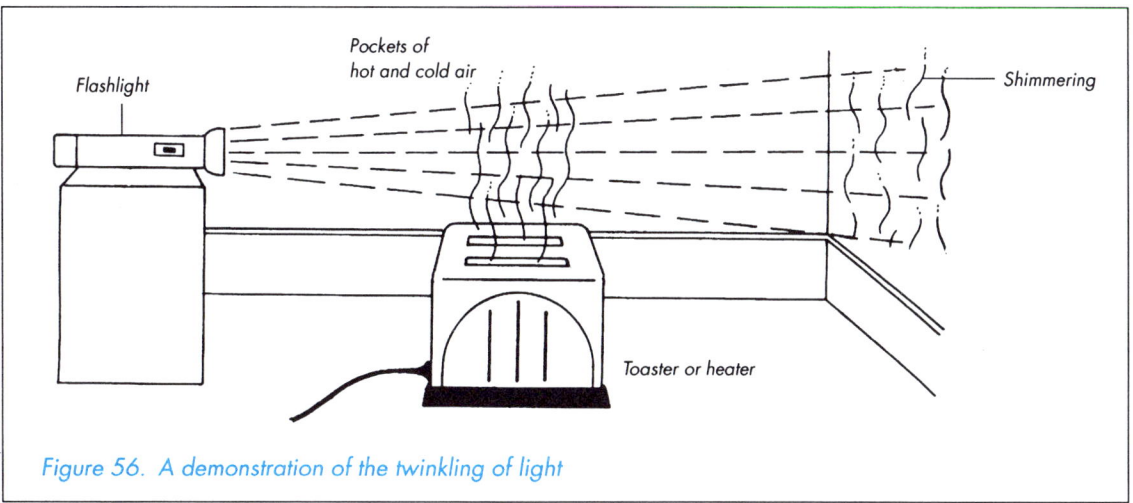

Figure 56. A demonstration of the twinkling of light

16. Dust Clouds in Space

All the stars we see in the sky—and billions more we cannot see because they are too faint—belong to the Milky Way galaxy, a huge family of some 200 billion stars moving through space. Our sun, Earth, and the other planets of our solar system are like a tiny speck quietly tucked away in one of the outer suburbs of the galaxy, about two-thirds of the way out from the center. Here is a region containing millions of hot stars, dust, and gas, and pinwheeling away from this are great spiral arms, which likewise contain billions of stars, dust clouds, and gas.

The dust and gas are part of the structure of the galaxy. Where the dust and gas particles are thicker, they show as dark patches, dust lanes, or clouds within the Milky Way. Like a curtain or veil drawn across the sky, they dim or block the light of stars beyond.

The Horse-Head Nebula in the constellation of Orion (Figure 57) is such a dense cloud of dust and gas, while just by the two brightest stars of the Southern Cross is the Coal Sack (Figure 58), a dark mass of dust and gas that blocks the light from faraway stars and so dims our view of the sky. Clouds of gas and dust called nebulae, which absorb light, seem to be present in much of space between the stars.

You may have noticed that fog dims and reddens the headlights of an approaching car. In a similar way, one of the effects of dust clouds in space is to make light from distant stars dimmer and redder than it really is.

The Dimming Effect of Haze and Fog

What you need: plastic sheets of different colors; balloons; electric lamp

Figure 57. Nebulae are great clouds of gas and dust found throughout the systems of stars. The Great Nebula in Orion is typical of gaseous galactic nebulae.

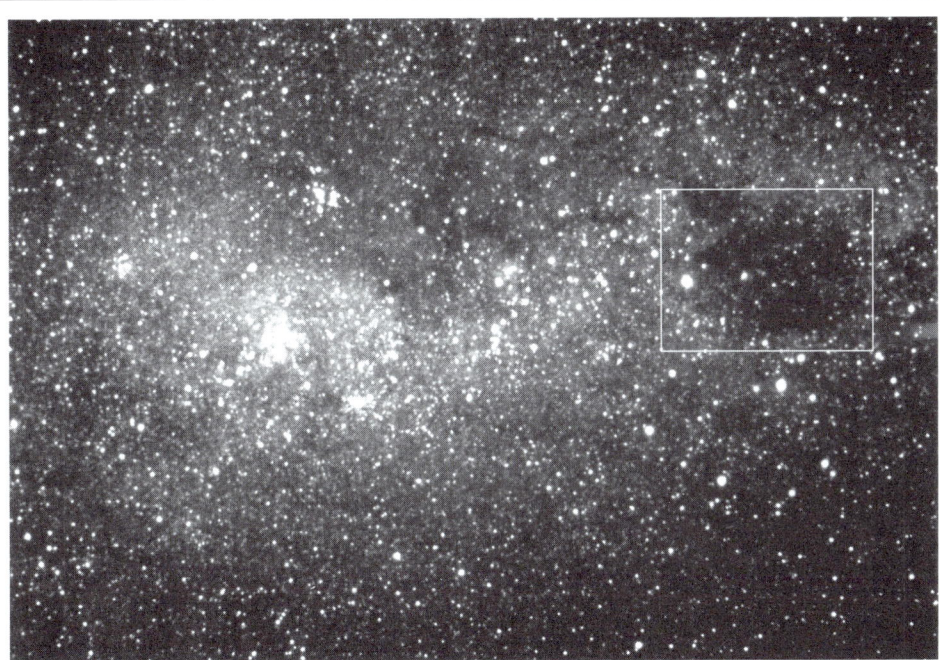

Figure 58. The Coal Sack (see box) is a dark mass of gas and dust that borders the two brightest stars of the Southern Cross, Alpha Crucis and Beta Crucis. It can only be seen in the southern hemisphere.

1. Switch on the electric lamp and look at it through a piece of dark plastic (see Figure 59a). How does the plastic affect the amount of light coming to your eye? How is this like astronomers looking at distant stars through masses of gas and dust out in space?

2. Try this with different colored plastics. Does the color of the plastic make any difference? Does the thickness? Try two thicknesses.

3. Blow up a dark-colored balloon and look at the light through it (Figure 59b). What happens to your view of the lamp as you slowly let air out of the balloon? Does the size of the lamp change? Does the color change? Does the lamp disappear altogether? How does the color of the balloon affect what you see? Does the shape matter? What happens when you blow up the balloon more?

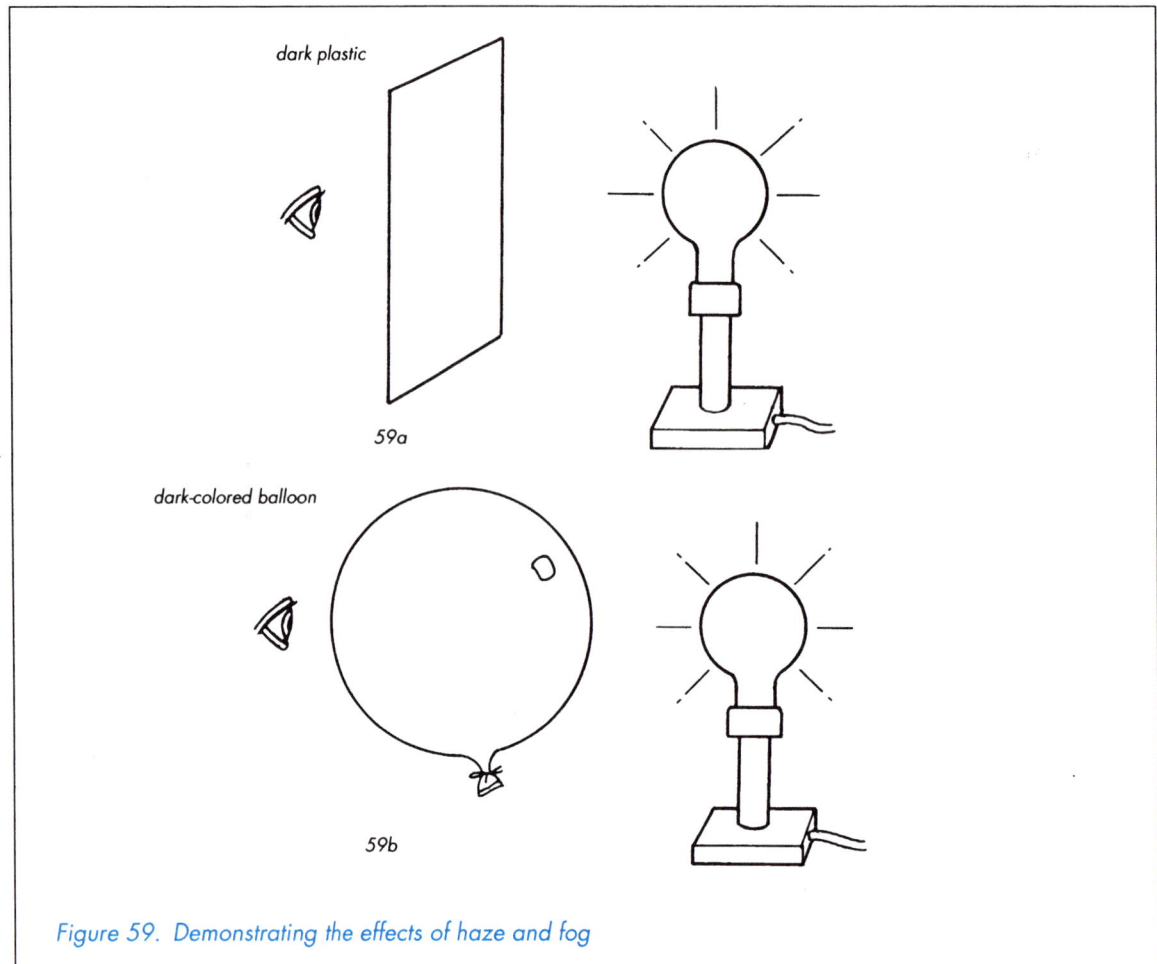

Figure 59. Demonstrating the effects of haze and fog

4. Seen through a fog, a car's headlights look red. See if you can find out why. If the fog becomes thicker, what happens to the light? If the fog lightens, what happens? If you move farther away from the headlights so that you are looking through more fog, what happens to the light?

5. At the center of the Milky Way galaxy, there are enormous amounts of gas and dust and the light is dimmed a thousand billion times. This means that astronomers cannot see into the center of our own galaxy. But radio astronomy is helping them to see into this fascinating region. Find out how.

17. Why Is the Sky Dark at Night?

A German astronomer named Wilhelm Olbers believed the universe contained such a large number of stars and galaxies that they could not be counted. Each star gives out light and some of this light reaches Earth no matter how far away the star is (Figure 60).

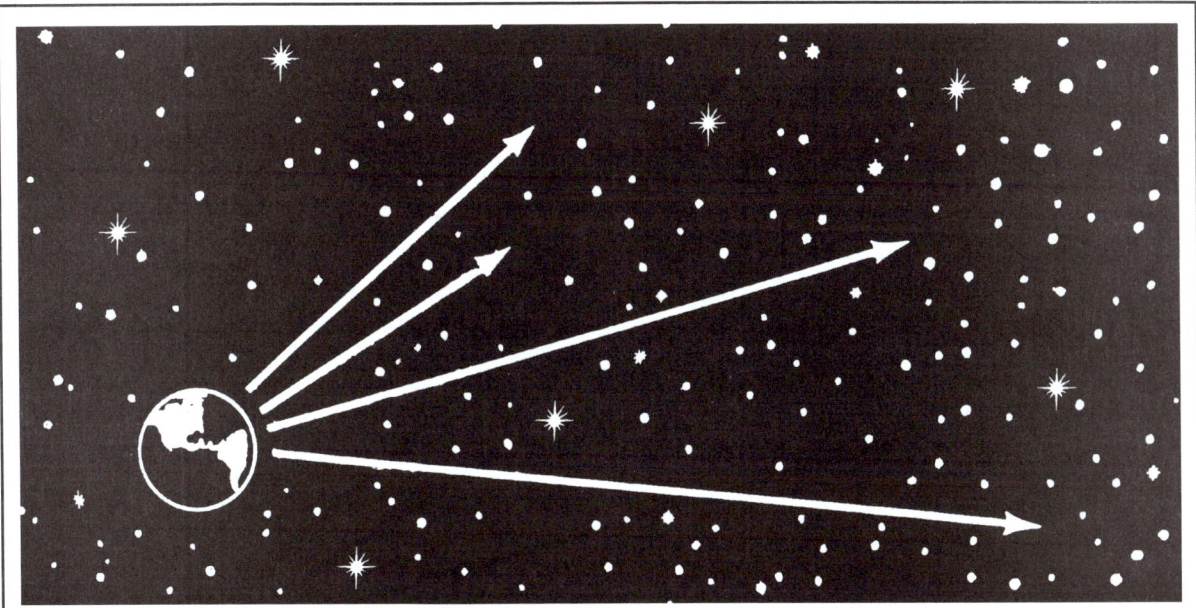

Figure 60. Olbers's paradox is that whichever way we look far out into space there is bound to be a star. In that case, why does the sky appear dark?

Olbers went on to say that if light from all these stars—so many that they could not be counted—was arriving at Earth from every direction, then the sky at night should be brilliantly bright. This is because wherever you look in space there is bound to be a star, and this would make the sky as light as day everywhere. The fact that this idea does not work and that the sky is dark at night is sometimes known as Olbers's paradox.

Part of the answer to this paradox lies in the fact that the universe is expanding. Because the universe is moving away from us, the light from stars is reddened; the farther away a star or galaxy is, the redder or darker the light. As energy has been taken away from the light, we do not see the distant star or galaxy in its true brightness. Very distant galaxies may contribute no light at all to the night sky.

The sun is another reason. As the sun sinks below the horizon, the rays slant through more and more atmosphere so that more and more light is absorbed. With the reddening of the sky at sunset, more and more light is taken away, the sky becomes dark with light from the stars, and planets sparkle like brilliant gemstones against the velvet black of night.

How Light Is Absorbed

What you need: aquarium or other glass or plastic container; flashlight or projector; milk; white paper or card for screen, sodium thiosulphate (photographer's hypo or fixative); vinegar; stirrer

1. Fill the aquarium with water and stir in a little milk. Then shine a beam of light from a flashlight or projector through the water so that it falls on the screen (Figure 61). What is the color of the light on the screen? How has the light been absorbed? What happens when you add more milk? Describe any color changes. How is this light like passing to us from the stars far out in space? **Note:** Before going on to the next step, empty and rinse out the aquarium.

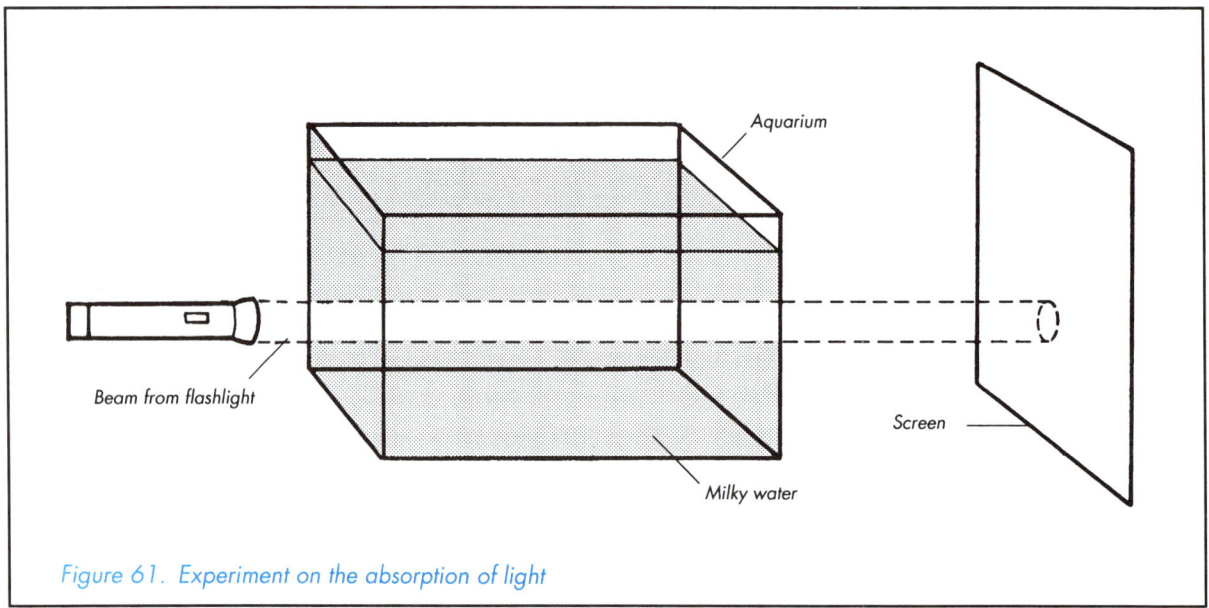

Figure 61. Experiment on the absorption of light

2. Make up a weak solution of sodium thiosulphate in your aquarium. Use 4–5 tablespoons of thiosulphate per liter of water and stir to dissolve. Now stir in one teaspoon (5 ml) of vinegar per liter. What do you notice about the liquid? As the liquid becomes denser, what happens to the color of the light on the screen? How does the color of the light change when seen from the side? How does this show us that tiny particles take away light?

3. How do your experiments help you to see why the sky is dark at night? How does the idea of an expanding universe play a part?

18. Algol—the Demon Star

> *The great beauty of astronomy is not what is incomprehensible in it, but its comprehensibility—its geometrical exactitude.*
>
> —William Hale White
> *Religion and Art of William Hale White*
> by Wilfred Stone

The sun, moon, and stars held a great fascination for the Arabs, who were among the early astronomers. The Arabs noted that one bright star in the constellation Perseus (Figure 62) seemed to wink at them every three days. This, they thought, was a bad omen, so they named the star *al ghul*, meaning the "ghoul" or "demon" star.

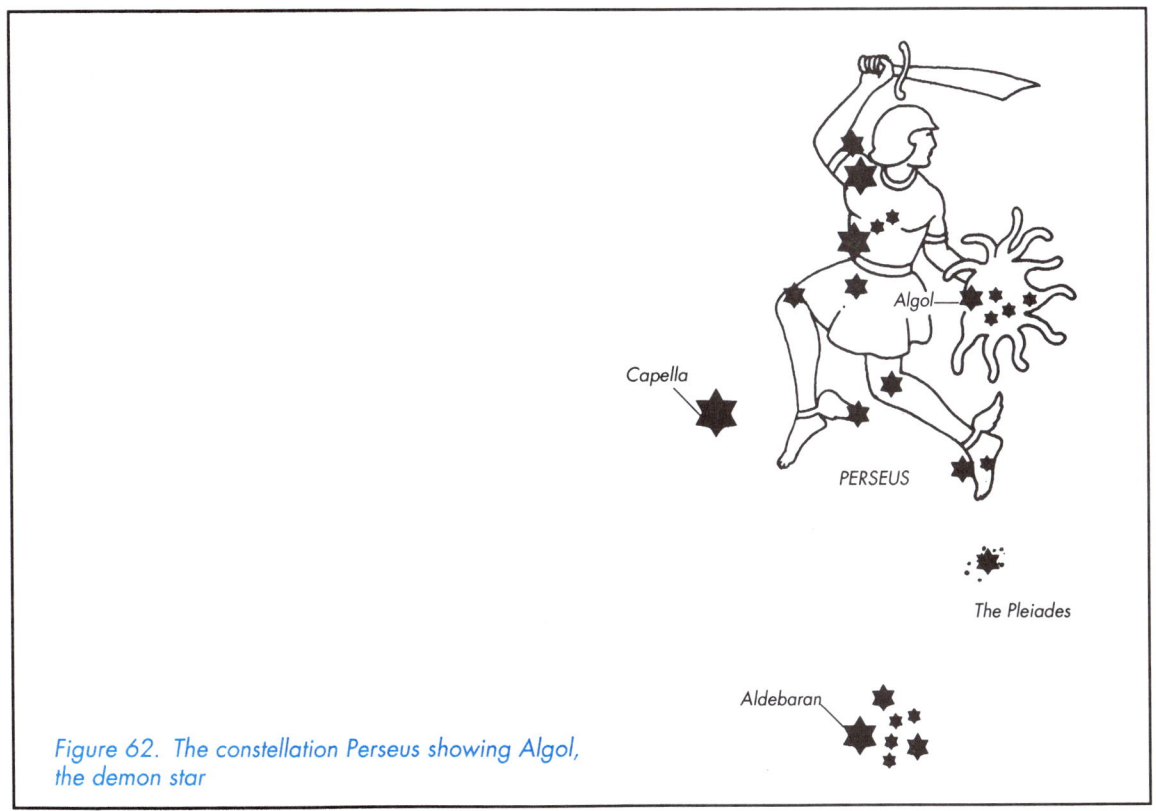

Figure 62. The constellation Perseus showing Algol, the demon star

In 1783 John Goodricke, an English astronomer, was first to put forward the idea that the wink or change in light was caused by a darker star in orbit around a brighter one. This meant that one star was eclipsing the other and cutting off the light for a time.

Stars such as these are called variable stars, as their light is constantly varying. Pairs of stars, also known as double stars or binaries, are very common in space. The two stars stay as a pair rotating in space, rather like a pair of dumbbells rotating about their joining bar (Figure 63).

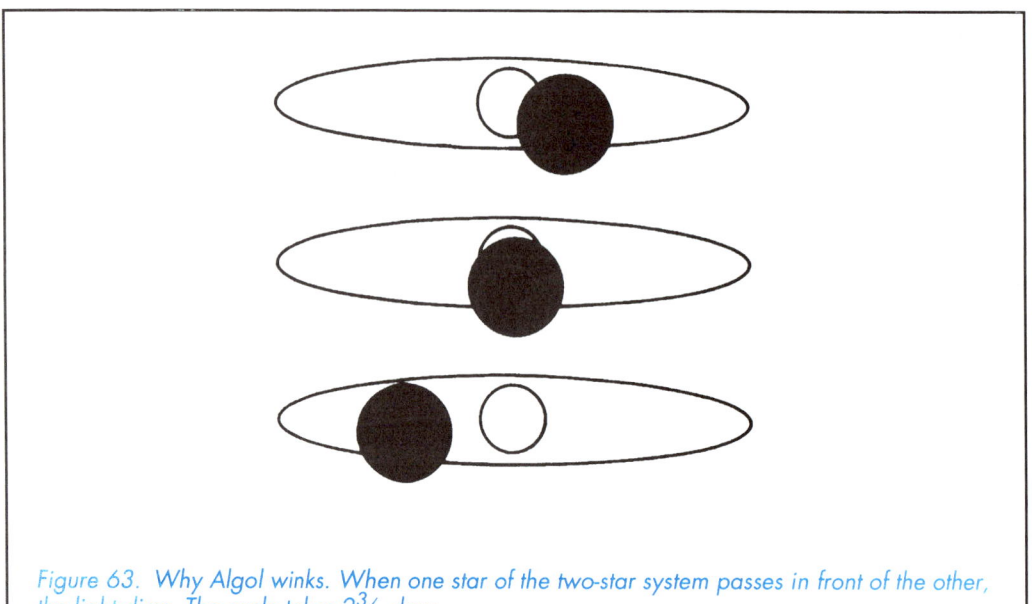

Figure 63. Why Algol winks. When one star of the two-star system passes in front of the other, the light dims. The cycle takes $2^3/_4$ days.

Because the light from Algol is changing, it is possible to draw a light curve. The curve shows how the light varies with time because one star passes in front of, or eclipses, the other during each orbit.

Variable Stars

You can make a model to show how the light varies when one star eclipses or passes in front of another.

What you need: reading lamp with 75–100 watt lamp to represent the brighter star of the pair; a ball about 10 cm across on a string—the second star of the pair; a light meter or camera with built-in light meter.

Do this experiment in a darkened room.

1. Stand about 2 meters from the reading lamp. If you are using a camera, look through it at the pointer on the scale of the light meter. Adjust your distance from the lamp to give you about a half-scale reading of the pointer (Figure 64). What is the reading shown?

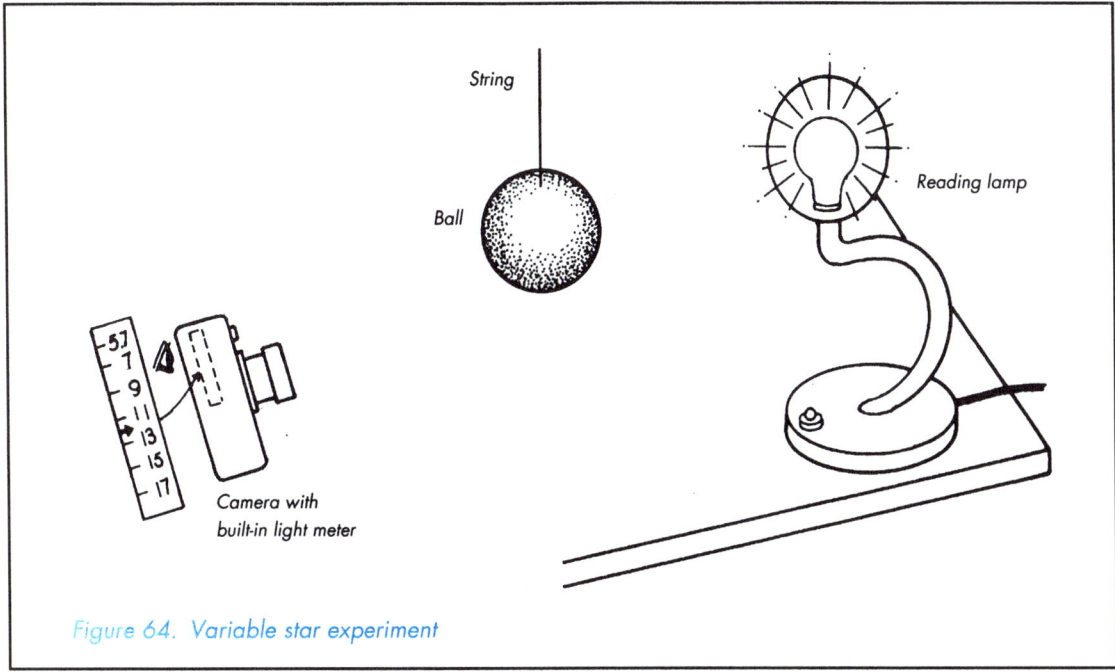

Figure 64. Variable star experiment

2. Have a partner move the ball between the lamp and the camera, about halfway between. What happens to the light reading? What is the value now? Why the change? What is the term that describes the two stars in this position? What actually does happens when Algol winks? How often does the wink take place?

3. Have your partner move the ball in a circular path (orbit) at an even speed around the lamp. Do this 4–5 times. What happens each time the ball passes between you and the lamp? How is this like what is happening to Algol?

19. Space Navigation

People have drawn maps since very early times, yet even today we do not know exactly how far apart the continents are, or where some islands are. Some scientists think the continents are drifting so that the distances between them are always changing. Where a place is on the face of the earth—its latitude and longitude—is important in navigation.

One instrument used to tell us where we are on Earth is the sextant. By sighting on the sun or a star we are able to find our position at sea. A very accurate clock called a chronometer (radio and satellite signals are now used) is used to give longitude. Where the lines of latitude and longitude meet on a map gives the place where the readings were made.

Spacecraft can tell their position in space using a similar system. The spacecraft sights on a known object—such as a star, the sun, or another satellite—at a certain time and so is able to check its position in space. If necessary, the spacecraft can correct its own flight course. The first *Mariner* space probe to Mars flew by the planet in December 1962. During its 8½ month journey, *Mariner's* sensors were locked onto the bright star Canopus so that the spacecraft could navigate its way through the inky blackness of space.

Make a Sextant

You can make a simple sextant and use it to determine your latitude.

What you need: protractor; drinking straw; paper clip; thread; adhesive tape; atlas or globe

1. Using tape, attach the drinking straw to the flat edge of the protractor. Tie a piece of thread to swing free from the center of the straight edge of the protractor. Tie a heavy paper clip to the end of the thread to act as a weight (Figure 65).

2. Go outside at night and look through the drinking straw at Polaris, the Pole Star (Figure 66).

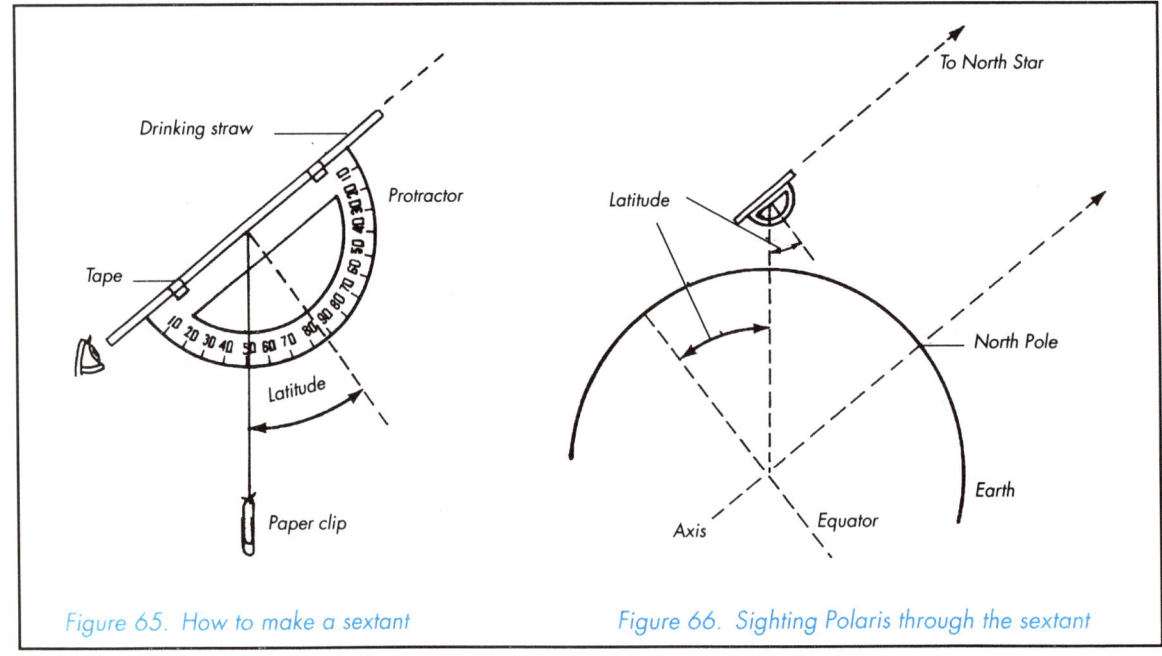

Figure 65. How to make a sextant

Figure 66. Sighting Polaris through the sextant

3. Have a partner note the number of degrees from the center of the protractor scale to the vertical string. How many degrees do you find? How does this compare with your latitude from your atlas or globe?

20. Finding Direction by the Stars

On any clear night the stars shine on high, like tiny beacons showing the way to the sailor or explorer. One of the bright stars used for navigation was Sirius, the Dog Star. The Polynesians were skillful navigators and knew that Sirius in its path across the sky passed directly over Vanua Levu, one of the islands of the Fiji group. Sirius, then, was the clue to direction.

Using Sirius as a lodestar (guide), they could travel along a great circle course (line of longitude) and were certain to arrive at their destination. For example, when they sighted Sirius directly overhead, they knew that Vanua Levu was close at hand. There was also a lodestar for sailors in the northern hemisphere. When Polaris the Pole Star was abeam on their right hand, they knew their ship was heading west—toward the sunset. Polaris is almost directly over the North Pole. If you drop a vertical from Polaris and move in that direction you are traveling due north.

In the southern hemisphere there is no bright Pole Star. But there is a point in the sky the equal of a Pole Star. To locate this point, called the Celestial South Pole, use the Southern Cross. A line drawn from the head to the foot of the Cross always points to the same spot in the sky. Due to the rotation of the earth, the Cross and other stars seem to revolve around this point. If we think of the earth as spinning on an axis like a knitting needle, then one end of the axis points to the Celestial South Pole, the other end to Polaris, the Pole Star.

The *Mariner 9* spacecraft needed a bright star at a wide angle away from the sun for its 167-day journey to the planet Mars. Canopus, the second-brightest star in the sky, met this need. Sensors on the spacecraft tracked Canopus and the sun; this ensured that the solar panels faced the sun, and that the earth antennae pointed earthward. Space engineers could then send instructions to the spacecraft to make certain it took the right direction through space to the faraway planet.

Which Way Is North?

What you need: Star (and constellation) Finder (see pp. 6–7) to help you find any of the stars and constellations mentioned here that you are not sure of.

Using the stars to tell direction

1. Find the Big Dipper and the two stars in the bowl opposite the handle; these are the Pointers (Figure 67). Draw a line from the bottom star through the upper one and it brings you to the Pole Star, Polaris. If you drop a vertical line from Polaris and walk toward it, in which direction are you traveling? Can you explain why?

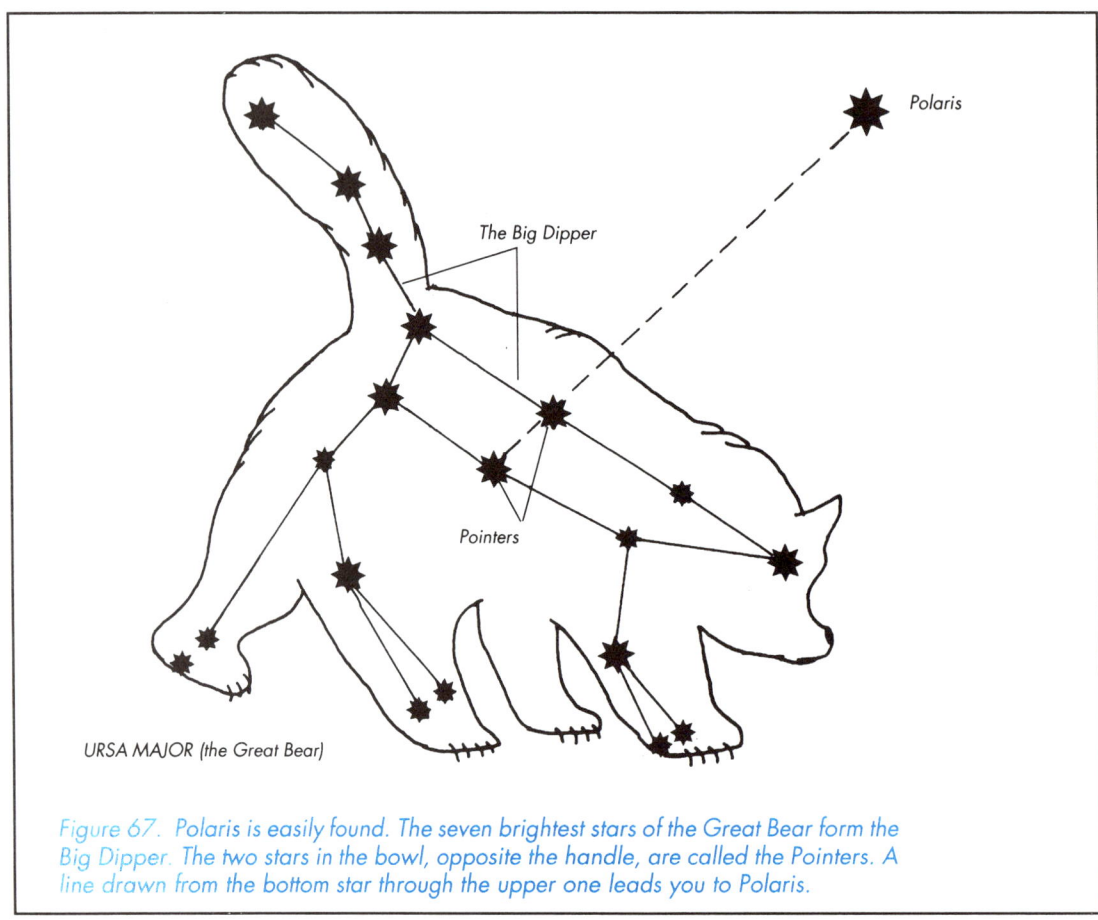

Figure 67. Polaris is easily found. The seven brightest stars of the Great Bear form the Big Dipper. The two stars in the bowl, opposite the handle, are called the Pointers. A line drawn from the bottom star through the upper one leads you to Polaris.

2. If you were at the North Pole looking up at the sky, how would the stars seem to be moving? What is the point in the sky directly above the Pole?

Using a watch to find direction

In the northern hemisphere, point the hour hand at the sun. The direction halfway between 12 o'clock and the hour hand is a north-south line (Figure 68).

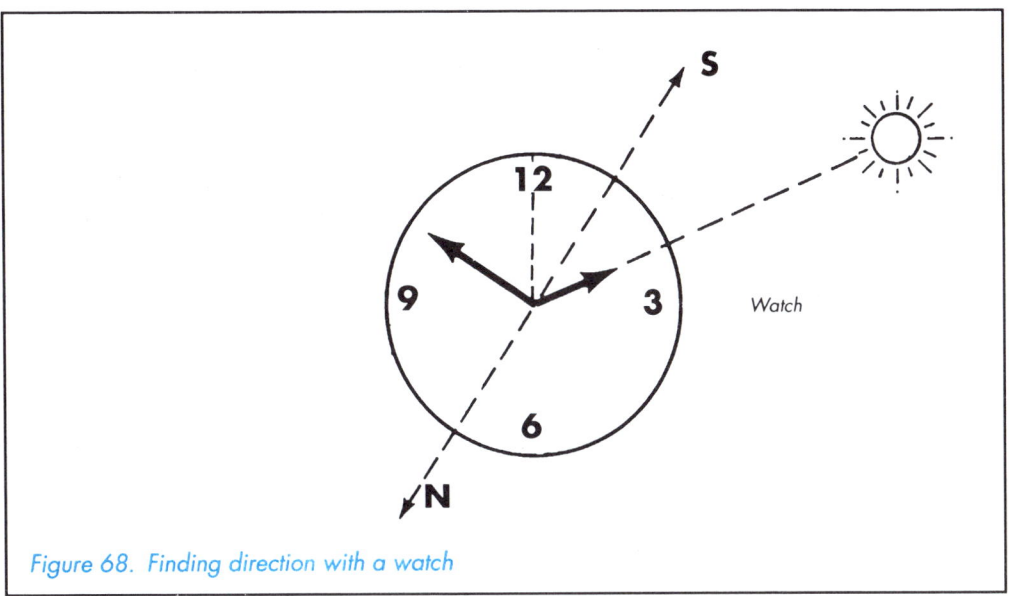

Figure 68. Finding direction with a watch

21. Comets

> *When beggars die, there are no comets seen;*
> *The heavens themselves blaze forth, the death of princes.*
>
> —Shakespeare, *Julius Caesar*

"A comet is a bright star with hair streaming from it" is one way our forefathers described these visitors from space. They saw the tail as hair streaming beautifully across the sky. Most comets are best viewed through a telescope of low power and wide field, but now and again one is bright enough to be seen with the naked eye.

All comets have the same makeup—a head surrounded by an atmosphere or coma, and a tail that grows as the comet nears the sun. The nucleus within the head is thought to be composed of dust, bits of rock, ice, and frozen gases such as ammonia and methane (marsh gas). As a comet gets closer to the sun, its brightness increases. Brightness also depends on how near to Earth its path takes. In 1910, Halley's Comet came so close that the earth passed through its tail and the comet was a very bright object indeed. But in the 1985–86 visit, the comet was some 60 million kilometers distant, brightness was much less, and the tail was nowhere near us (Figure 69).

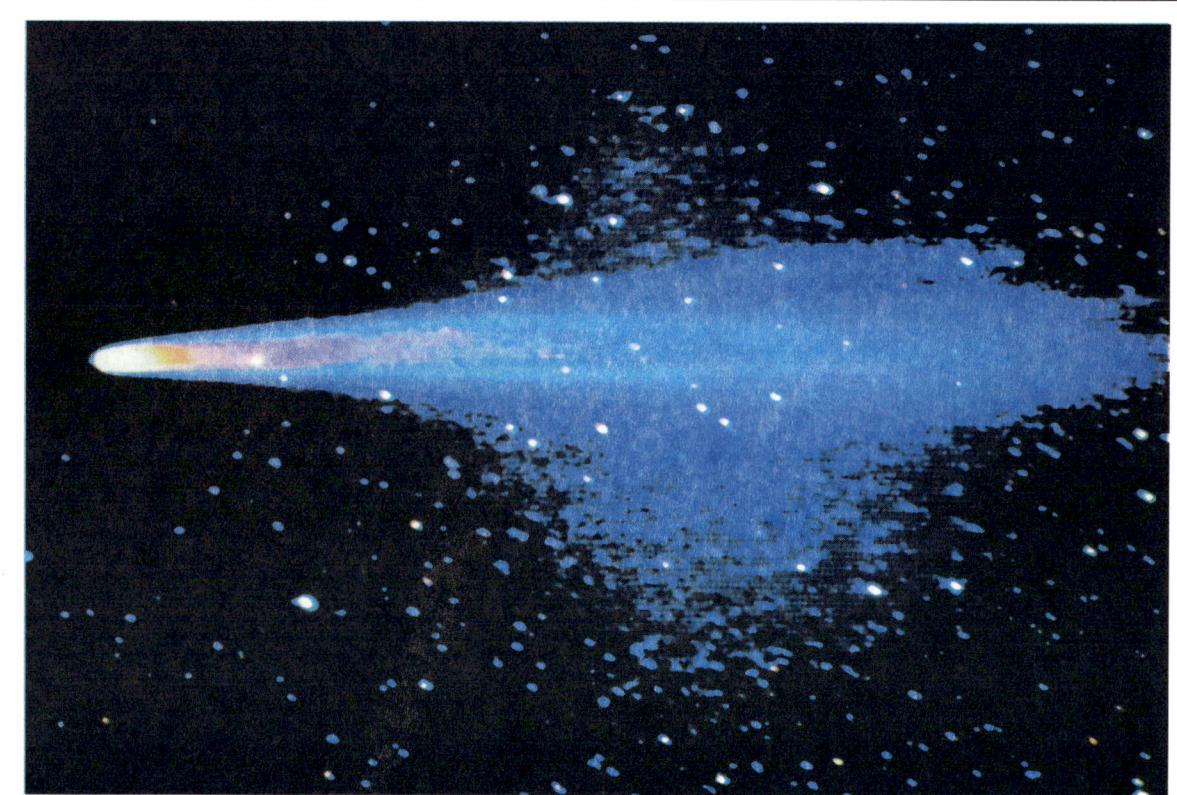

Figure 69. Halley's Comet as it passed close to Earth in 1986

Astronomers think that the sun and its family of planets formed from a nebula, a great whirling merry-go-round of gases out in space. The particles in the nebula came together due to gravity, then grew and grew to produce the sun and the planets. The inner planets, being nearer the sun, do not have much snow and ice; but the outer planets are mainly frozen matter; this is more like what comets are made of. So comets are looked on as materials left over from the formation of the solar system. The Dutch astronomer Jan Oort thinks there is a vast cloud of comets far outside the solar system. The gravity tug of a nearby star disturbs the young comets in the cloud; they enter the solar system and head for the sun. Comets are thought to be destructive and may have caused the death of the dinosaurs some 65 million years ago. Due to inertia (mass) and speed, a comet striking the earth would cause a mighty explosion. A cloud of dust over the earth would cut off the sun's light and heat, and all life would probably perish. (On a smaller scale, this might have happened in Siberia in 1908 in what is known as the Tunguska Event.)

On March 14, 1986, the *Giotto* spacecraft flew within 500 kilometers of the nucleus of Halley's Comet and carried out scientific experiments. The results of these will add greatly to our knowledge of these mysterious visitors from space.

As a comet approaches the sun, frozen matter sublimes off and outgassing occurs. It follows from this that each time a comet goes around the sun, it loses matter. This means that comets are not with us for too long, so new comets must constantly replace the old.

Some Properties of Comets

What you need: ruler; ammonium chloride; test tube; burner; glass; card; coin; water; strip of water; shuttlecock; modeling clay; knitting needle; chalk; plastic pen top; plastic basin; thick plastic bag; earth; sand; pebbles; molasses; about two cups of crushed dry ice (to crush, wrap lumps of dry ice in thick newspaper and pound with a hammer)

Subliming

Some substances change directly from the solid to the vapor state without becoming a liquid—that is, unlike most substances, they do not melt. Ammonium chloride is well known for this property.

1. To show sublimation, put a teaspoonful of ammonium chloride into a heat-resistant test tube and warm it over a small flame. Watch the test tube carefully (Figure 70). What happens to the solid at the bottom of the test tube? Does it disappear? What forms in the upper, cooler part of the test tube? This is called the *sublimate*. What happens if you heat the sublimate?

2. Another common substance that sublimes is solid carbon dioxide, also called dry ice. It is dry because it changes from solid to vapor without any liquid state. This change occurs at the low temperature of –78.5°C; for this reason, dry ice is used in cold storage equipment. **Caution:** Dry ice burns, so wear gloves to handle it. Place a piece of dry ice in a small dish in front of you. Describe what happens. Explain the meaning of the terms *fusion* and *sublimation*. Make a list of the uses for dry ice.

3. Air fresheners, used to sweeten the air in rooms in the home, depend on the principle of sublimation. Can you explain how?

4. How does subliming take place in the life of a comet? In what ways does this affect a comet such as Halley's Comet?

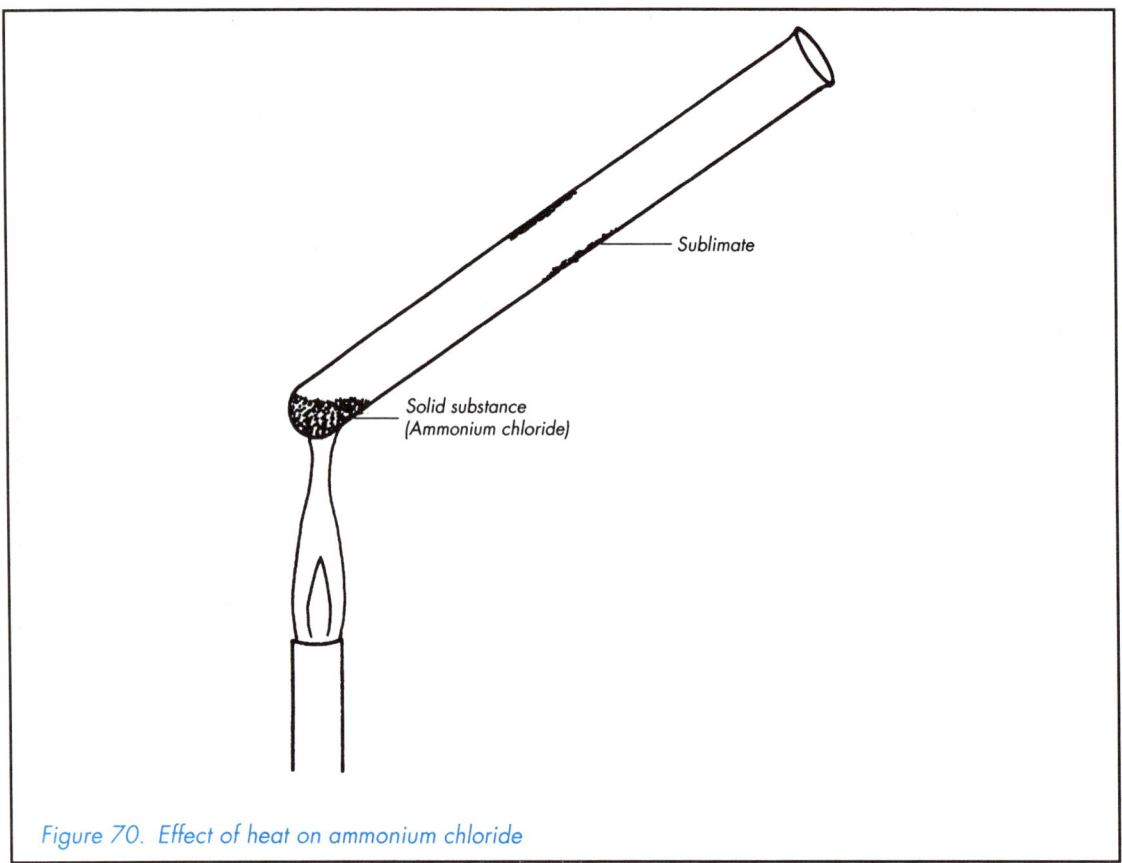

Figure 70. Effect of heat on ammonium chloride

Inertia

The tendency of a body to maintain a state of motion is called inertia. A bowling ball thrown along a lane tends to keep moving because of its inertia. It is difficult to push a car from a rest position because of its large inertia or mass. Once it starts moving, the inertia of the car makes it difficult to stop.

The masses of comets are thought to lie between 100 million tons and 100,000 billion tons. Even though this makes them less than a hundred millionth of the earth's mass, they still have considerable inertia. Comet fragments striking planets and moons cause huge craters due to their mass and speed. Comets travel in their orbits because of their inertia.

1. To show inertia, place a 10-cent piece on a card over the top of a glass (Figure 71). Now give the card a sharp flick. What happens to the card? To the coin? How does this show inertia?

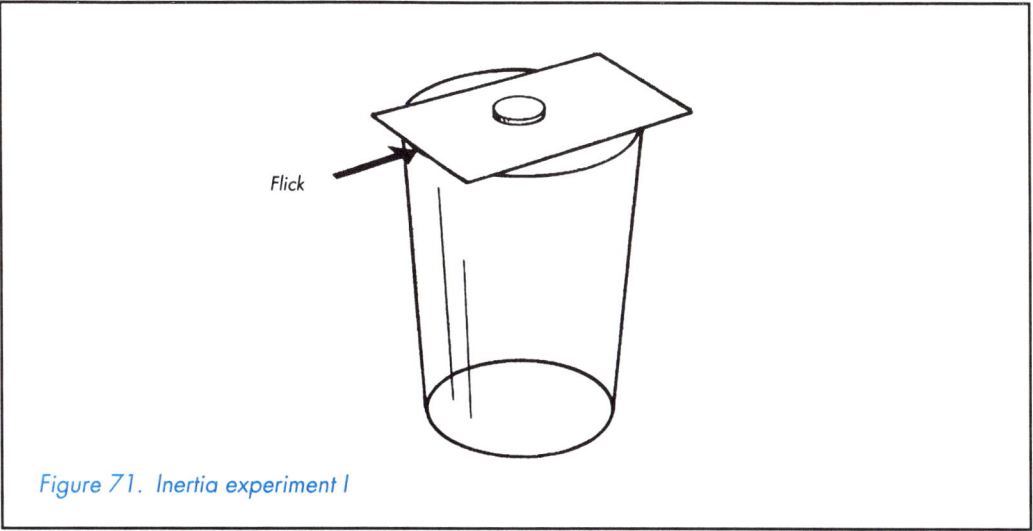

Figure 71. Inertia experiment I

2. Place a glass full of water on the end of a strip of paper (Figure 72). Move the paper slowly. What do you see the glass do? Now give the paper a sharp jerk. What happens? How is inertia at work? How does inertia keep Halley's Comet traveling over its long ellipse?

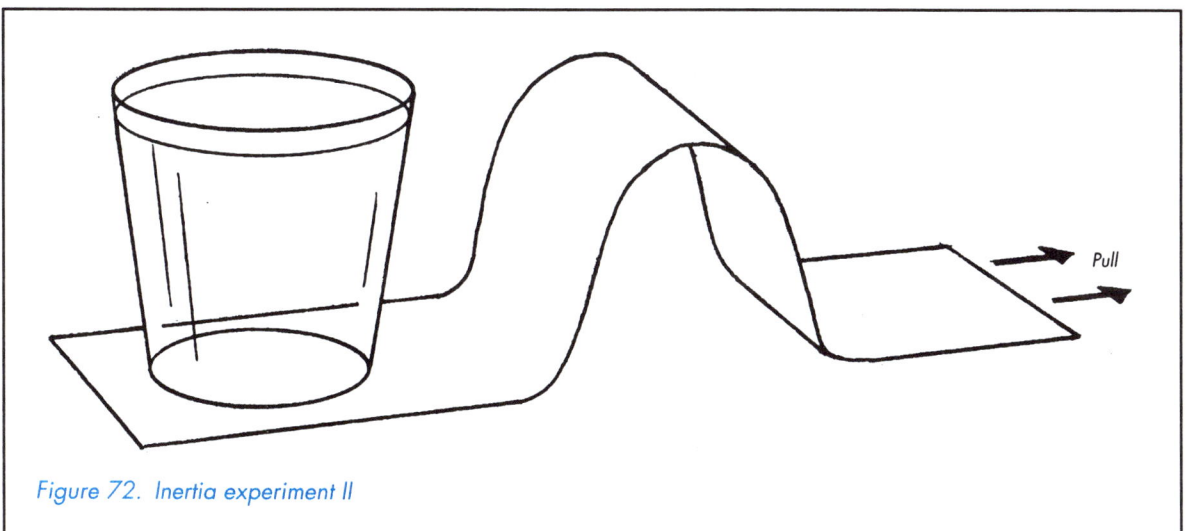

Figure 72. Inertia experiment II

Model comet

You can use a shuttlecock to make a model of a comet. The round end of the shuttlecock becomes the head of the comet, while the vanes sticking out behind are the tail. Find the balance point as well as you can by balancing the shuttlecock on one finger.

Press the plastic top of a felt-tip pen into a small piece of modeling clay and stick the opposite side of the clay ball onto the balance point. Now support the shuttlecock on a fine knitting needle, making sure it balances and rotates freely (Figure 73). Your model comet is now ready to try out. You just need a day with a strong wind or breeze blowing, to represent the solar wind.

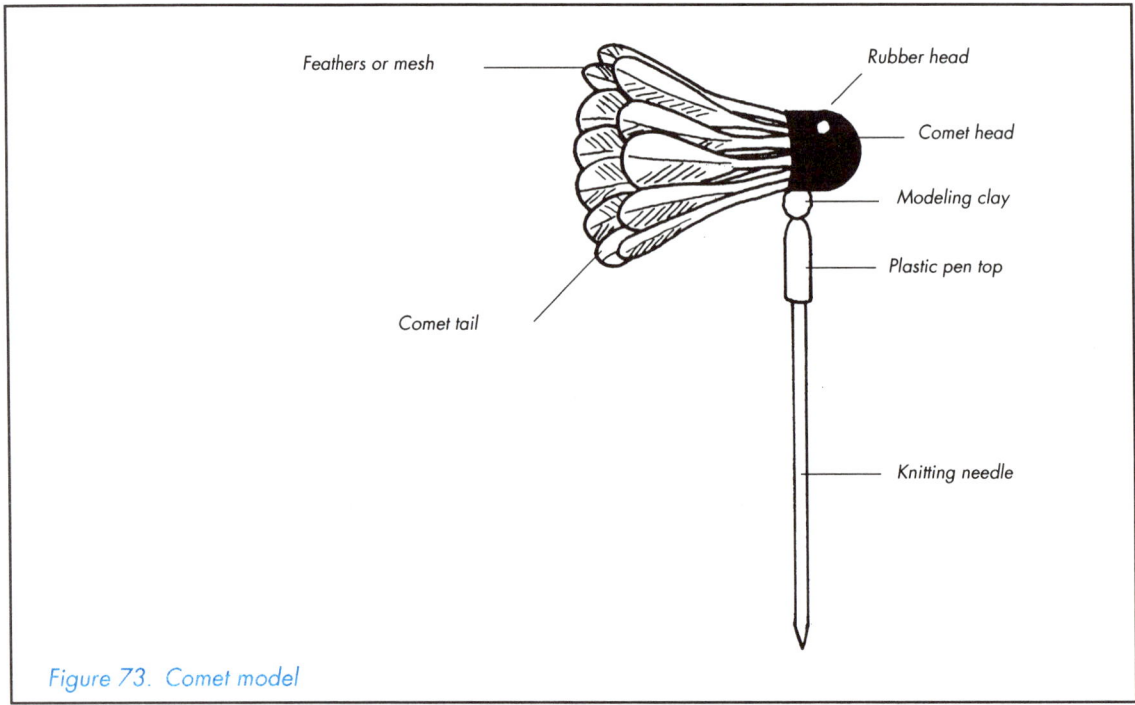

Figure 73. Comet model

Chalk out one end of a parabola on a large area of asphalt, facing into the wind. This represents the comet's path in space.

Holding the knitting needle with the model comet in one hand and away from your body, walk along the parabola into the "solar wind" (Figure 74). In what direction does the tail point?

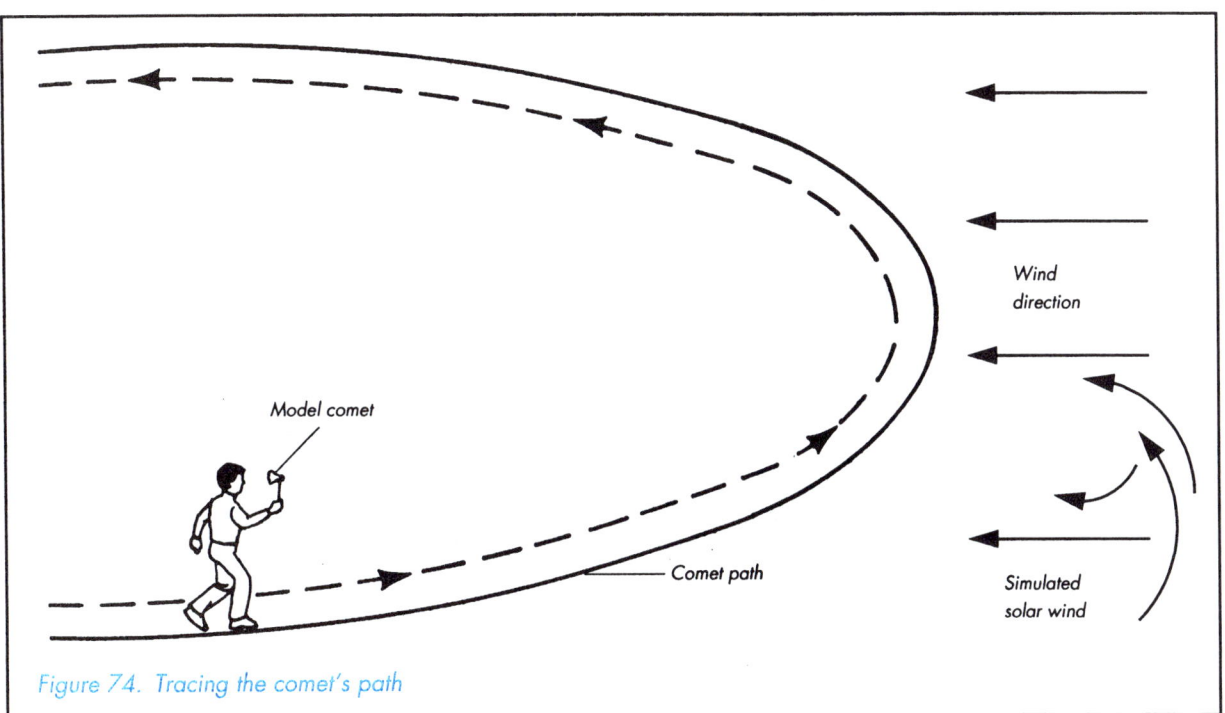

Figure 74. Tracing the comet's path

Continue walking around the curve of the parabola. How does the model comet change direction? How is this like an actual comet?

As you round the curve of the parabola and start walking away, what happens to the direction of the tail?

Look at photographs in books of Halley's Comet as it moves around the sun. How do they compare with your own observation?

Outgassing from a comet head

To show outgassing, mix up your own version of a comet head. Line a plastic basin with a plastic sheet or heavy plastic bag (Figure 75). Pour in about 600 ml of water (1¼ pints). Add some earth, sand, a few pebbles, and a teaspoon of molasses as organic matter; mix.

Now add two cups of crushed dry ice. **Caution:** Dry ice burns, so wear gloves to handle it. While stirring well, form the mass into a roundish comet head. It will soon be completely frozen. Remove the plastic sheet to display the "comet head."

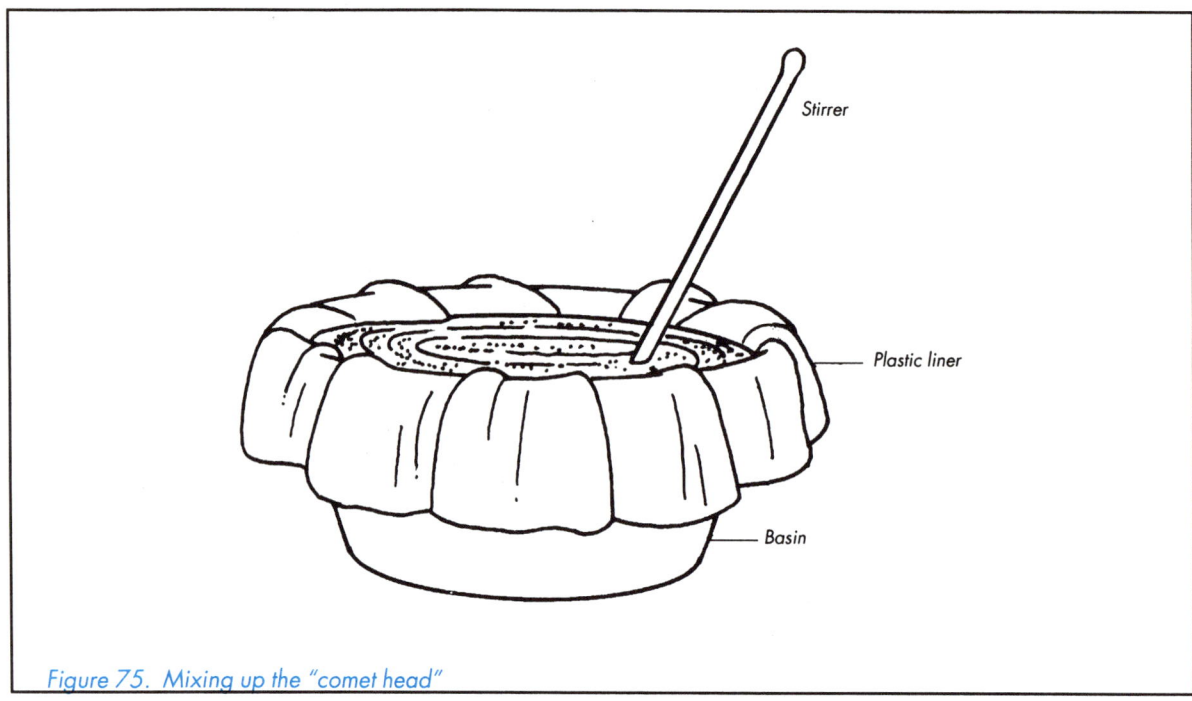

Figure 75. Mixing up the "comet head"

As heat is absorbed from the surroundings, the solid carbon dioxide will begin to sublime, changing directly from its solid state to a gas. How is this like what happens to Halley's Comet as it nears the sun? What do you see happening? What do you hear? What is meant by outgassing? What happens as the dry ice sublimes away? As the water-ice melts, what are you finally left with?

Name _____   Date _____

Halley's Comet

You can measure the orbit of Halley's Comet. Figure 76 shows the elongated orbit of Halley's Comet. The scale used in the diagram is one inch (2.5 cm) = 1,000 million kilometers (625 million miles).

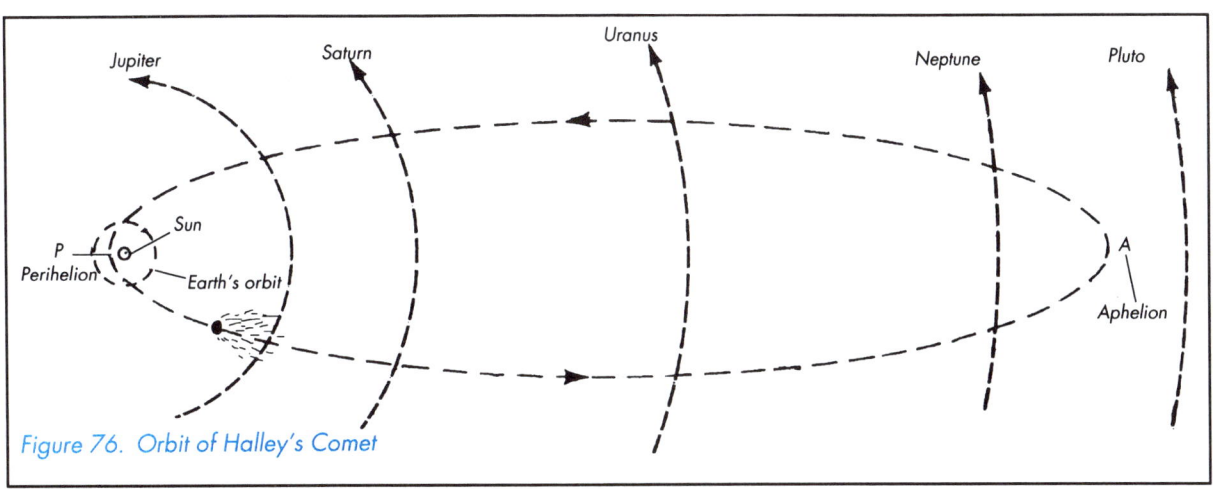

Figure 76. Orbit of Halley's Comet

Measure the distance from *P* (perihelion—when the comet is closest to the sun) to *A* (aphelion—when the comet is farthest from the sun). Now fill in the answers to the questions below.

Distance from perihelion to aphelion = _____ cm (_____ in)

1. What is the distance in kilometers from *P* to *A*? _____

   What is the distance in miles from *P* to *A*? _____

2. Between the orbits of which two planets does the aphelion lie?

   _____ and _____

3. At perihelion, Halley's Comet is 88 million kilometers from the sun. How far from the sun is it at aphelion? _____ kilometers _____ miles

4. Perihelion is between the paths of the two planets closest to the sun. Name them. _____ and _____

5. How many years does Halley's Comet take for one journey around its ellipse?

   _____

6. When will Halley's Comet next appear in Earth's skies? _____

7. Find out what happened when fragments of Comet Shoemaker-Levy rained down on Jupiter in July 1994.

© 1995 J. Weston Walch, Publisher   73   Astronomical! 44 Activities, Experiments, and Projects

22. Night and Day

Just as a top spins on a rod through its center, so the earth spins on its axis. One end of the axis is the North Pole, the other end the South Pole. Because the earth is round like a ball, only half of it is lighted at once. The side of the earth that faces the sun gets its light from the sun. The side of the earth facing away from the sun is dark.

But as the earth is spinning, these sides are not always the same—they are changing all the time. Whether it is day or night, every place on the earth is constantly moving. The earth makes one rotation on its axis every 24 hours.

The earth also revolves or travels through space around the sun. It takes the earth one year to complete the journey once around the sun. We have $365\frac{1}{4}$ days and nights in this time.

The Spin of the Earth

You can show how the spin of the earth gives us day and night and also how the earth travels around the sun.

What you need: strong frosted electric lamp to represent the sun; a globe of the earth (or you can use a white ball with equator, tropics, Arctic and Antarctic circles sketched in); a pin; a stool

1. Hold the globe of the earth at the same height and a little over a meter away from the "sun." Turn it slowly on its axis. What do you notice about one half of the earth? What about the other half? What causes day and night?

2. Stick a pin perpendicularly into the globe to show the place where you live (Figure 77). How does its shadow change in length as the earth turns on its axis? What name do we have for the time when the shadow is shortest?

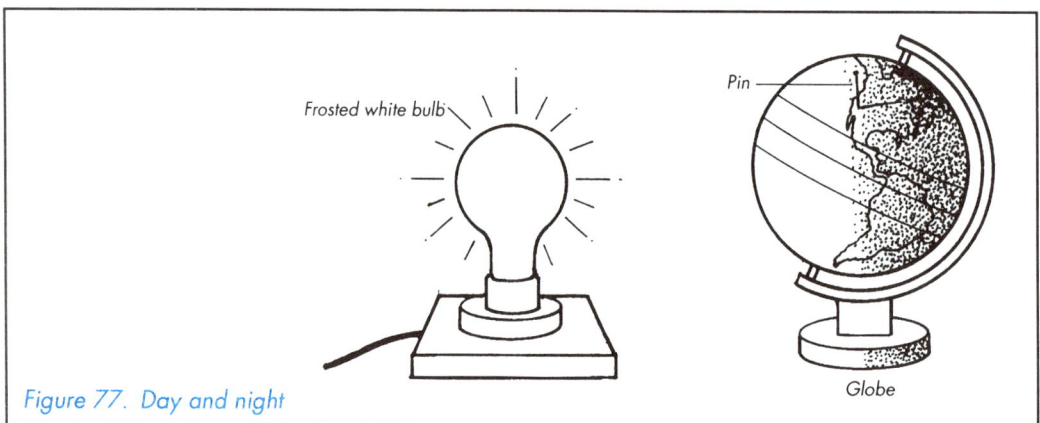

Figure 77. Day and night

3. Now walk with the earth in a circular path around the "sun." Be sure you keep the earth's axis always pointing in the same direction (Figure 78). Which position gives the greatest length of day? Which gives the least? Can you show two positions where day and night have the same length? What name do we have for these? When do they occur? Find out the meaning of the word "solstice." When do the solstices take place?

Figure 78. "As the world turns"

Chapter Two

A Star's Life

23. Star Birth

> *The heavens declare the glory of God and the firmament proclaims his handiwork.*
>
> —Psalm 19

In the constellation of Orion, a line of faint stars make up the sword hanging from the Mighty Hunter's belt. Even with the naked eye, one of the stars in the middle of the sword has a fuzzy appearance. This "star" is not a star at all; it's a huge cloud of molecules of gas and dust, some 15 light-years across, called a nebula. Star formation is actively taking place in the Great Orion Nebula and many young stars are found in this area. All are unstable, with the result that their light output varies rapidly in an irregular manner.

The problem with the molecular cloud is that the gas and dust are so dense that astronomers have not been able to see what's going on inside it. But now astronomers can see into the nebula using the light of infrared or heat radiation.

Using a new British telescope, the James Clark-Maxwell Telescope, or JCMT, astronomers have been able to tune into groups of molecules deep within the gas and dust clouds. Mauna Kea in Hawaii is at an especially high altitude—4,145 m (13,600 feet)—and the air is very dry. Since water vapor blocks infrared, the telescopes at Mauna Kea are especially suitable for infrared work.

By observing heat sources embedded within the gas and dust of the nebula, scientists have succeeded in putting together the story of star formation. Dust and gas clouds start to collapse and condense into a number of cores. Within the cores, molecules of gas and dust contract further because of the gravity pulls of the gas and dust molecules upon one another. The JCMT infrared telescope revealed these stars which become hotter and hotter as they shrink and more material clumps onto them. Temperatures at the center of the contracting masses rise to 15,000,000°K, which is high enough to start the thermonuclear or hydrogen bomb activity in the core. The ignition of the nuclear fires marks the moment of birth. The radiation pressure of the hot gases pushing outward now balances with the pull of gravity inward and the young protostar stops contracting.

Remnants of the original dust cloud still surround the young star; out of this swirling mass, planets may form. Violent winds may blow away from the young star, dispersing the remaining nebula into space.

The Power of Attraction

You can demonstrate how particles condense or clump together when an attractive force acts on them.

What you need: sodium thiosulphate (hypo); test tube; water; burner; piece of clear glass or plastic; iron filings; magnets; horseshoe magnet if available; books; plastic comb; puffed rice or puffed wheat, crushed to powder

Solidifying solution

1. Dissolve 25 grams of hypo crystals in as little water as possible. Heat to boiling, then set aside to cool. To witness molecules clumping together, give the test tube a sharp tap on the side. What do you see taking place? If the solution is truly supersaturated, it should all clump together or solidify at once. If this does not take place, your solution is too dilute and you need to reheat it to boil off some of the water.

2. Lay the piece of glass or plastic on the books as in Figure 1. Sprinkle the iron filings evenly over the glass.

   Bring one end of a magnet under the glass (Figure 2). Describe how the iron filings behave. Do they come together or condense? Do they form clumps? Try moving the magnet around. Do the clumps grow in size? How is this like the particles in nebulae far out in space forming clumps because of an attractive force acting on them? Try this using a horseshoe magnet as well.

Model of collisions between gas clouds

1. Try using two magnets as shown in Figure 3. Bring the "clouds" together. How is this like nebulae, giant clouds of gas and dust, colliding in space? How do you think this might favor star birth?

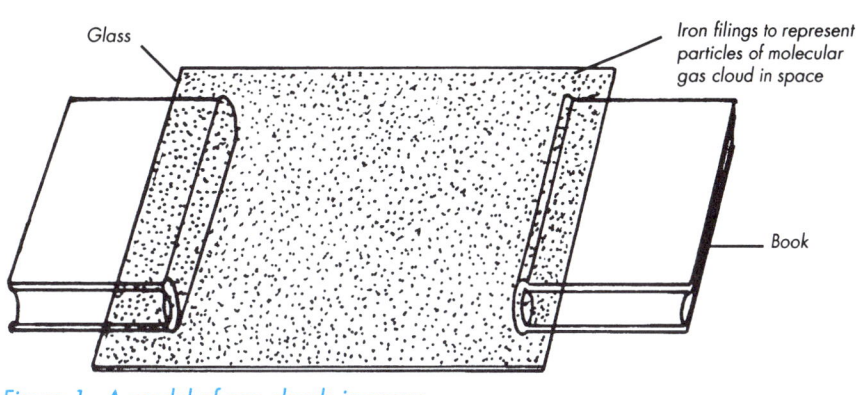

Figure 1. A model of gas clouds in space

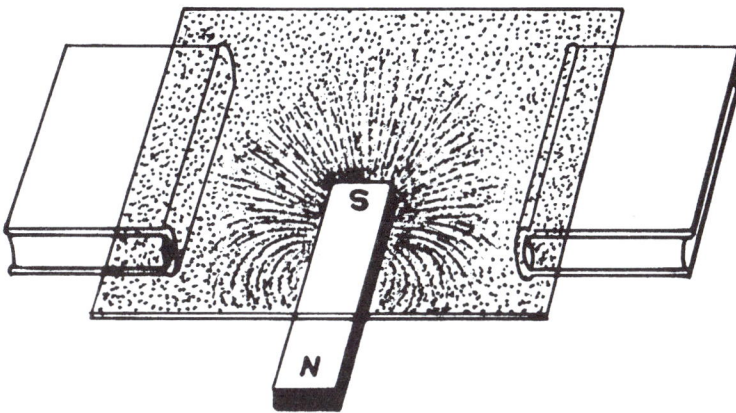

Figure 2. A demonstration of attractive forces on particles

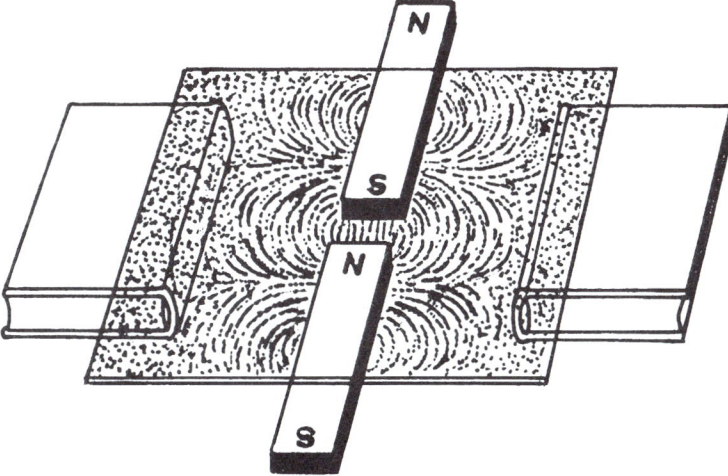

Figure 3. A model of colliding nebulae

2. Pass a comb several times through your dry, un-oiled hair, then hold it over the crushed cereal. Describe what takes place. Could this be like particles in a nebula attracted together? (Do this experiment on a dry, cold day in winter. It will not work when humidity is high.)

3. How do your experiments help you to picture star birth when clouds of gas and dust condense far out in space due to gravity?

24. The Sun As a Star

The sun is a great sphere of glowing gases at very high temperature (Figure 4). It is the source of all life. Without its light and heat, nothing would grow, not a creature could exist.

Figure 4. Although the chemical constitution of the sun is similar to that of Earth, it is so hot that it remains completely gaseous.

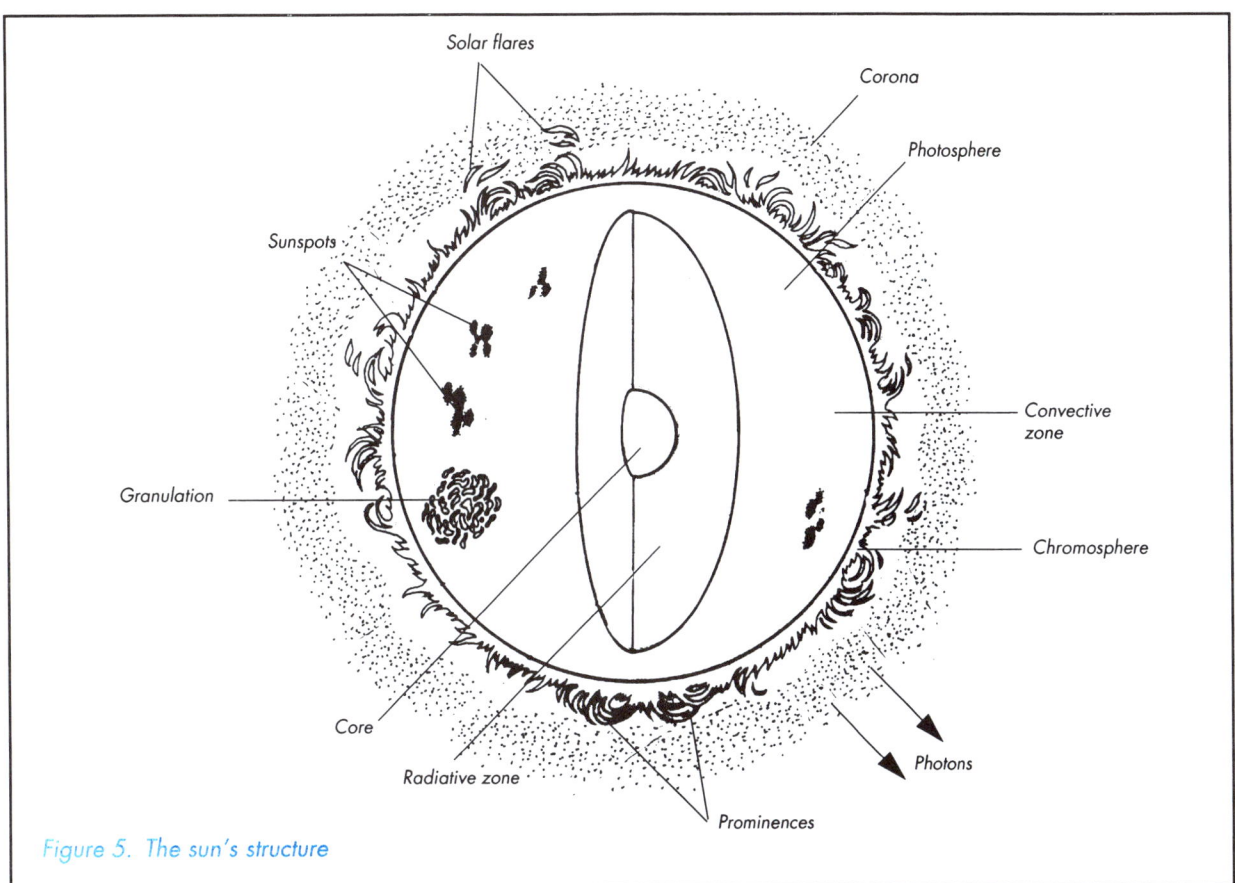

Figure 5. The sun's structure

Using an instrument known as a spectroscope, scientists have discovered the presence of enormous quantities of hydrogen and helium in the sun. When four hydrogen atoms fuse together, a helium atom is formed. The mass of the helium atom so formed is slightly less than that of the four parent hydrogen atoms. The mass that seems to be lost changes into energy. This is the source of the sun's tremendous energy. Measurements show that, during nuclear explosions, the temperatures developed are the same as those of the sun. In this furious process, scientists estimate the sun's loss of mass at over four million tons per second. Yet the sun is likely to maintain its temperature for another 35 billion years without noticeable loss.

The corona is the outer part of the sun's atmosphere (Figure 5). Seen during an eclipse, it reaches millions of kilometers into space. Its temperatures are about 2,000,000°K, the hottest observable temperatures in the universe. The chromosphere lies below the corona and can be seen during solar eclipse. It is red in color and is mainly hydrogen gas. The photosphere is the bright surface of the sun. Its temperature is 6,000°K. In the convective zone, gases whirl about. In the sun's core at temperatures near 15 million°K, nuclear reactions take place, the energy passing outward through the radiative zone.

Sunspots are great storms that rage furiously on the sun. They usually appear first in pairs towards the high latitudes, then more appear closer and closer to the sun's equator. With time the spots begin to die away; then the next cycle begins again in the higher latitudes. On an average the complete cycle takes about $11\frac{1}{2}$ years. Sunspots are related to periods of increased solar activity, which have a marked effect on the earth's environment. Solar prominences are great clouds of incandescent gas that shoot out 300,000 km from the sun's surface, then curve gracefully back into the sun's disc. Strong magnetic fields may be involved. Solar flares, sudden brilliant outbreaks that occur near sunspots, are also related to the sunspot cycle. From the flares, great eruptions shoot out 500,000 km from the sun at speeds of 400,000 km per hour.

Seen through a modern solar telescope, the sun's surface appears grainy, the granules changing in brilliance as you watch them. Each granule is about 1,000 km across and represents gas bubbling up over the sun's surface like water boiling in a kettle. Great outbursts on the sun—sunspots and solar flares—result in increased output of X-ray and ultraviolet radiations. These enter our atmosphere and interfere with long-distance communications. Scientists today are sending instruments aloft in rockets and satellites in order to solve some of these problems of electrical communication. The signals radio telescopes receive from the sun may reveal some of the sun's secrets and how it is able to influence the earth.

Radiation as a Source of Energy

What you need: hand magnifier; sheet of paper; fruit can; camphor or candle; three pots with potting soil; peas

1. Hold the hand magnifier in bright sunlight with a sheet of paper behind it. Move the paper to and fro until there is a bright spot on it. All the sunlight which falls on the lens is brought to this spot. Try using a bigger hand magnifier. Is the spot brighter? Explain why. What happens to the paper? What rays of the sunlight does the lens concentrate at the spot?

2. Take the fruit can and hold it over a piece of burning camphor, which burns with a very smoky flame (or use a burning candle). In this way, coat the sides of the can with soot. Then add water to fill the can and place in the sunshine. After an hour or so, put your hands in the water. What can you say about the temperature? How has heat been gained? Repeat the experiment using a shiny can. Which can is the better absorber of the sun's heat? Explain why.

3. Plant five or six pea seeds in the soil of each pot. Put one pot where it gets sunlight, stand a second in a dark corner, and put the third in a cupboard where it gets no light at all. Which seeds show the best growth? What do you notice about the ones in the dark corner?

Name _____   Date _____

Talking About the Sun

1. Choose the correct words from the list to complete the paragraph about sunspots; write them in the spaces provided.

   ultraviolet   eleven   dark
   high   equator   long-distance
   eruptions

   Sunspots are giant _____ on the sun's surface. Being less bright than the rest of the sun's disc, they appear as _____ areas. Sunspots generally appear in the sun's _____ latitudes. Then more appear toward the sun's _____. They occur in cycles every _____ years or so. Sunspots shoot into space vast quantities of charged particles called ions and electrons, as well as _____ radiation. Sunspots interfere with _____ communication. They also cause the aurora of the polar regions.

2. "Give me the splendid silent sun with all his beams full-dazzling,
   Give me juicy autumnal fruit ripe and red from the orchard."

   These lines are by the poet Walt Whitman. He sees the majesty of the sun in the sky. To him the sun meant life and light and the wonder of all growing things.

   Write some lines of your own in which you express the same ideas.

   _____
   _____
   _____
   _____
   _____

© 1995 J. Weston Walch, Publisher   Astronomical! 44 Activities, Experiments, and Projects

25. Hot Breath of a Red Giant

In about five billion years the sun will have used up the hydrogen at its core and will enter the red giant stage of its life history. As the core compresses due to gravity, heat will be generated. This will set the hydrogen in the surrounding layers burning. The sun will balloon out into a bloated red giant 40 times its present size. Mercury, Venus, and Earth will be destroyed as the sun swells to beyond Earth's orbit.

The hot breath of the red giant will affect the outer planets and their moons. Europa, Callisto, and Ganymede, orbiting Jupiter 770,000,000 kilometers from the sun, will have kept their frozen cover during the sun's colossal outpouring of energy. But as the sun enters the red giant stage, the ice-covered moons will begin to melt. If the ice of Europa is pure water-ice, it will take hundreds of millions of years to melt. If the ice is a water-ammonia mix, it will melt sooner as its melting point will be lower. Once the ice crust on Europa has melted, the moon will be covered by fog and cloud drifting across a vast expanse of water.

Because a red giant is so swollen, the outer layers of gases are very thin and the surface density is very low. By contrast, the core of a red giant is very dense and hot. Gases escape from the surface of the red giant and drift off into space. Red giants are cool stars with surface temperatures of around 3,000°K (Figure 6).

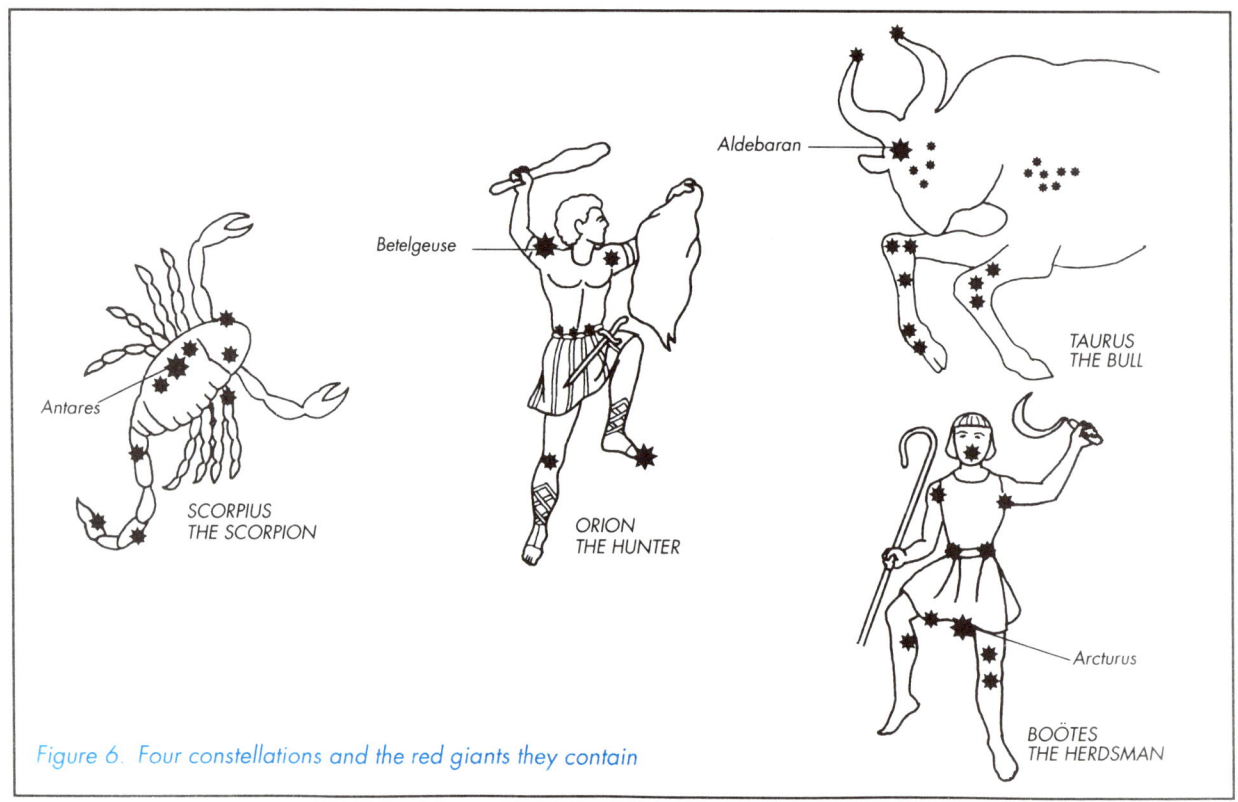

Figure 6. Four constellations and the red giants they contain

Expanding Gas

In this experiment you will show how heat expands gases and sets up movements in gases, and you will see how this is important in the red giant stage of a star's life.

What you need: medicine dropper or small bottle; wood ash, chalk dust, or talcum powder; hot water; convector heater or reading lamp; two paper bags; thread; stick; adhesive tape; candle; matches; wire

1. Make a wire holder for the dropper and place it under hot water, or use the small bottle (Figure 7). What do you see? What is the effect of heat on the gases of air in the dropper or bottle? Is the density of the gas different? If so, how?

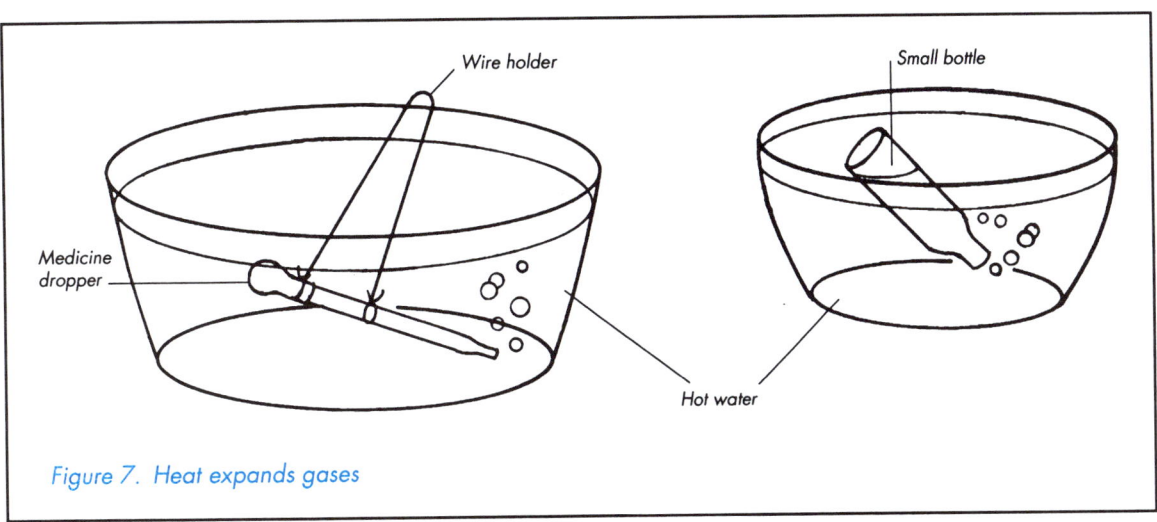

Figure 7. Heat expands gases

2. Sprinkle some wood ash, chalk dust, or talcum powder above a convector heater or reading lamp. Watch the tiny particles; what do you see them doing? What does this tell you about the effect of heat on particles of air (Figure 8)? How could this be like the particles in the outer layers of gases in a red giant?

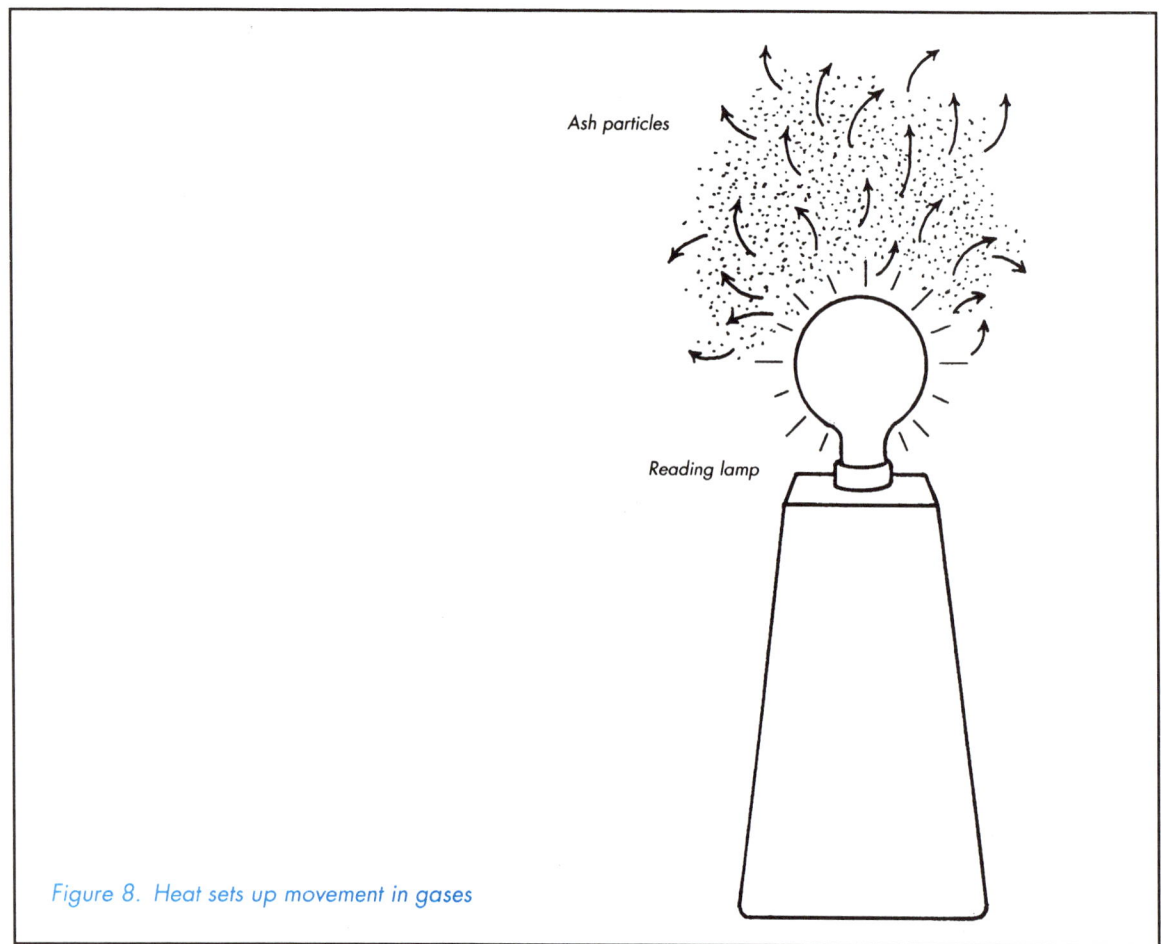

Figure 8. Heat sets up movement in gases

3. Arrange the stick and paper bags as in Figure 9, making sure they balance.

4. Hold one bag steady and bring the lighted candle below it. What does the heat of the candle do to the gases of air in the bag?

5. Now take away the candle and release the bag. What happens? How is the bag able to overcome gravity? How has heat affected the air in the bag? Can you relate this to what happens in a red giant?

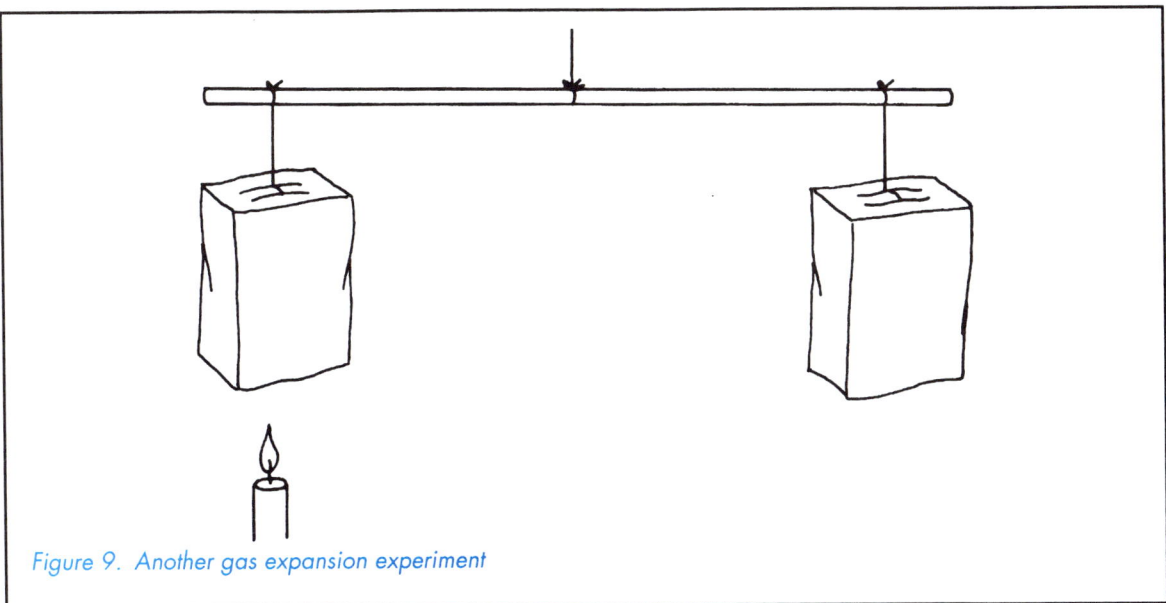

Figure 9. Another gas expansion experiment

26. White Dwarfs

A star ends its life as a white dwarf, a neutron star, or a black hole. Locating these objects in the sky is not easy. In the end, it was gravity that found them out.

Telescopes such as that at the Royal Greenwich Observatory have studied the stars for over 100 years, plotting their courses across space. A lone star, it was thought, would follow a path in a straight line over the sky. But the German astronomer Friedrich Wilhelm Bessel, studying the path of Sirius the Dog Star across the heavens, found that it wobbled its way through space as if pulled by an invisible force—a nearby star. Therefore there must be a companion star in orbit around Sirius. But why couldn't anyone see it?

In 1862 Alvan Clark, American astronomer, turned a powerful new telescope on Sirius and was the first to see Sirius B, the pup companion to Sirius, the Dog Star (Figure 10). Astronomers discovered some strange features about the pup. It was as heavy as an ordinary star, yet it shone with a dim light, which meant it was very small.

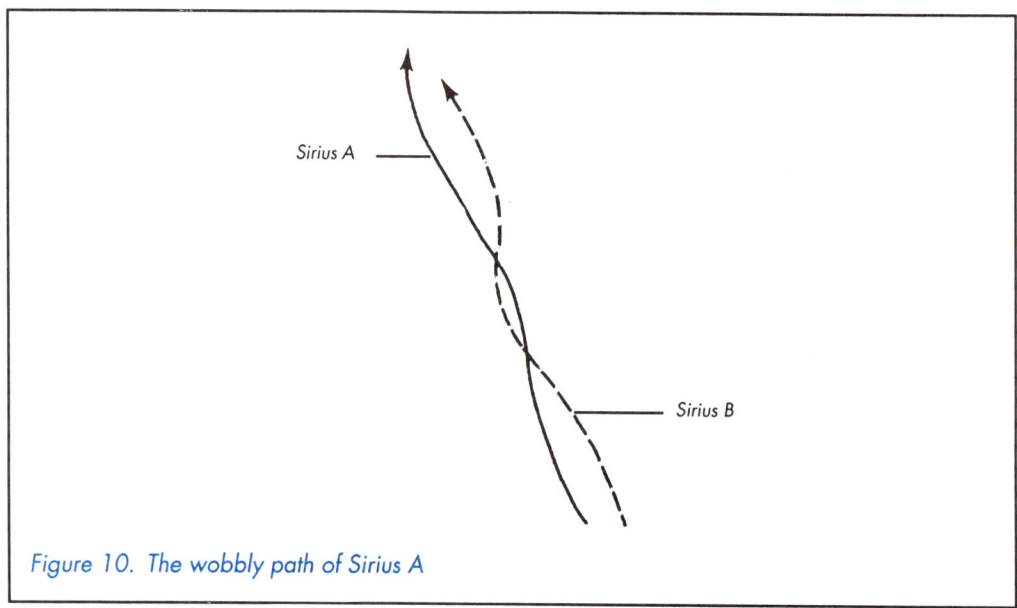

Figure 10. The wobbly path of Sirius A

Astronomers call such stars white dwarfs. Sirius B was the first of many white dwarfs to be discovered (Figure 11). These stars are extremely heavy and dense so they generate a very powerful gravity field. The atoms are very tightly packed together. A cupful of white dwarf material would weigh as much as two 747 Jumbo Jets. Because the particles are so compressed the star is white-hot—thus the name, white dwarfs. A white dwarf is the corpse of a dead star, the core of a star the size of the sun that has collapsed due to gravity when its fuel ran out. The aging star, in its death throes, throws away its atmosphere, which the telescope reveals in the sky as a beautiful planetary nebula. At the heart of the nebula is the white dwarf at a temperature of 50,000–100,000 K. The star has no energy source and leaks its heat away into space, eventually ending up as a cold, black cinder.

Figure 11. Through a telescope, Sirius B shows as a small dot close to its much brighter companion Sirius A.

Compression and Heat

You can show how pressure affects the melting point of ice and that compressing particles together sets heat free.

What you need: two ice cubes; block of ice; loop of fine brass or steel wire with heavy weight attached; loop of thicker wire with same size weight; bicycle pump; bicycle tire and tube

1. Squeeze two melting ice cubes together. What happens? How is pressure helping? What happens when you squeeze snow together? Why it it hard to make snowballs when the temperature is much below freezing (Figure 12)?

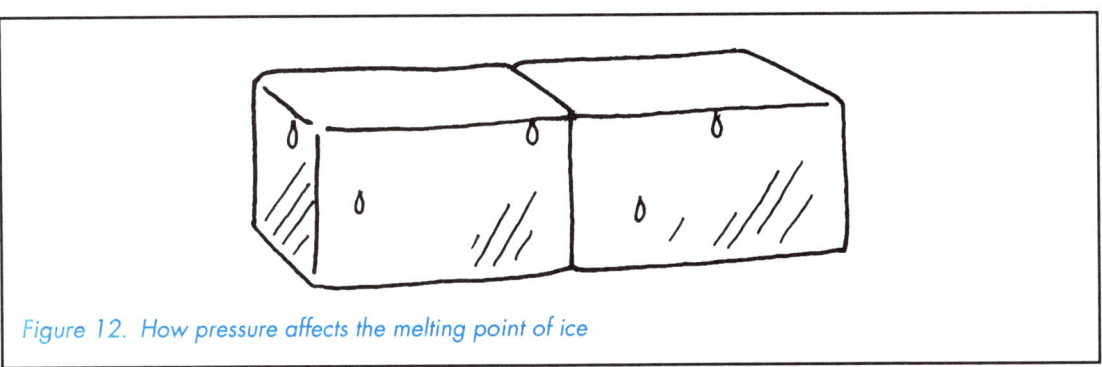

Figure 12. How pressure affects the melting point of ice

2. Place the ice block over the sink with the fine wire loop around it with the attached weight. What do you see happen? The pressure decreases the melting-point of the ice, the ice melts under the wire, and the resulting water refreezes above it. Can you now explain why the wire cuts through the ice but leaves a solid block?

3. To help with the concept of pressure and its part in melting the ice, use another loop of thicker wire carrying the same size weight, and start both wires at the same time. What do you find?

4. To find how compression causes heat, try pumping air into a bicycle tire, holding your hand over the end of the pump. What do you notice about the end of the pump (Figure 13)? Can you explain this in terms of particle theory? **Note:** As you push the pump handle down, the air particles within bounce off it with increased speed. The increased speed means an increase in the energy of the particles, which shows itself in an increase of temperature. Explain now why the compressed particles of a white dwarf make the star white-hot.

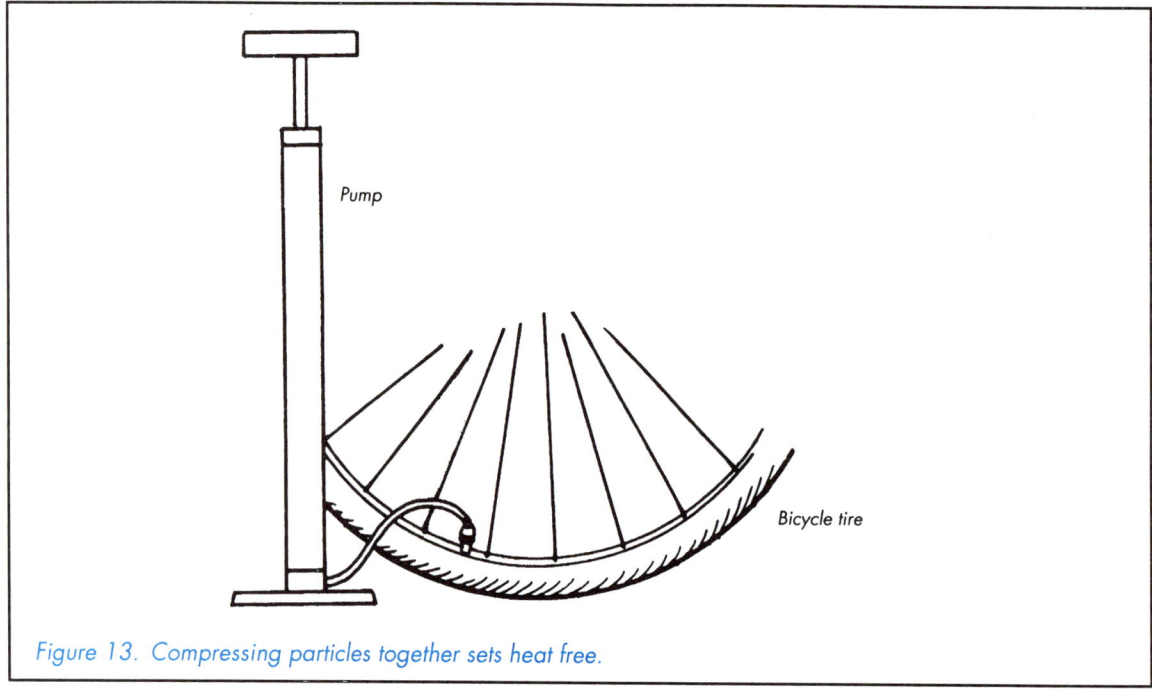

Figure 13. Compressing particles together sets heat free.

27. Supernovae—Stars That End with a Bang

Very massive stars end their lives in tremendous explosions in which most of the star's mass is ejected into the surrounding space at very high speeds. These are supernovae; all that is left of the original star is its core, which becomes a neutron star or pulsar (Figure 14).

Supernovae exploded in our galaxy in 1604, 1572, 1181, 1054, and 1006. The supernova of 1054 was observed by Eastern and Arab astronomers, who recorded it as brighter than the planet Venus. It was visible in full daylight for 23 days.

The Crab Nebula (Figure 15), a gaseous remnant of the 1054 supernova, lies in the constellation Taurus about 4,000 light-years away. It covers an area of about 7- by-12 light-years. At the center of the Crab Nebula is a pulsar only a few kilometers in diameter with a mass roughly the same as the sun. It pours forth radiation at all wavelengths from radio to X rays and gamma rays. Its total brightness is 25,000 times that of the sun.

Figure 14. The supernova in the Giant Magellanic Cloud. The bright object in the center lower part of the photo is the Tarantula Nebula. Just above and to the left is the supernova.

The pulsar rotates 30 times every second and was originally the dense central core of the exploded supernova. It is bound to the nebula by magnetic fields which act as a brake on its rotational spin, slowing it down by a tiny fraction each day. The rotational energy lost is emitted as radiation by electrons spiraling in the magnetic fields.

Supernovae are divided into two main types. In a Type I supernova, the white dwarf in a binary star system draws so much from its red giant companion that it collapses to a neutron core. When material falls in from the outer layer of the star, it rebounds off the dense core. The shock wave from this collision blows off the star's outer layer of gas (Figure 16). In a Type II supernova, the process is similar, but the star is a supergiant near the end of its active lifetime. When the core becomes too massive to support itself, it collapses to a neutron core (Figure 17). The two types also differ in their brightness and in the rate at which they decline from maximum brightness.

Figure 15. The Crab Nebula is assumed to be the remnant of a supernova first observed in 1054. The supernova was visible in daylight for 23 days and at night for almost two years.

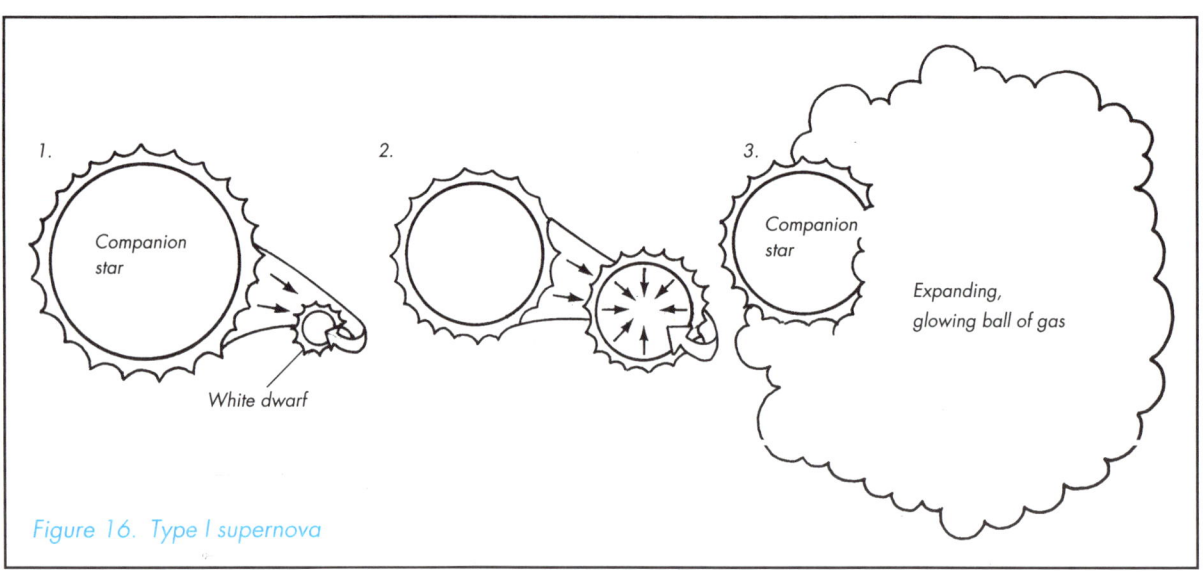

Figure 16. Type I supernova

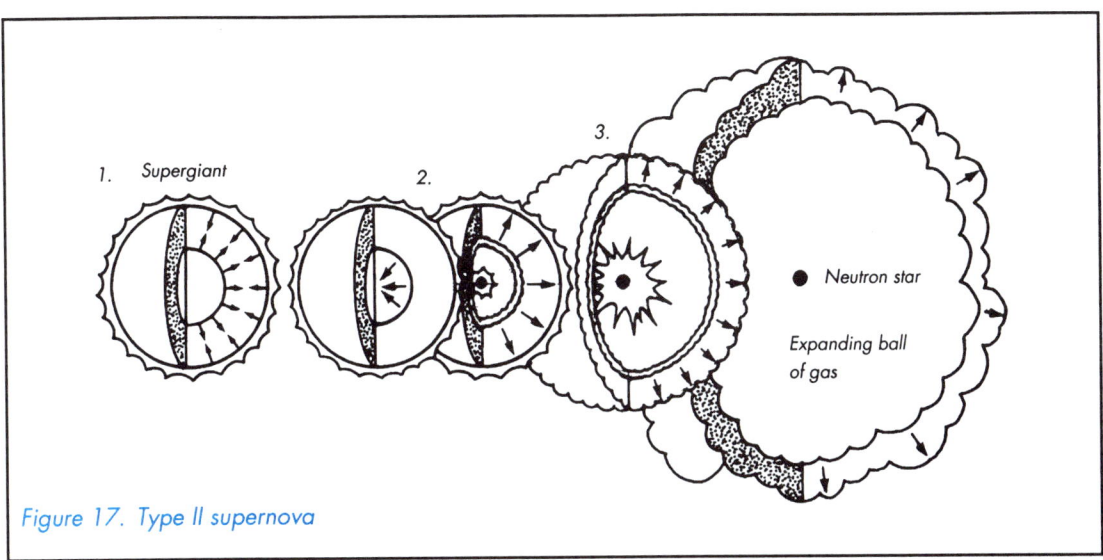

Figure 17. Type II supernova

One of the many showpieces of the southern sky is the beautiful Eta Carinae Nebula. It takes its name from the famous star Eta Carinae. In 1843 this star blazed forth to become the second brightest star in the sky. This outburst had been preceded by considerable variations in brightness over a 16-year period.

The outburst was followed by violent fluctuations until the star gradually faded to well below naked-eye visibility. Over the last few decades it has again risen to reach naked-eyed limits. Many astronomers believe that Eta Carinae will again explode as a supernova.

Material ejected by Eta Carinae fills space around the star and glows from the light of many very bright stars in this region, many of which are candidates for supernovae explosions as they are consuming their fuel at a tremendous rate. Future supernovae in our galaxy are likely to come from faint but massive stars that are members of binary systems.

The nearest supernova to our galaxy exploded in 1987 and is known as 1987A. It is situated in the Large Magellanic Cloud and was the first comparatively near supernova to be studied with modern instruments. The intense studies made of this object provided a useful check on current theories now accepted as valid.

One problem in observing supernovae is that they are obscured for a time by the gas and dust ejected in the explosion. The only method of penetrating this cloud is by infrared methods. Although the clouds are usually opaque, it is possible to see through them at infrared wavelengths. As the atmosphere screens out most of the incoming infrared radiation, satisfactory observations can only be made from high-altitude observatories or orbiting telescopes such as IRAS (infrared astronomical satellites).

Observing Supernovae

You can demonstrate magnetic spinning and braking and show how dust clouds in space (simulated by a balloon) block the astronomer's view.

What you need: aluminum or copper cup; nail; knitting needle; wood or plastic base; modeling clay; horseshoe magnet; string; copper disc with hole drilled at center; plastic top of ballpoint pen; white balloon; tissue paper

1. Attach the knitting needle to the base with modeling clay (Figure 18). Use the nail to make a dimple at the center of the base of the metal cup. The cup must spin freely when supported on the point of the knitting needle.

2. Hang the horseshoe magnet from the string as shown, then spin the magnet so that the string is twisted. Now let the string untwist, holding the magnet just above the cup. What does the cup do? In which direction does it turn?

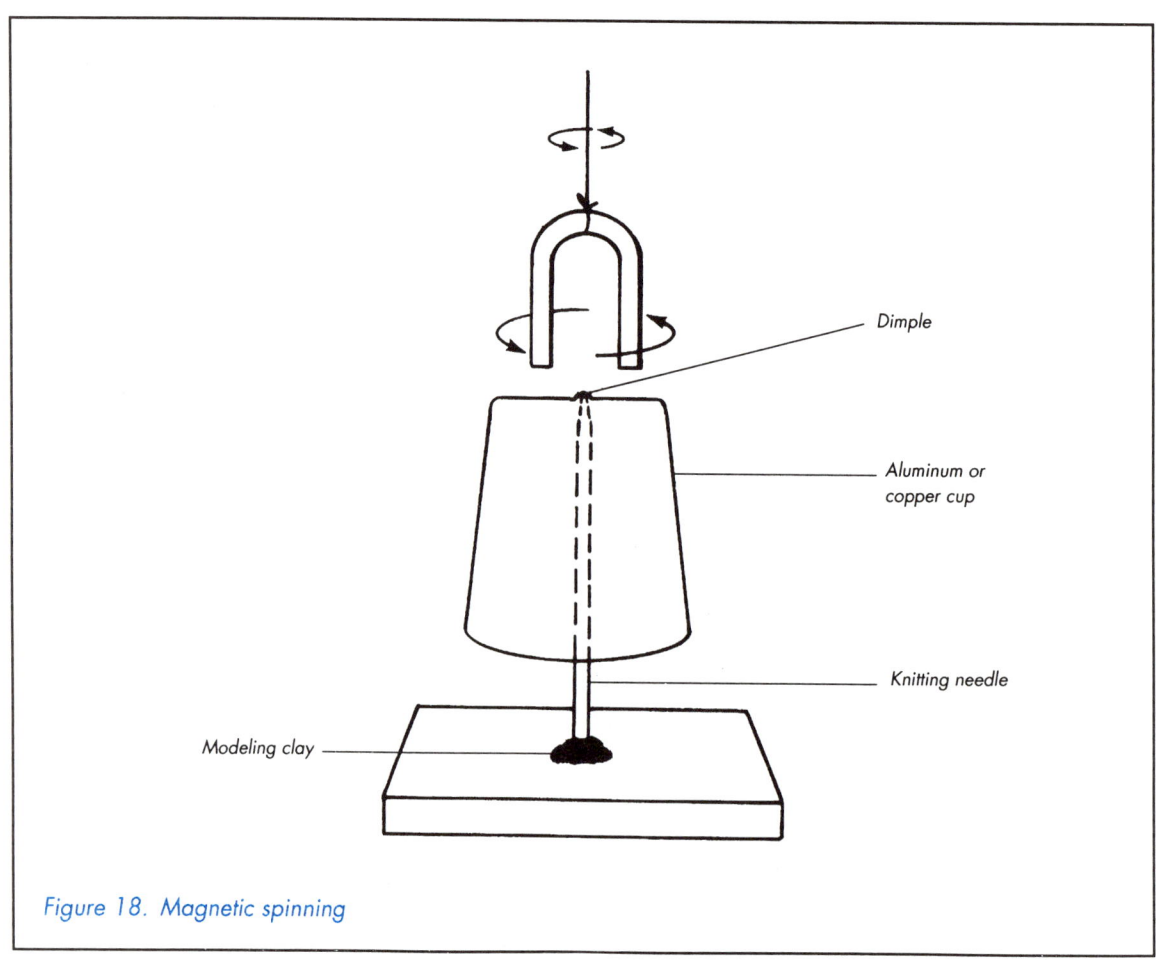

Figure 18. Magnetic spinning

3. The movement of the cup is set up by eddy currents. What are these? What is the part played by the horseshoe magnet?

4. Use the arrangement shown in Figure 19. Spin the disc, then hold the horseshoe magnet so that the disc is spinning between its poles. What do you notice? How are magnetic fields involved? How do magnetic fields act to brake the spin of a rapidly rotating neutron star?

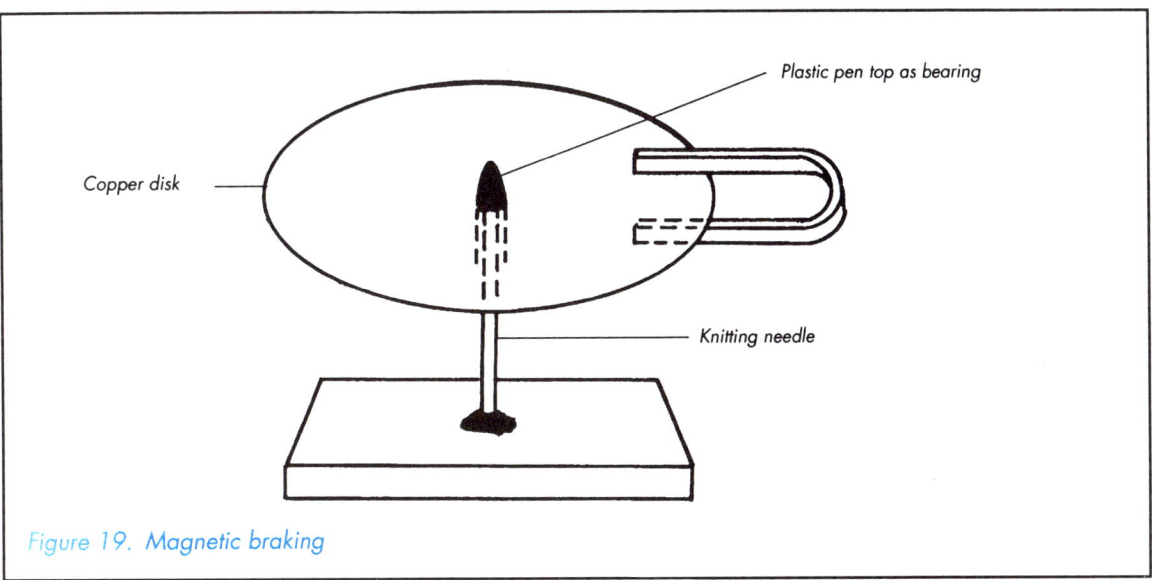

Figure 19. Magnetic braking

5. Switch on the lamp and look at it. What is the color of the light coming to your eyes? Now look at the lamp through the blown-up balloon (to simulate a gas cloud). Is the light changed in any way?

6. Now slowly let some air out of the balloon, observing the lamp through it as you do so. Describe any changes in the appearance of the lamp. Does blowing up the balloon more have any effect?

7. Look at the lamp through different thicknesses of tissue paper (to simulate gas blown off). How is the light affected in each case? How is this like the problem of observing supernovae?

28. The Pulsar Puzzle

In 1966 scientists using a new radio telescope near Cambridge, England, discovered a strange new signal from outer space. Whenever the telescope looked in a certain direction in the sky, it detected a regular series of pulses, rather like a Morse code signal. The extreme regularity of the pulses and their fixed direction in the sky eliminated the possibility of local radio interference. So the scientists assumed the signals were messages from an alien civilization in outer space. They named the source LGM 1, for Little Green Men No. 1.

Further studies disproved any ideas that the signals were from a planet or space station in orbit around the sun, as no effects due to orbital motion were detected. Soon after, with the discovery of sources LGM 2, LGM 3, LGM 4, it was obvious that this explanation was not correct either. Why had no one found the pulses before? Quite simply, it was because no one had looked.

The radio telescope used by the Cambridge scientists had been operating only two months and was the first radio telescope designed to detect rapidly changing signals. It consisted of over 2,000 aerials—each rather like a home TV antenna—covering an area of 1.6 hectares and tuned to a frequency of 81.6 megacycles.

Researchers were using the telescope to study the radio equivalent of a star's twinkling. This twinkling or scintillation is caused by small pockets of hot and cold air being blown between the star and the observer's eye. In a similar way, a small radio source will scintillate as clouds of electrically active gas move across the line of sight. Study of the variations tells us something both about the clouds and about the winds moving them. The Cambridge telescope was intended to study changes in the solar wind between and beyond the planets. The discovery of pulsars was a fortunate accident.

The telescope had been designed and was directed by Professor Antony Hewish of Cambridge University, while the actual operation was carried out by a young Ph.D. student named Jocelyn Bell. She first saw the pulsar signals and persisted in studying them, looking through more than 6 km of paper charts, searching for scintillating radio sources.

A pulsar is a kind of lighthouse in space and is in fact an extremely powerful beam of radiation shining from a point on a spinning neutron star. We see a pulse whenever the beam shines in our direction.

A neutron star is the remains of a heavy star, two to three times heavier than our sun, which has used up its nuclear fuel and collapsed under its own weight. When the star collapses, it explodes in an awesome explosion known as a supernova. Huge clouds of gas thrown off the star are so bright as to outshine an entire galaxy. A neutron star is left behind as a remnant. The matter in the core of the star is compressed down to such enormous densities that the parts of a normal atom are crushed into one another and become neutrons. The density of a neutron star is so great that a teaspoon of neutron star matter on Earth would weight a million tons, and a pin made of it would be heavier than a battleship. A neutron star also increases its spin and its magnetic field, the latter building up to a thousand billion times greater than Earth's.

Because the neutron star is both magnetic and spinning, it acts as a great dynamo out in space, and this powers the light and radio waves that flash through space. Some 150 pulsars are known, rotating between 642 times a second and once every two seconds. The time of rotation is very stable and rivals the accuracy of the very best atomic clocks. Sometimes, however, a pulsar shows a glitch—a sudden change in its spin. This is the result of a starquake, a sudden cracking and movement of the crust of the neutron star similar to the familiar earthquake.

Six pulsars are known within the remnants of old supernovae. The most famous are in the Crab and Vela nebulae (Figure 20), which exploded in A.D. 1054 and about 10,000 years ago, respectively. In 1987 a supernova was reported in the Great Magellanic Cloud; studies of this supernova appear to confirm the creation of pulsars in such explosions.

Figure 20. A pulsar is a "lighthouse in space" that originates from a neutron star. The arrow points to a pulsar in the Crab Nebula.

Model Pulsars

You can make a lighthouse model and a dynamo model to demonstrate the action of a pulsar.

What you need: ball with supporting string attached; mirror; flashlight; horseshoe magnet; wood base; brass rods 3 mm × 12 cm; 20–22 gauge copper wire; hookup wire; switch; tape; flashlight batteries

1. Fix the mirror, representing the rotating hot spot on the pulsar, to the ball (neutron star) with tape (Figure 21).

2. Have a partner hold the end of the string and spin the "neutron star" with the flashlight rays shining on it. Describe what you see. How are the pulses of light you see like the pulses of radiant energy beamed out from the hot spot of the rapidly rotating neutron star?

3. Try varying the speed of rotation from once per second to many times per second. Try this also with a flashlight set spinning (Figure 22). Find out how the rapid pulses are measured. What instrument do scientists use?

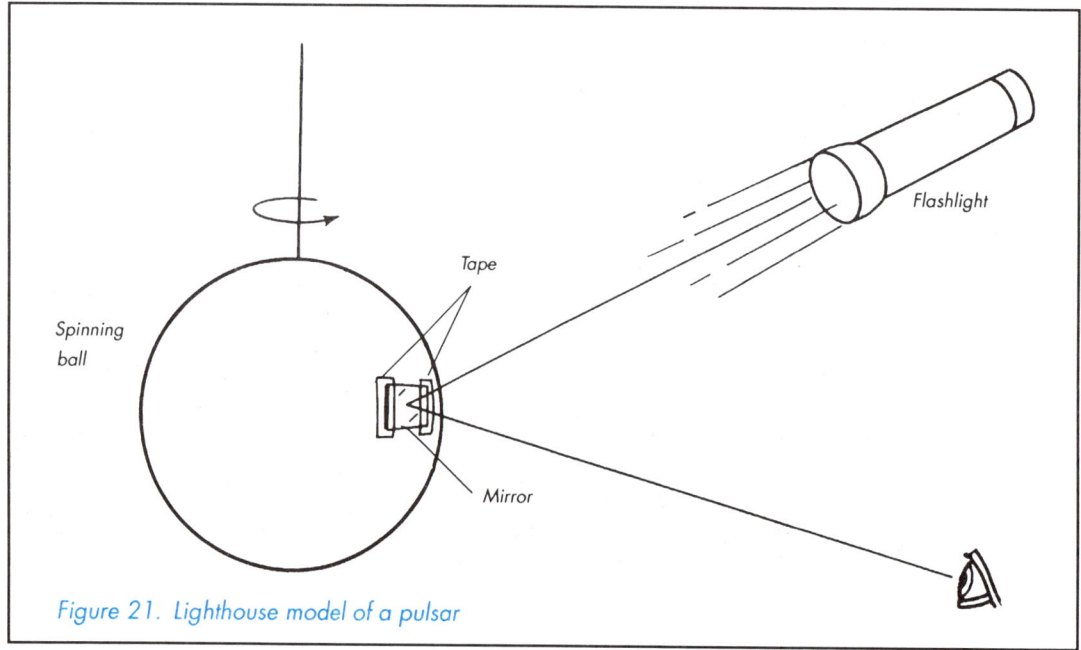

Figure 21. Lighthouse model of a pulsar

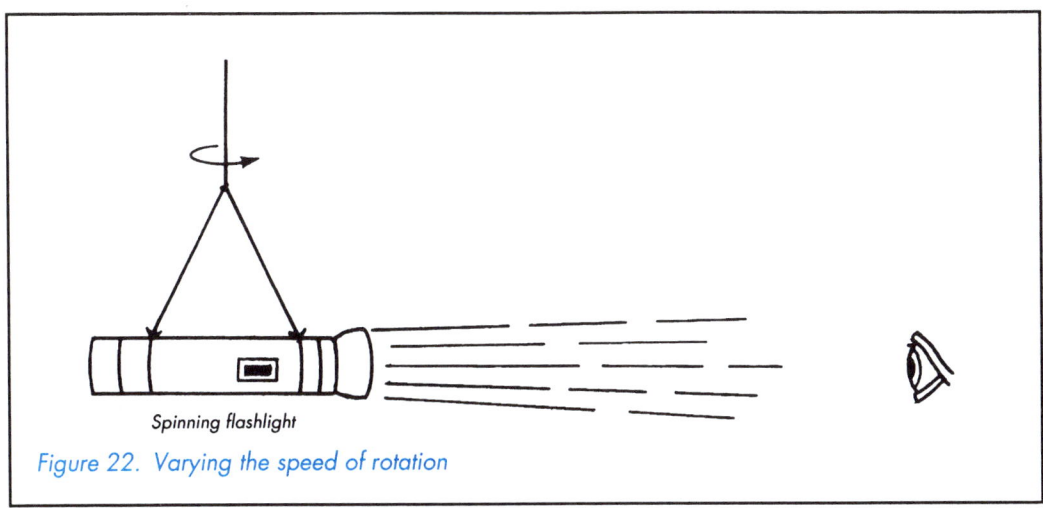

Figure 22. Varying the speed of rotation

4. To demonstrate the dynamo action of a pulsar, use the setup shown. The two brass (nonmagnetic) rods act as rollers along which a piece of 20–22 gauge bare copper wire can roll when you close the switch and current flows through the wire in a magnetic field (Figure 23). The copper wire must be clean and straight with no kinks in it so that it can roll freely. Make sure the brass rods are clean for good electrical contact; clean with emery paper if necessary.

5. Close the switch and release. What happens? What is the dynamo action? Try reversing the battery terminals or the poles of the magnet. How is the direction of the movement affected? **Note:** Don't leave the switch closed, as the short circuit is a heavy draw on the battery.

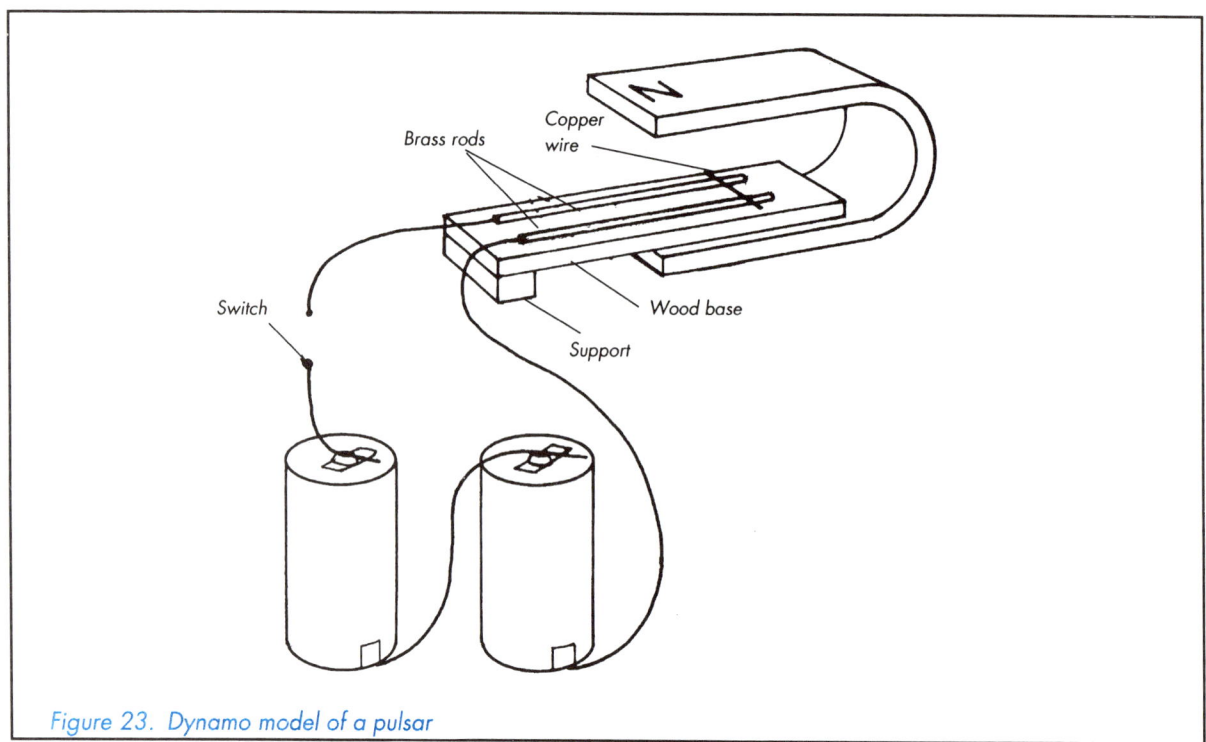

Figure 23. Dynamo model of a pulsar

29. Black Holes

The star that exploded and made the Crab Pulsar was 15 times more massive than our sun. When an even heavier star explodes it leaves behind a stranger-than-fiction corpse: a black hole—an object whose gravity field is so intense that not even light photons can escape from it.

To escape from our earth's gravity pull, the *Pioneer* deep space probes had to reach a speed of 7 miles (11.2 km) per second. To escape from the sun's more massive gravity, you would have to reach a velocity of 400 miles (640 km) per second. But these are minor values when compared with highly compressed stellar corpses such as neutron stars and black holes. The escape velocity from a neutron star would be half the speed of light—90,000 miles (144,000 km) per second. And if Earth were compressed down to a marble 2.5 cm across, the escape velocity would rise to the speed of light—186,000 miles (3×10^5 km) per second (Figure 24).

It seems an incredible destiny. The giant stars of the universe, visible from distant galaxies, become so compressed that gravity becomes overwhelming, the star shrivels away to zero size, and gravity becomes infinite. The region around the hole is black and empty—hence the term "black hole."

Astronomers look for black holes in binary systems where the black hole is in orbit around an ordinary star. The gravity of the hole is so intense that material is drawn off the companion star and sucked into the cosmic drain. In this process, the material is furiously heated and emits radiation such as X rays which can be detected by satellites. One very likely candidate for a black hole is Cygnus X-1. Swirling gases appear to be swallowed up by a black hole.

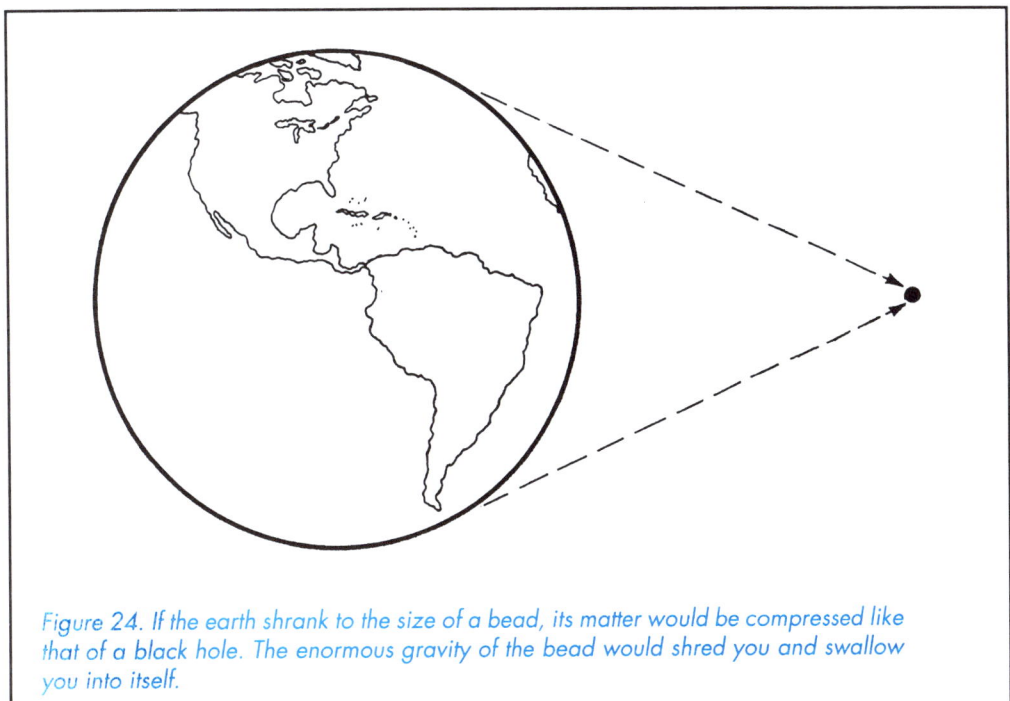

Figure 24. If the earth shrank to the size of a bead, its matter would be compressed like that of a black hole. The enormous gravity of the bead would shred you and swallow you into itself.

Many astronomers think that black holes might affect the future of our universe. The universe is expanding, carrying the galaxies with it, but will it continue to expand forever? This depends on whether there is enough matter, and therefore enough gravity, to act as a brake, halting the expansion and even reversing it. At some time in the future we may have a shrinking universe rather than an expanding one.

Astronomers believe that shortly after the big bang, a generation of supermassive stars was created. These stars would have died as black holes. In the future, space telescopes in orbit will look back so far in space and time that they will search out these first-generation superstars and see them as they were before they collapsed as black holes. If such stars existed, it is the massive gravity fields of their corpses that pervades the whole of the universe and will in the end decide its future.

Some scientists believe that radiation can escape from a black hole. Stephen Hawking has investigated the appearance of two virtual particles within the hole (particles of short life that scientists cannot detect directly but the effects of which can be measured). One of these is drawn in by the gravity of the hole and the other escapes.

In another analysis described by Roger Penrose, a body traveling in a part of the black hole called the ergosphere (Greek *ergos* meaning "work") breaks into two pieces. One of these pieces falls into the black hole, and the other comes out again with more energy than it went in with. Some of the rotational energy of the black hole gets added to the part that emerges. The black hole thus becomes a very efficient energy-conversion machine.

A futuristic picture is also given of a civilization living around a rotating black hole. Every day, trucks take their refuse down into the ergosphere and deposit it. The returning trucks bring back the energy equivalent of this waste to provide the energy needs of the civilization; the black hole becomes a tremendous powerhouse out in space. Thus black holes, rather than being something from which nothing can escape, may become tremendous sources of energy.

Radiation in Space

You can experiment with radiation, the transmission of radiant energy by electromagnetic waves through space.

What you need: candle; square of black hardboard; 100-watt electric lamp; radiometer

1. Light the candle and place your hand beside the flame. Explain why you can see the flame and feel the warmth. Note that the waves are longer than the visible red and are called infrared. Heat is not transferred through space. The radiant energy must first be absorbed before it turns to what we describe as heat.

2. Repeat the experiment with a 100-watt electric lamp. Are your findings the same?

3. Place the piece of black hardboard between your face and the lamp for 2–3 minutes. Have the black side facing the lamp and about 5 cm from it. Explain why you can no longer see the lamp or feel the heat. Touch the black hardboard. What do you notice about it? Explain why.

4. Place the radiometer about 30 cm from the lighted candle. Do the vanes move? Repeat with the lamp. Describe what happens (Figure 25). What is the radiometer receiving from the candle and the lamp?

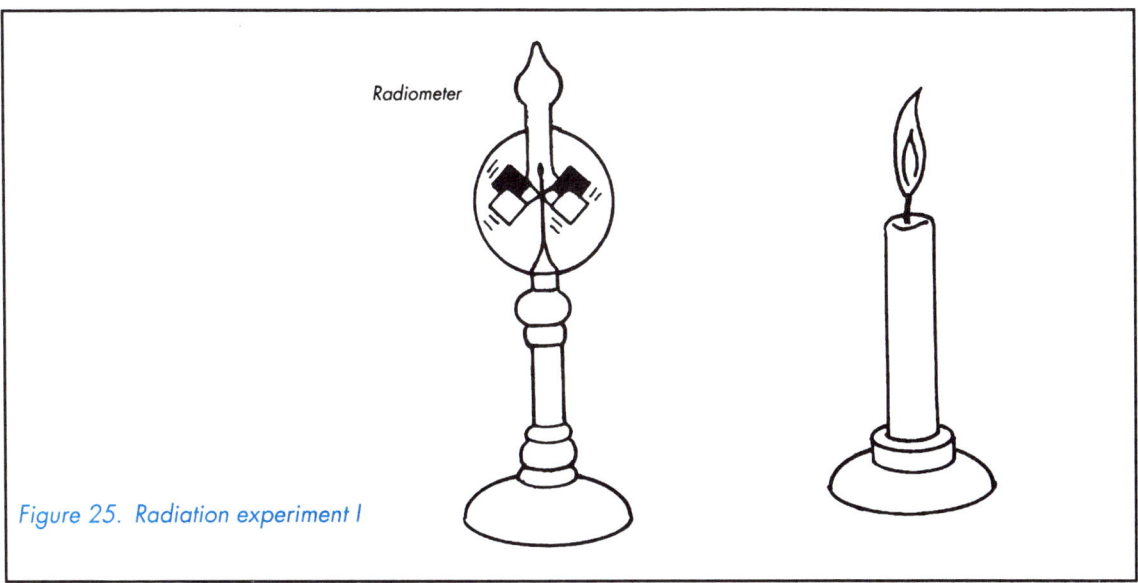

Figure 25. Radiation experiment I

5. Put the radiometer in the direct rays of the sun. Describe how it performs (Figure 26). What is the source of the energy that causes the radiometer to spin? Cut off the sun's rays with the square of black hardboard. What happens to the radiometer? How is it affected by shadow?

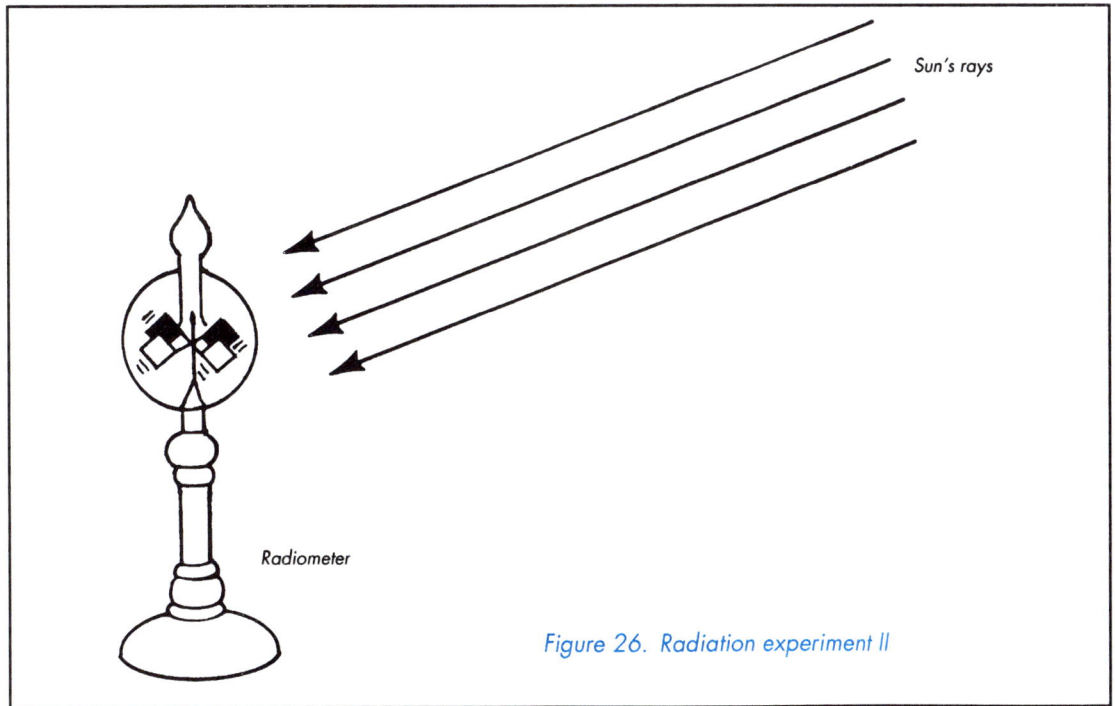

Figure 26. Radiation experiment II

6. Find out why the radiometer spins. Write a paragraph on your findings.

Chapter Three

The Planets

30. Mercury

> *Do there exist many worlds, or is there but a single world? This is one of the most noble and exalted questions in the study of Nature.*
>
> —Albertus Magnus, 13th century

Mercury, Venus, Earth, and Mars are the inner members of the sun's family. They make up a group of four rocky planets, quite unlike the great, outer gas planets. During its journey around the sun, Mercury's shape changes; like the moon, it goes through phases. Because Mercury is small—about half as big as our moon—and close to the sun, it is difficult to see. The best time to see Mercury is when it is far from the sun, as an evening star or morning star.

On the sun side of Mercury, temperatures reach a scorching 350°C. At night it drops to –170°C. This is because there is no atmosphere to trap the heat. A Mercury year, the time for one trip around the sun, is 88 days, while one rotation on its axis takes 58.7 days.

Mercury has an iron core, enough to supply all Earth's needs for millions of years. The planet's surface is like the moon's, with highlands showing many craters and great smooth plains with few craters.

Planet Orbits

What you need: sheet of glass or plastic about 50 cm square; three clamps; strong bar magnet or electromagnet; ball bearing or other steel ball; cardboard; paper; string; two pins; pencil; level

1. Arrange the glass, clamps, and magnet as shown in Figure 1. Level carefully so that the steel ball does not run off when placed anywhere on the glass plate. Mount the magnet under the center of the glass and as close to it as possible.

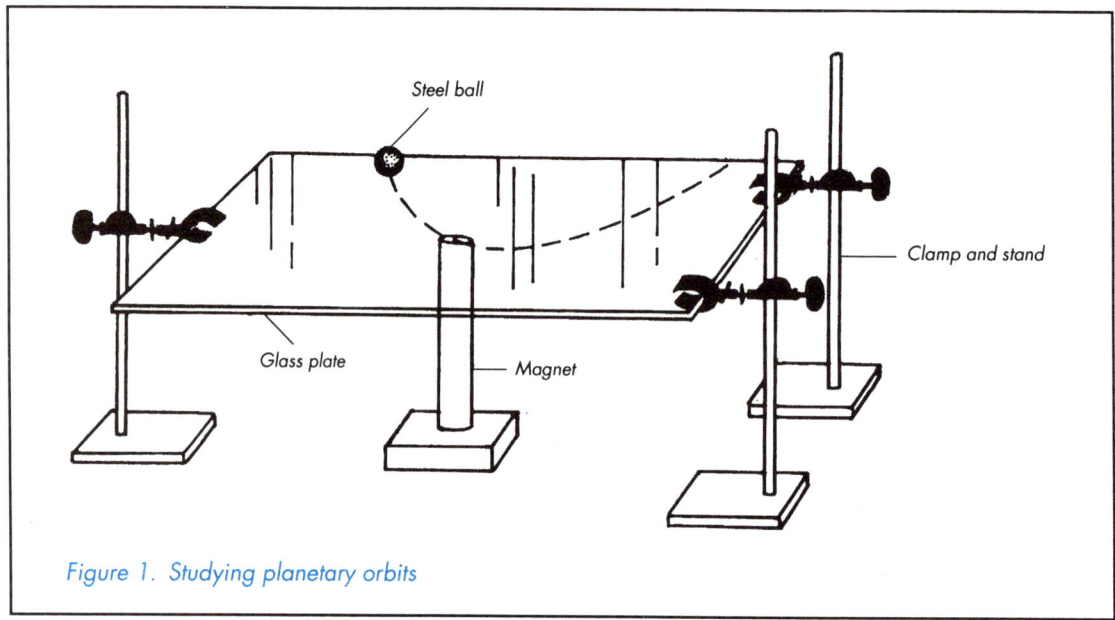

Figure 1. Studying planetary orbits

2. Roll the polished steel ball slowly across the glass; note that its path depends on its speed and its distance from the magnet. With a little practice you should be able to produce curves like that shown.

3. Experiment with slower speeds and see if you can produce closed orbits.

4. If the ball represents a planet and the magnet the sun, when would the planet move fastest? In the solar system, which planets move at higher speeds, the inner or the outer planets? Can you say why?

5. The word "ellipse" is often used to describe planet or satellite orbits. You will get a good idea of what an ellipse is like by drawing one. To do this, place a loop of string loosely around two firmly fixed pins (Figure 2).

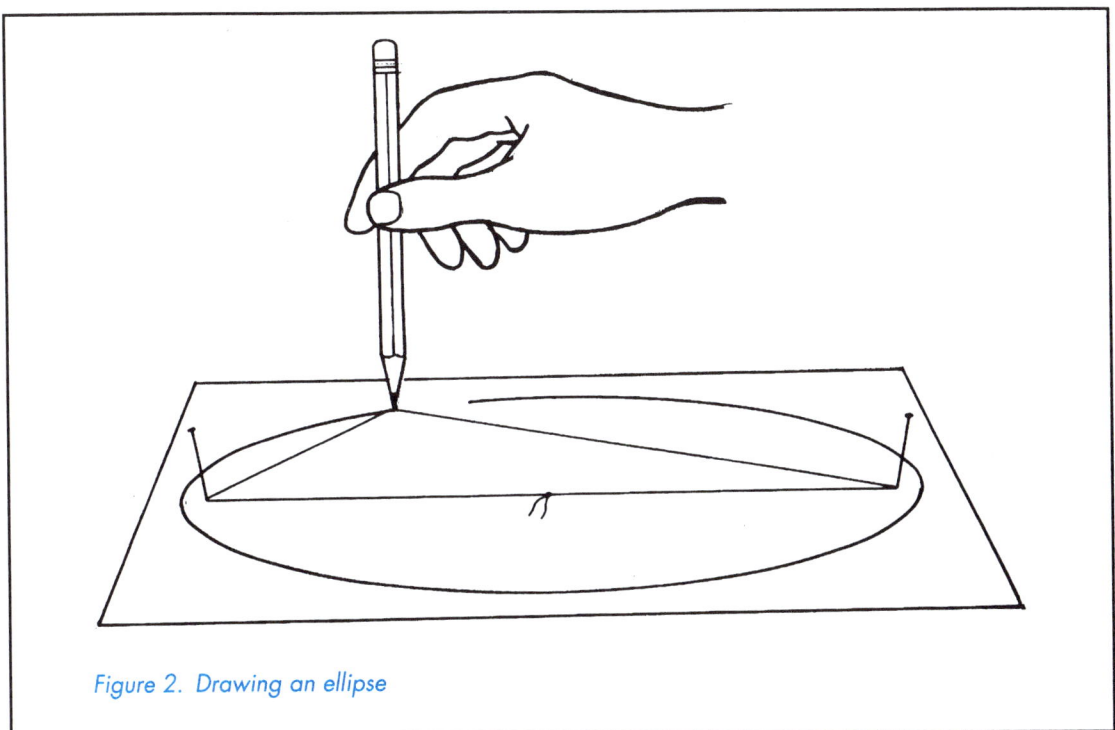

Figure 2. Drawing an ellipse

Draw the string tight with a pencil, then move the pencil along the path that keeps the string tight, as shown in the diagram. The two pins are at points known as the foci (singular—focus) of the ellipse. How would you describe the shape of an ellipse? Try drawing ellipses with the pins a little farther apart, then a little closer together. How does the shape of the ellipse change?

31. Venus

While Venus is about the same size as Earth, spacecraft studies show that it is a very different world. The atmosphere is mainly poisonous carbon dioxide and its clouds contain sulfuric acid. The atmosphere of Venus traps the heat from the sun like the glass of a greenhouse. Surface temperatures reach 475°C, hot enough to melt lead. Pressure is 90 times that of Earth.

Some photos show the surface of Venus thick with rocks, possibly due to meteorites striking the surface. Other photos show smooth surfaces without rocks, which may be lava flows.

Venus, the brightest planet, can be seen even in the daytime; it is best observed in early evening or just before dawn, and so is called the evening star or morning star.

On rare occasions, Venus shows up as a tiny black bead moving across the face of the sun. Astronomers call this a transit (Figure 3).

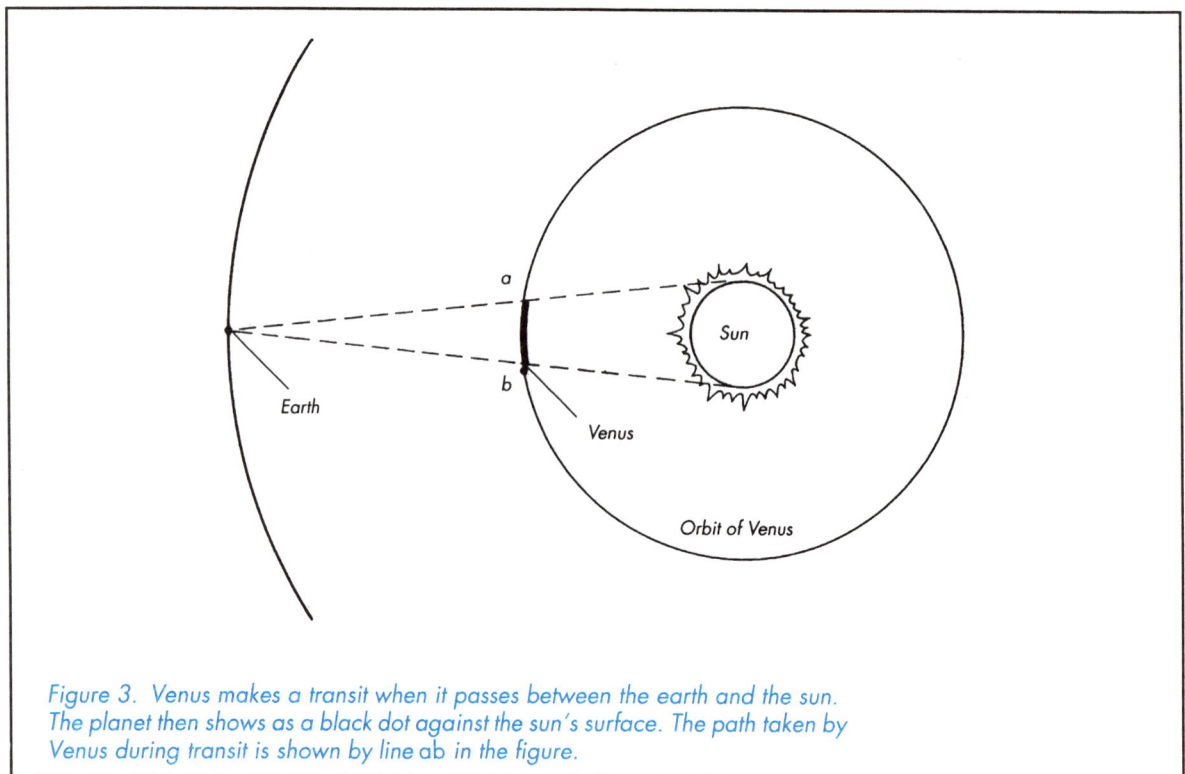

Figure 3. Venus makes a transit when it passes between the earth and the sun. The planet then shows as a black dot against the sun's surface. The path taken by Venus during transit is shown by line ab in the figure.

The Transit of Venus

You can demonstrate a planet in transit.

What you need: bead tied to thread; reading lamp; cardboard with support; scissors

1. Suspend the bead (Venus) between the bright reading lamp (sun) and the piece of cardboard (Earth).

2. Stand about three meters from the "sun's" face and have a friend move the thread with its attached "Venus" slowly across the "sun's" face. Describe how the "transit of Venus" appeared to you.

3. Cut or punch two holes in the cardboard, one at the center and another somewhere toward the outer edge. Look through the holes, moving from one to the other as your friend moves the bead as before. How is this like what observers do? (Remember that the cardboard represents Earth.)

4. Find out anything you can about the 1769 transit of Venus.

5. The word "transit" has other meanings in astronomy. What are they?

6. What things about Venus are similar to those on Earth? What things are different?

32. Earth: Rotate and Revolve

The earth is by no means a perfect sphere. As early as 1673 it was reasoned that due to the rotation of the earth on its axis, a centrifugal effect (a moving away from the center) would cause a bulge at the equator and a flattening at the poles. Due to this, the pull of gravity varies from place to place over the earth's surface.

As the flattened poles are 21 kilometers closer to the center of the earth than the equator, the pull of gravity is stronger there. A man weighing 100 kilograms would weight about 100.5 kilograms at the poles.

Earth also revolves in space around the sun. The curved orbit is caused by a centripetal force acting on it—the gravity pull between the sun and Earth (or other planet).

Rotate and Revolve

What you need: water; round balloon; screw eye; hand drill; string; soft ball tied to strand of elastic; top, or cardboard disc 10 cm across; plastic pen cap

1. Place the balloon under the tap and fill it with water.

2. Attach the screw eye to the hand drill. Tie off the neck of the balloon and hang it from the screw eye.

3. Revolve the hand drill, steadying the balloon with your hand if needed. How does the shape of the balloon alter as it rotates? What is happening to cause the change in shape? Can you relate what you see to the rotation of the earth on its axis? How does rotation affect shape at the equator? At the poles?

4. Swing the ball around your head (Figure 4). What happens to the size of the circle as you spin the ball faster? When is the rubber band pulling hardest on the ball? How is this like the earth revolving around the sun? What force holds the earth in its path?

Figure 4. Revolving

5. Spin the top or the cardboard disc on the pen top as shown (Figure 5). Which is rotating, the spinning ball or the top? Which is revolving?

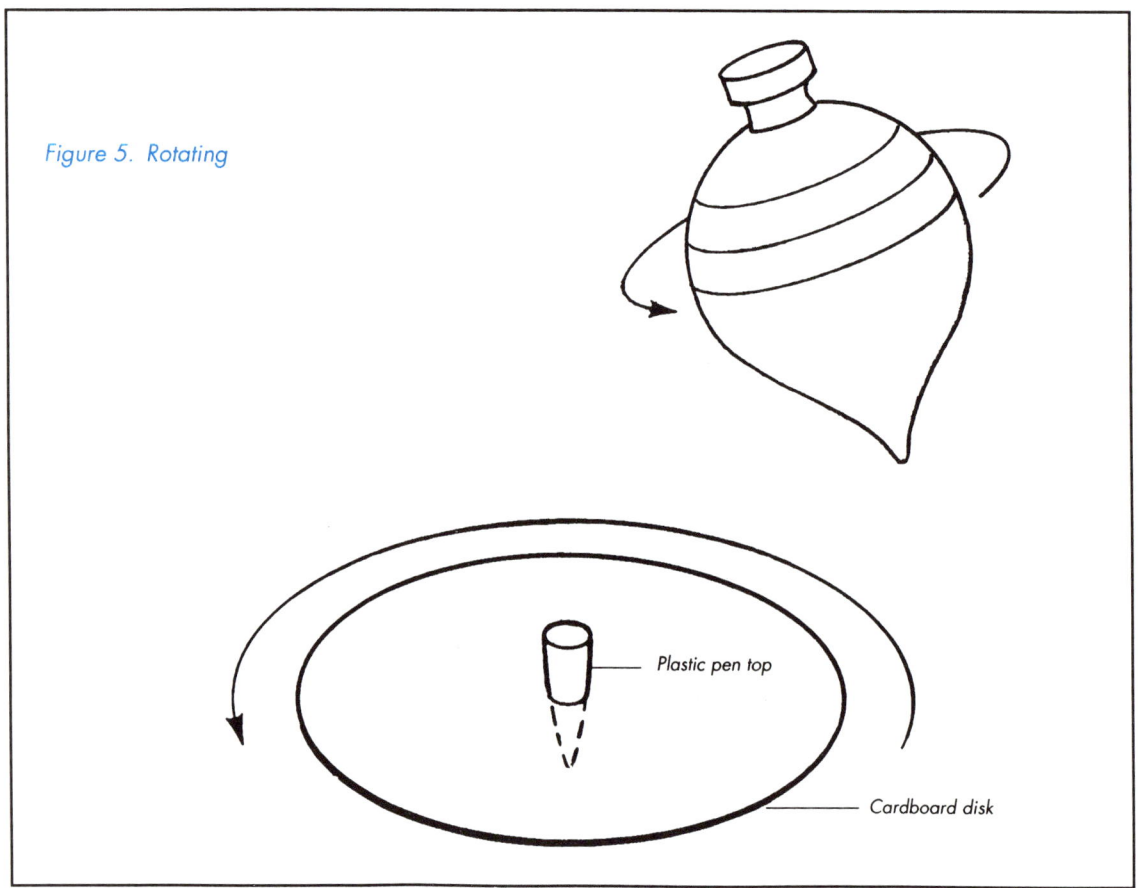

Figure 5. Rotating

33. Mars: Making the Red Planet Green

Some scientists believe that Mars can be made habitable, but with an atmosphere only a hundredth as dense as Earth's and summer temperatures of –60°C (Antarctic winter), the difficulties would be great. Yet Mars has about 1,200 cubic miles of frozen water in its polar ice caps; there is also water in the planet crust as ice. The soil of Mars contains key elements for life—hydrogen, oxygen, carbon, nitrogen, phosphorus, and sulfur. Scientists would aim to give Mars an Earthlike atmosphere, as the planet is massive enough to retain it for tens of millions of years. This could be done in five stages, beginning in the year 2015.

Stage 1 (2015–2030): First human beings arrive for a year and carry out agricultural experiments. Temperature –60°C.

Stage 2 (2030–2080): Warming begins as orbiting solar mirrors warm the polar ice caps, sprayed with black soot to reduce reflected heat loss. Carbon dioxide, oxygen, nitrogen, and water vapor freed from crust with other gases give a greenhouse effect. Temperature now –40°C.

Stage 3 (2080–2115): Rivers flow from melted ice; tundra and plant life present. Clouds develop. Sky turns from pink to blue. Temperature –15°C.

Stage 4 (2115–2130): Small seas form with plankton to absorb carbon dioxide. Evergreen forests form. Temperatures at freezing point.

Stage 5 (2130–7210): Towns, farming, and industry develop. The air is fully breathable. Mars is now very Earthlike. Temperature 10°C.

Ecology and Mars

Look at some of the problems scientists are studying in relation to establishing human colonies on Mars.

What you need: three test tubes with stoppers; two aquarium snails; two pieces of aquarium plant; plant cuttings; soil in cloth; jars; funnel; wood splint; a clear or light-colored round balloon; two paper bands; books; core with hole; two thermometers

Ecology for a new planet

All living things are dependent upon one another. This state of balance seen throughout is known as ecology. To demonstrate this, fill each of the three test tubes to within 2–3 cm of the top with water. Place an aquarium snail in the first test tube, a piece of aquarium plant in the second, and a snail and a piece of aquarium plant in the third (Figure 6). In which test tube does life continue for the longest period? Why?

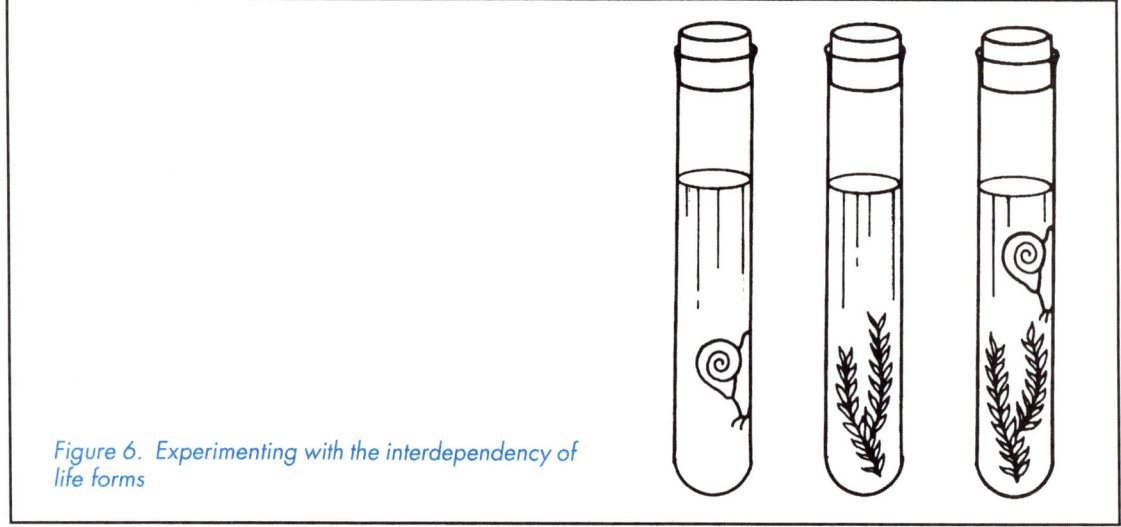

Figure 6. Experimenting with the interdependency of life forms

The greenhouse effect

Carbon dioxide and water vapor are key atmospheric gases. They allow the sun's shortwave heat rays to pass through but trap the long waves radiated by the earth. They act like the glass of a greenhouse. Using two books, the thermometers, the balloon, and two bands of paper, set up the demonstration as shown in Figure 7. Place both the thermometers in sunlight and take temperature readings after a few minutes. Which thermometer shows the higher temperature? How is the heat trapped?

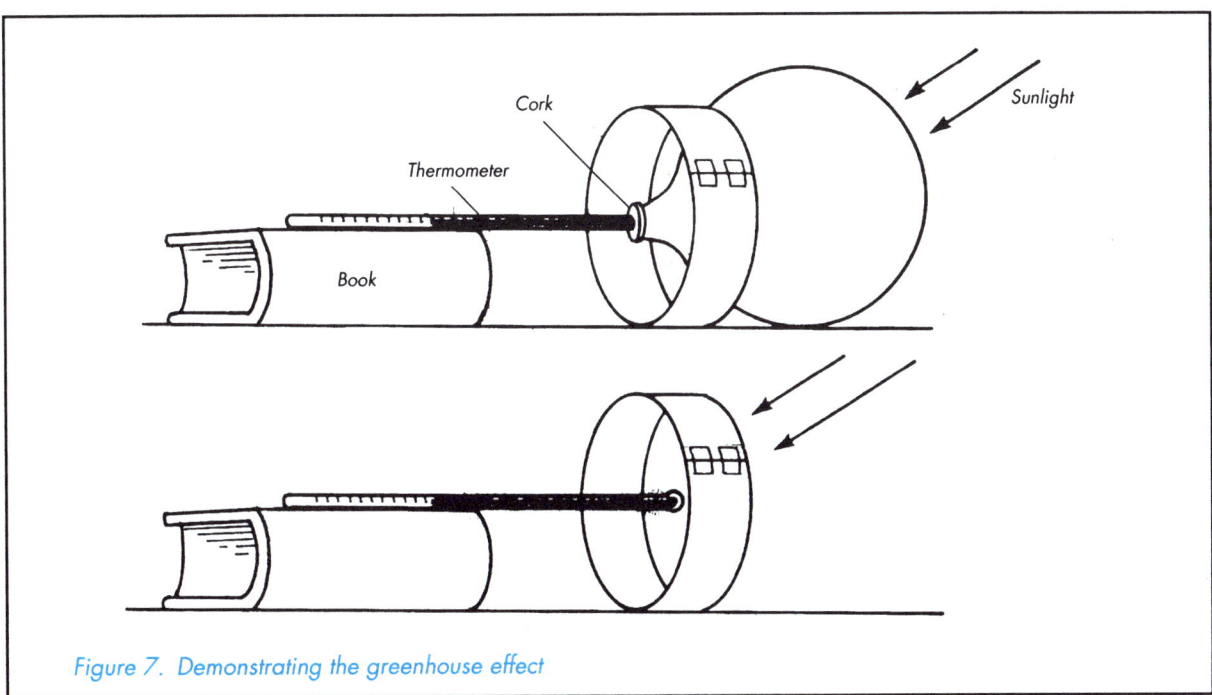

Figure 7. Demonstrating the greenhouse effect

Plants need minerals

Pour a jar of water over the soil in the cloth and collect the water that washes through. Pour plain water into another jar. Arrange plant cuttings in jars as shown in Figure 8 and examine after one week, then two weeks. What do you see? How are minerals important for plants?

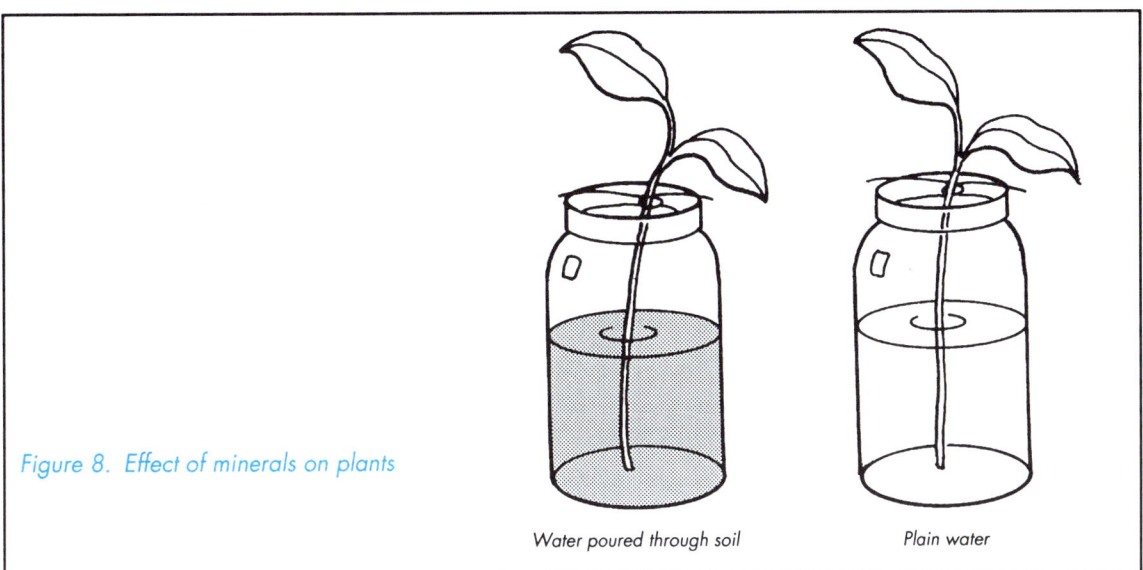

Figure 8. Effect of minerals on plants

34. Jupiter: The Giant Planet

In March 1979, *Voyager 1* passed within 280,000 kilometers of the giant planet Jupiter and its 14 moons, and found an amazing variety among them (Figure 9). The closest approach of the spacecraft was to Io, innermost of the large Jovian moons, and photographs were taken from 14,000 kilometers. Two other large Jovian moons, Ganymede and Callisto, seemed to be covered with water-ice; everywhere there were giant, frozen craters. The moons had no atmosphere.

Figure 9. Jupiter and its four planet-size moons, called the Galilean satellites, as photographed in 1979 by Voyager 1 *and assembled into a composite picture. The moons are not to scale but are in their relative positions. The moons are Io (upper left), Europa (center), Ganymede, and Callisto (lower right).*

Some astronomers describe Jupiter and its satellites as a solar system in miniature. Just by Jupiter's cloudy surface, *Voyager* discovered a ring of rock particles a few kilometers thick and several thousand kilometers wide, similar to the rings around Saturn but too fine to be seen from earth. Amalthea, the closest of the Jovian moons, showed as a tiny object 130 kilometers wide and 225 kilometers long, its tapering shape pointed at Jupiter by the planet's gravity pull.

The photographs of Jupiter showed it clad in a magnificent Joseph's coat of many colors in bands of yellows, browns, and oranges. It is marked with a Great Red Spot (Figure 10) some 50,000 kilometers across, a great seething cauldron of gases erupting on the planet's surface. In 1660, astronomer Gian Domenico Cassini described a spot on Jupiter which may have been the Great Red Spot. He used it to determine the planet's rotation period. Jupiter's atmosphere is mainly hydrogen, with smaller amounts of methane, ammonia, helium, and some other molecules.

Figure 10. Jupiter's Great Red Spot is some 50,000 kilometers across.

The *Pioneer* spacecraft showed a tremendous magnetic field around Jupiter. High-energy electrons and protons are trapped in the magnetic lines of force, so that Jupiter has radiation belts around it like Earth's Van Allen belt (named after discoverer James Van Allen). Pictures sent back by *Voyager* confirm that the planet is covered by great belts of clouds. These form bands which move at various speeds and show disturbances, related no doubt to the currents set up by the planet's rapid rotation. Jupiter has a diameter of over 140,000 kilometers (11 times that of Earth); it rotates in less than 10 hours, as compared with Earth's 24. The planet takes 12 years for one journey around the sun.

Jupiter emits three different types of radio waves, which on a radio set sound like static or atmospheric noise. We receive more radio noise from Jupiter than we get from any other source except the sun.

As *Voyager* soared away from Jupiter, it photographed a wonderful aurora over the planet's pole, as well as flashes of light in the atmosphere. This may have been lightning and may prove the most exciting discovery of all. Under the action of an electric discharge such as lightning, organic molecules—the forerunners of life—can form out in space.

Jupiter Model

You can make a model of Jupiter and demonstrate its magnetic field and radiation belts.

What you need: two pieces of light cardboard about 20 cm square; black paper; art materials; paste; string; bar magnet; iron filings; scissors; magnetic compass; two books; drawing compass; sewing needle; thin slice of cork; bowl of water; sheet of glass or clear plastic

1. Draw a 10-cm (4")-diameter circle on the card to represent Jupiter. Note that the equatorial diameter is greater than the polar. Why? Can you show this on your model? Paste the circle onto the black paper for background. Then use crayons or paints to draw in stripes or bands in shades of yellow, brown, and orange. At times Jupiter shows olive-green and blue markings; show these also. Include the Great Red Spot, which changes in color and size. What can you find out about this spot?

2. Cut a strip of cardboard about 20 cm (8") long. Crease this strip about 1 cm ($3/8$") from each end. Glue these sections of the strip to the model, leaving about 1 cm ($3/8$") on each side of the equator. The strip should form an arc above "Jupiter." Press four pellets of modeling clay onto this strip to represent the Galilean satellite moons of Jupiter—Io, Europa, Callisto, and Ganymede. Io and Europa are inner, the other two are outer; try to show this on the model. Label the moons. Find out about Galileo's discovery of them.

3. Hang your model of Jupiter on the wall and view it with half-closed eyes from 2–3 meters away. Note the colored bands (what do they represent?), the Great Red Spot, the greater diameter at the equator, and the satellite moons. Compare your model with color pictures in books from your school library. Why do you think Jupiter was named after the King of the Gods?

4. Place the glass or clear plastic across two books as shown in Figure 11. Draw a circle on the other piece of card about the same in diameter as the length of the bar magnet; place on top. Place the bar magnet under the glass or clear plastic as shown. Now lightly sprinkle iron filings over the card. Gently tap one corner of the card. What do the iron filings do? How is this like Jupiter's magnetic field reaching out into space many times the diameter of the planet? Find out what you can about the magnetosphere of Jupiter.

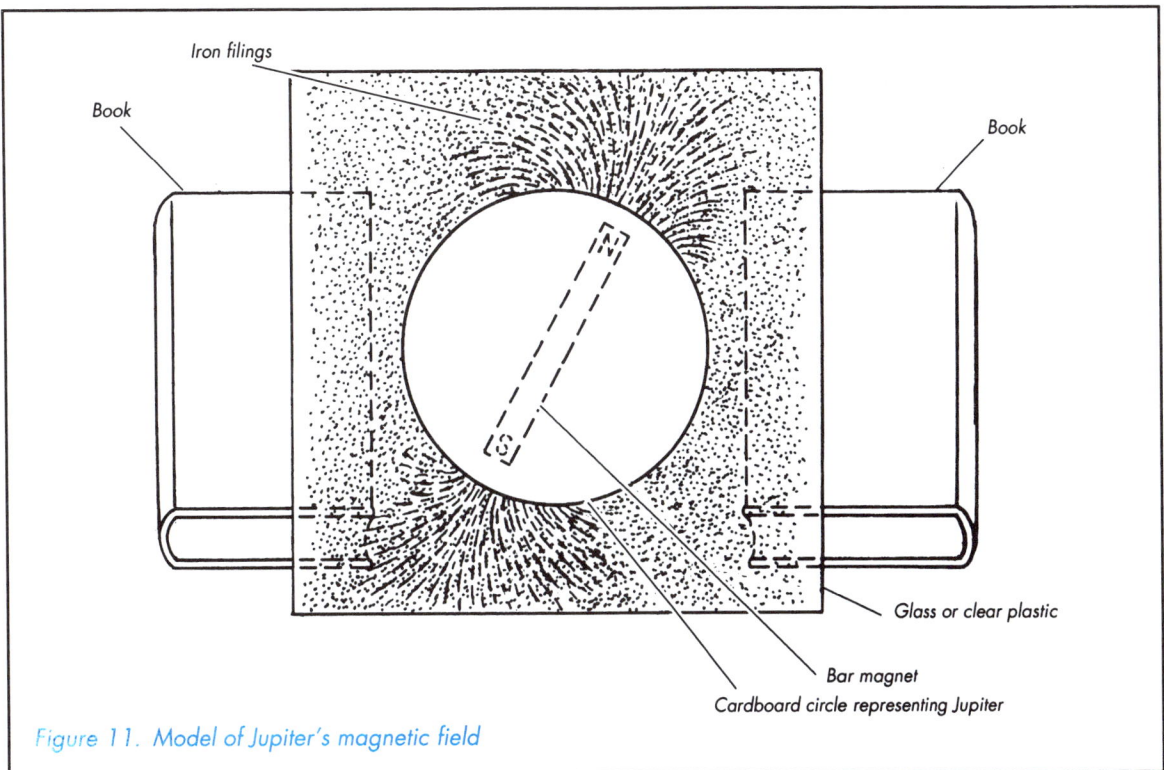

Figure 11. Model of Jupiter's magnetic field

5. You can show how particles from the sun trapped in Jupiter's magnetic field spiral from pole to pole; that is, you demonstrate the radiation belts of the giant planet. Find out about Earth's Van Allen belt. To do this, magnetize the sewing needle by stroking it about 20 times in one direction only. Then push the needle through the thin slice of cork and float it in a trough of water. Place the bar magnet as shown in Figure 12. How does the needle move? Place the needle/cork at different places in the trough. Does the needle take different paths? Try a second needle of opposite polarity to the first. Remove the first needle, and place the second one where the first one came to rest. Compare the paths of the two needles. What does this tell you about the lines of force? How is this like the radiation belts of Jupiter?

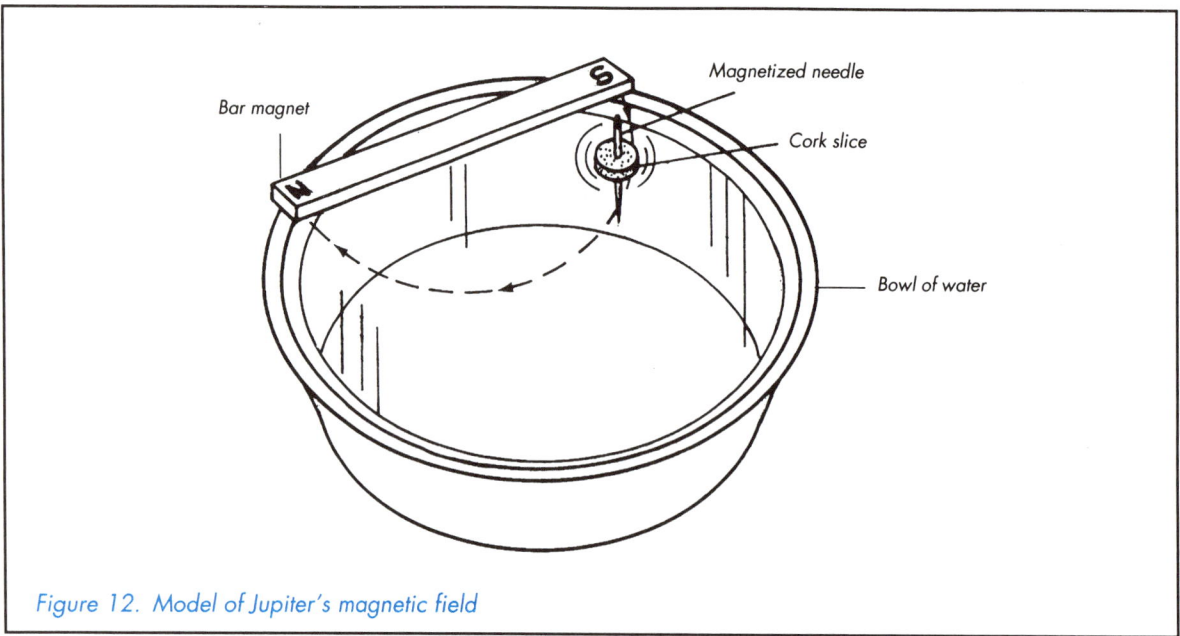

Figure 12. Model of Jupiter's magnetic field

6. Mars is over 200 million kilometers from the sun, and Jupiter is over 800 million kilometers distant. Yet Jupiter appears to us much brighter than Mars in the night sky. How do you explain this?

35. Io: Jupiter's Incredible Moon

In 1610 Galileo looked through his telescope at Jupiter and saw four bright points of light in orbit around the planet. These four satellite moons of Jupiter are named Io, Europa, Callisto, and Ganymede. They are known as the Galilean satellites in his honor. The pictures sent back from space by the *Voyager* spacecraft showed Io a waterless, rocky body with a surface of many colors and more than six volcanoes erupting at once. The gravity pull of massive Jupiter on Io, plus the pull of Europa and Ganymede as they pass it, causes Io's surface to rise and fall in a regular way like an ocean tide. (Scientists call the process "tidal pumping.")

The rise and fall generates tremendous heat through friction in Io's interior. The heat melts sulfur deep in Io; scientists think that sulfur dioxide gas detected by *Voyager* is the main force driving Io's volcanoes. As the sulfur gas erupts from the volcanoes, it cools quickly and condenses on the surface. This would explain Io's vivid orange, yellow, red, and black surface colors (Figure 13).

The eruptions on Io may send particles far and wide into Jupiter's magnetic field (also called the "magnetosphere"). *Voyager* detected particles of sulfur and oxygen in a band of ions shaped like a giant doughnut around Jupiter at the distance of Io's orbit. The ions are trapped in the band by the magnetic field lines along which they move. At Jupiter's north and south poles some ions spill out, giving brilliant displays of aurora. A faint ring around Jupiter discovered by *Voyager* is very likely due to the eruptions on Io. Measurements show that Io's eruptions throw out three tons of material into the doughnut daily; this represents less than a tenth of one percent of its mass for the next ten billion years.

Figure 13. On the surface of Io, a number of volcanoes erupting at once throw out tons of material every day.

Experiments with Sulfur

What you need: sulfur; test tubes; water; medicine dropper; beakers or glasses; wire; teaspoon; hand lens; saucer; burner; iron filings; magnet; cup; blue litmus

1. Put a little sulfur into a saucer and look at it through a hand lens. Describe the crystals.

2. Design an experiment to see if sulfur conducts an electric current.

3. Put a rice-grain of sulfur in a test tube and add a dropper of water. Does the sulfur dissolve? Does warming help?

4. Take a teaspoon of iron filings and two teaspoons of sulfur; mix them together well on the piece of paper (Figure 14). Look at the mixture through the hand lens. Describe what you see. Pass the magnet through the mixture. What happens? (Figure 15)

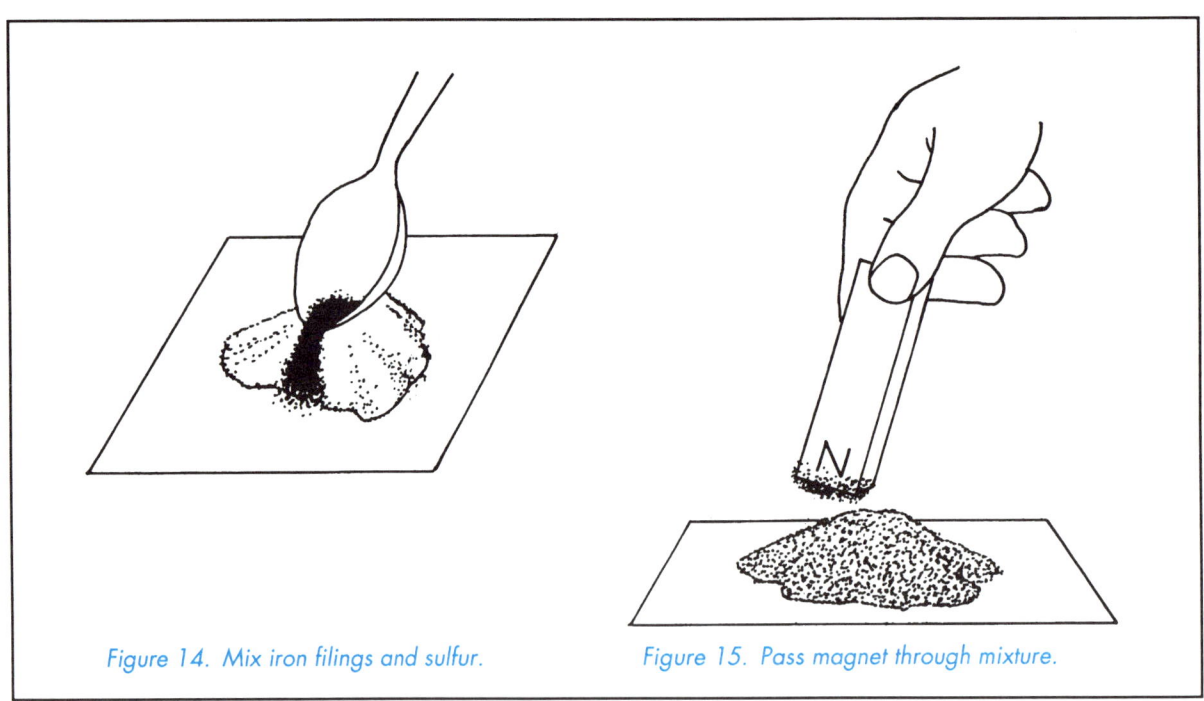

Figure 14. Mix iron filings and sulfur.

Figure 15. Pass magnet through mixture.

5. Remove the iron filings from the magnet and make another iron-sulfur mix. Place the mix in the cup and add a dropper of water—just enough to give a paste when you stir it (Figure 16). What do you notice about the cup? Explain why. What does the water form? What can you smell?

6. When the cup is cool, look at its contents (Figure 17). Can you now separate the iron from the sulfur? Why or why not? Find a name for the black powder you have made.

7. Put about 3 cm of sulfur into a test tube and heat it gently. **Caution:** Keep shaking the tube as you do this to avoid overheating at any one spot. What are the color changes as the sulfur melts? When you have a pale yellow liquid, pour some drops into some cold water in a beaker.

   Continue heating the rest of the sulfur in the test tube, noting changes in color and thickness. Heat until reddish-black and nearly boiling. Pour this into cold water also. Compare this sample with the earlier one. You have made plastic sulfur; the first sample was ordinary sulfur. Why the name "plastic" sulfur? What happens if you keep stretching it?

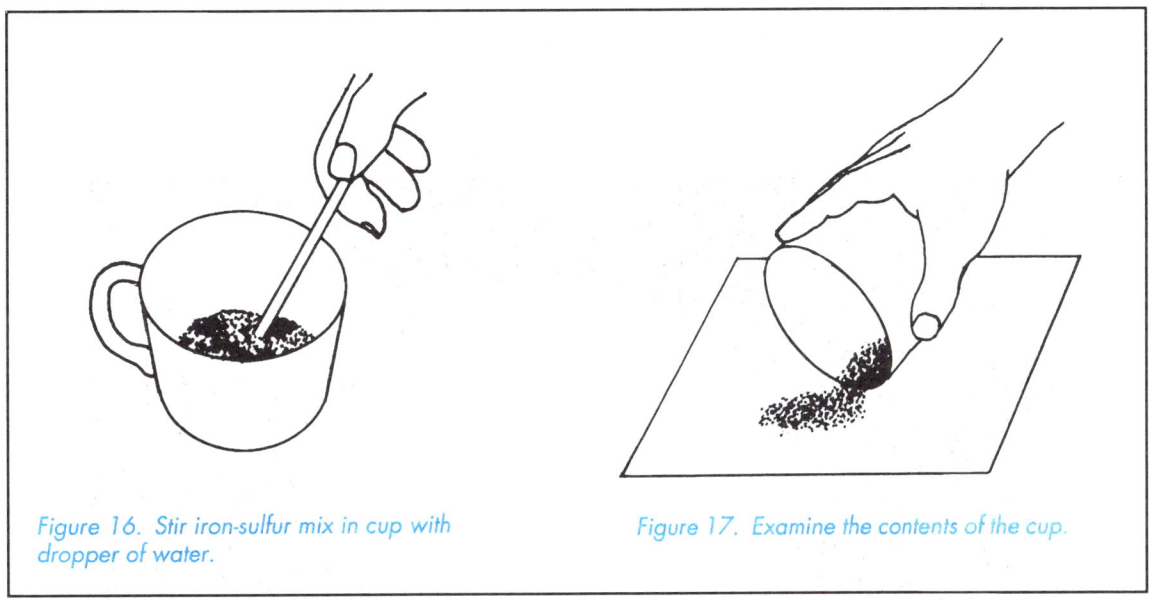

Figure 16. Stir iron-sulfur mix in cup with dropper of water.

Figure 17. Examine the contents of the cup.

8. Heat the end of a wire and dip this into sulfur; the sulfur will melt and stick to the wire. Hold the sulfur in the flame until it burns, then place the wire in a beaker containing a little blue litmus. Explain what happens.

9. List the reasons why you think sulfur should be classed as a nonmetal.

10. List the uses of sulfuric acid.

11. How is sulfur obtained from underground deposits?

36. Saturn: The Ringed Planet

Viewers of Saturn (Figure 18) are always fascinated by the serene beauty of this huge planet, with its equatorial diameter of 120,000 kilometers. Through a telescope we can see three main rings, the A, B, and C rings. A, the outermost ring, is separated from the brighter ring B by a dark band—the Cassini division, named after Cassini, the Italian astronomer who discovered it in 1675. The inner ring, C, is fainter than the other two.

The pictures sent to Earth by the *Voyager* and *Pioneer* spacecraft reveal the ring system in an entirely new light. This beautiful and complex system of multiple rings, intertwined and laced together in a pattern of supreme beauty, makes Saturn the most wonderful sight in the sky. The Cassini division shows as a region where the density of the ring particles is much less then elsewhere.

The rings are made up of countless tiny particles, ice crystals, and frosted rock, varying considerably in size. The particles orbit around Saturn's equator at different distances from the planet's cloud tops. The rings are 275,000 kilometers across but a slender 1 kilometer in depth.

Figure 18. As Saturn moves through its orbit, the rings are seen from different angles.

Saturn has some twenty satellites in orbit around it. The largest is Titan; with a diameter of 5,550 kilometers, it can be easily seen through a small telescope. Another satellite moon, Iapetus, is a puzzle, as its sides reflect light differently: One side reflects like dark rock, and the other like snow. Why this should be remains a mystery.

Saturn lies 1,427 million kilometers from the sun; though second largest in size of the planets, it has less mass than its smaller neighbors. It is made up of very light material, less dense than water; in fact, it would float (Figure 19).

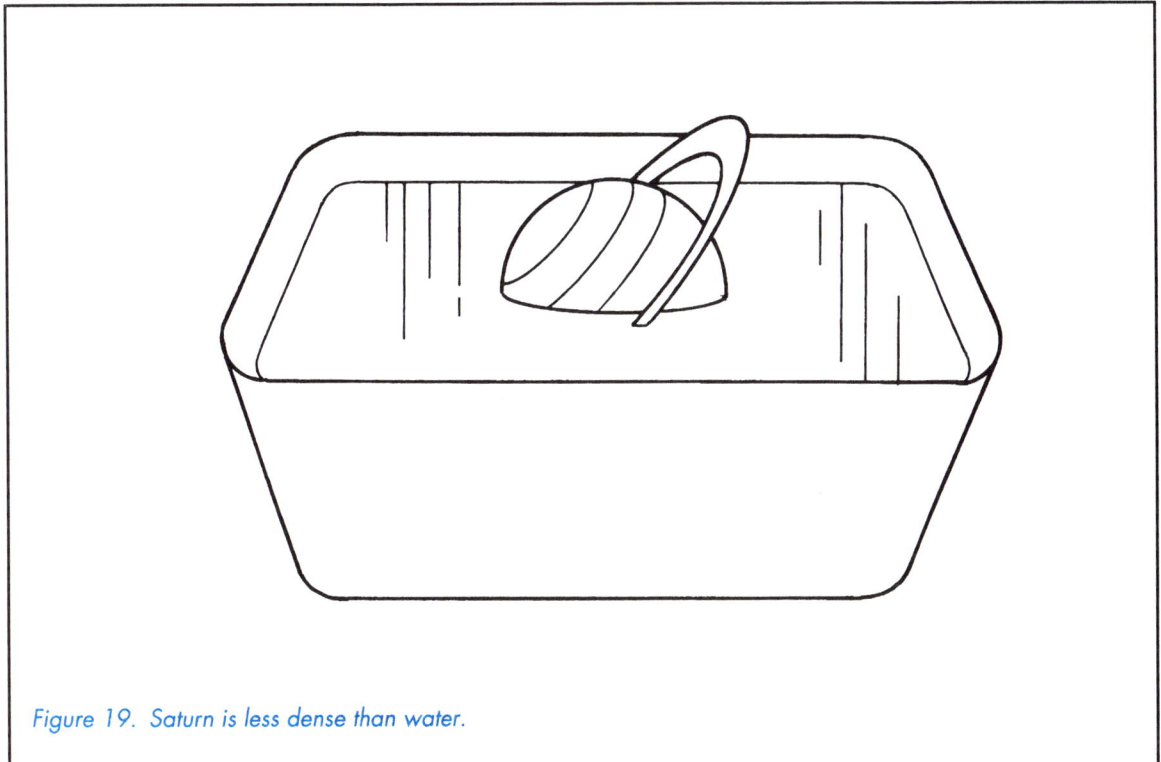

Figure 19. Saturn is less dense than water.

Saturn has a magnetic field and, like Jupiter, emits radio waves. Saturn's speed of rotation on its axis is about 10 hours; astronomers think the equatorial regions rotate faster than the poles. The planet takes 29.5 years for one orbit around the sun.

With a surface temperature of about −180°C, it would seem that most of Saturn's atmosphere is in the form of frozen crystals.

Features of Saturn

What you need: tennis ball; thin plastic sheet; refrigerator; flashlight; hand lens; table salt; basin of water; scissors; sand samples; sugar; washing soda; bath salts

1. Cut a doughnut-shaped collar from the plastic (to represent the rings) and fit this over the tennis ball (to represent Saturn). Place this in the basin of water. What happens? How is this like one of the features of Saturn? Explain.

2. Look at frozen crystals on the inside of a freezer. Shine a bright flashlight on them. Does the light reflect? How do you explain the glistening faces?

3. With a lens, look at some sea sand, fine river sand, and coarse river sand. Can you see clear crystals (quartz), and clay-colored crystals (feldspar)? Which contains most quartz—the sea sand or the river sand? Also look at substances like salt, sugar, washing soda, and bath salts with your lens. Try to sketch the crystal shapes. What might crystals have to do with the Rings of Saturn?

4. In what ways are Jupiter and Saturn similar? In what ways are they different?

37. Uranus

On January 24, 1986, *Voyager 2*, traveling at over 72,000 km/hr, sailed within 80,000 km of the blue-green planet's cloud tops. Because the Uranian system stands vertical, *Voyager* flew in and out of the Uranian family of rings, moons, and planet in a matter of hours, like a bull's-eye on a target. Of the five major moons, Miranda, the smallest, appeared as a fantastic fairyland of strange forms, craters, valleys, mountain ranges, fault lines, and even a possible ice flow. And all this was photographed in the murky light of deep space when the spacecraft was nearly 3 billion kilometers from the sun.

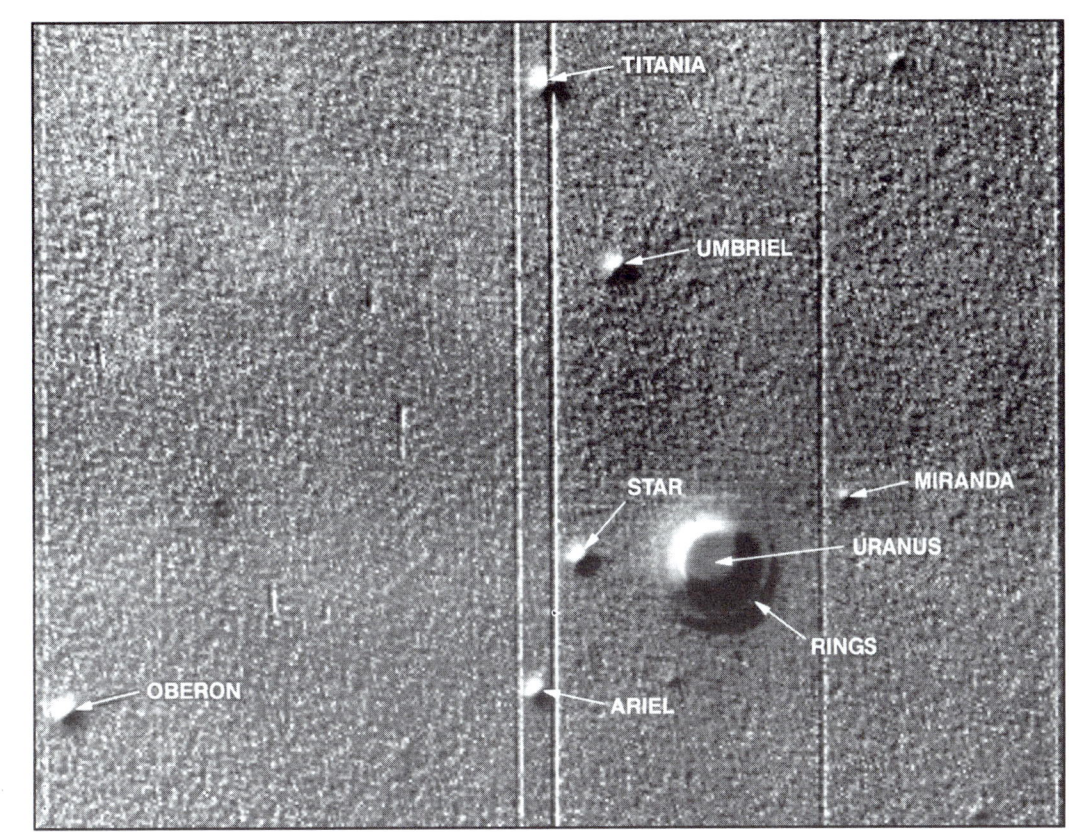

Figure 20. First definitive photo of the rings of the planet Uranus taken from Earth

The third-largest of the planets, Uranus is circled by at least nine charcoal-black rings (Figure 20). An odd feature of Uranus is that it lies on its side, axis tilted a full 95° (compare Jupiter 3°, Earth 23½°). Because Uranus travels the solar system in this strange position, one pole is sunlight for 42 years while the other is dark. Then, for the next 42 years, the situation is reversed. Currently, the sunlit southern pole is framed at the center of the nine rings (Figure 21).

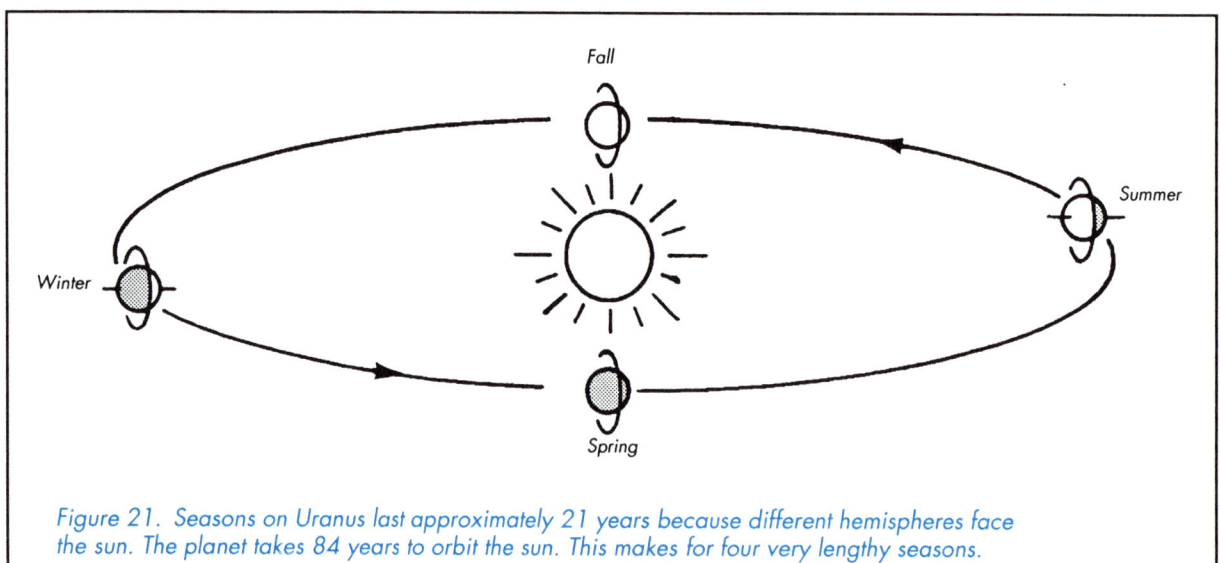

Figure 21. Seasons on Uranus last approximately 21 years because different hemispheres face the sun. The planet takes 84 years to orbit the sun. This makes for four very lengthy seasons.

What made Uranus topple over? One exciting idea is that it was struck by something about as big as Earth, traveling at about 65,000 km/hr. Such an explosion probably shot rock matter into space, and from this the moons formed. Due to the tilt of Uranus, the moons seem to follow a strange path. When the equator of the planet faces Earth, the moons appear to climb up the side, then drop over the top. Five moons were previously known, but *Voyager* discovered ten more—the largest being about 160 km in diameter, bigger than most asteroids.

An aurora had been seen on Uranus, so scientists believed a magnetic field would be present. Strangely, the Uranus magnetic field is tilted (Figure 22) and is not centered at the core of the planet as on Earth. One result of this is that the strength of magnetism on the surface of Uranus varies greatly from place to place.

Uranus spins in a direction opposite to Earth. Sometimes we see it rotating like the hands of a clock and at other times from top to bottom. The rings of Uranus are very thin; they were discovered in 1977, when astronomers saw a bright star blink through them before Uranus itself passed in front of the star.

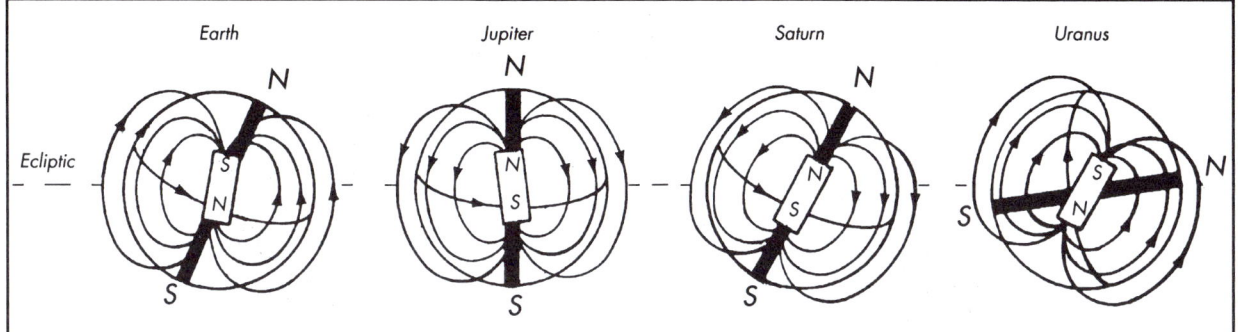

Figure 22. This diagram, not to scale, shows how a planet's axis of rotation (heavy lines) does not necessarily line up with its magnetic axis (bar magnets). In Uranus, the magnetic axis lies 55 degrees below the spin axis.

38. Neptune and Pluto

Neptune

Like Uranus, Neptune is a refrigerator. At nearly 5,000 kilometers from Earth, Neptune receives only one thousandth of the sunlight that falls on Earth (less than half what Uranus receives), yet its temperature is about the same as that of Uranus. This means there must be heat coming from Neptune's interior.

Low sunlight and a much higher level of internal heat must affect processes in Neptune's atmosphere. This is made up of hydrogen and helium with about 3% methane (natural gas). The methane absorbs the longer wavelengths of red light so that only the blues and greens are reflected to us. This gives Neptune a bluish-green color (Figure 23).

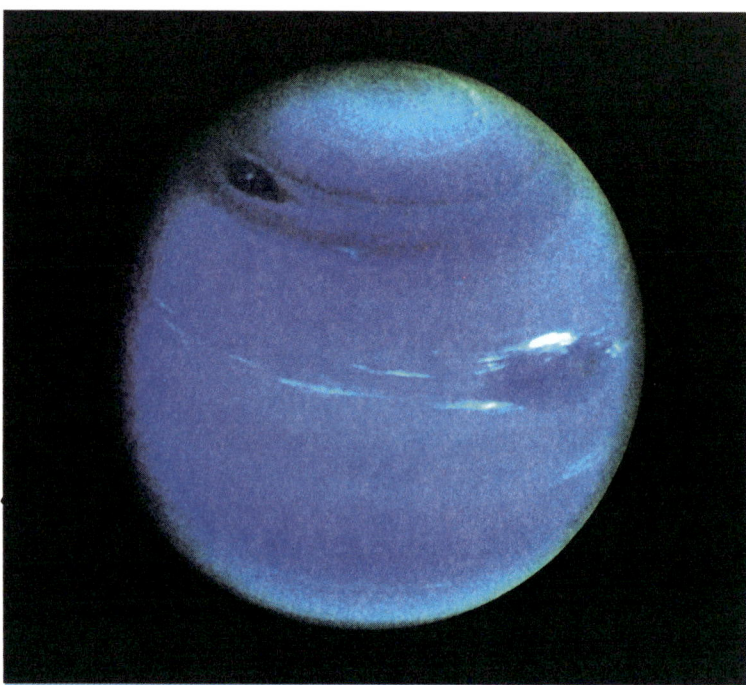

Figure 23. Neptune is seen by light reflected from the sun; its bluish-green color is due to absorption of the red, orange, and yellow solar rays.

Voyager 2 made its closest approach to Neptune on August 25, 1989. The pictures sent back by *Voyager 2* showed a Great Dark Spot—a violent storm area big enough to swallow Mars. Six unknown moonlets were discovered. The spacecraft also showed that Neptune has a magnetic field, and its cameras revealed cirruslike clouds of frozen methane gas. Five complete rings around Neptune were found.

Triton, Neptune's whitish moon, showed cliffs, faults, and craters. One crater, many hundred kilometers across, may have once shot forth frozen gases.

Who discovered Neptune? How was it discovered?

Pluto

In the largest telescopes, Pluto appears as just a speck. It was discovered on March 13, 1930, by observers at the Lowell Observatory in Flagstaff, Arizona. It is the smallest and usually the most distant planet, but its orbit is odd and it is currently closer to the sun than Neptune. With a temperature possibly about –230°C, no one could live on Pluto. Any air present would be frozen solid. Some think that Pluto may be an escaped moon of Neptune.

39. The Solar System

The solar system, which we now explore with satellites, is tiny when compared with the universe as a whole. At its heart is our nearest star, the sun. Around the sun nine planets revolve in near-circular paths or orbits. Closest to the sun is the planet Mercury, next is Venus, then Earth, Mars, Jupiter, Saturn, Uranus, Neptune, and finally Pluto.

The planets are held in their orbits by the sun's gravity and, except for Pluto, their paths lie nearly in the same plane. Planets closest to the sun are first to complete the round trip. Nearest the sun, Mercury takes 88 days; our Earth takes 365 days; distant Pluto takes 248 years for the journey once around the sun.

The sun is the source of heat and light for all the planets. We see them in the sky because of the light they reflect rather than because of any light they produce themselves. They shine in the sky because the sun is shining on them. As you might expect, planets close to the sun are warmer than those farther away. For example, where the sun shines on Mercury the temperature is about 500°C, whereas on distant Neptune the temperature is −200°C.

The planets have atmospheres, some more than others. Venus has clouds, Mars has little atmosphere, Jupiter has frozen gases.

Between the orbits of Mars and Jupiter are many minor planets, small bodies of rock we call asteroids. The largest of these, known as Ceres, is only 750 kilometers across. Many of the the asteroids are only one kilometer across.

1. Here are some interesting figures on what you would weigh on other worlds:

Earth	200 lbs	Saturn	187 lbs
Mercury	77 lbs	Uranus	159 lbs
Venus	181 lbs	Neptune	239 lbs
Mars	77 lbs	Pluto	11 lbs
Jupiter	509 lbs	Sun	5,560 lbs

You might want to illustrate these figures on a bar graph.

Model Solar System

You can make a mobile of the solar system to hang in your classroom (Figure 24).

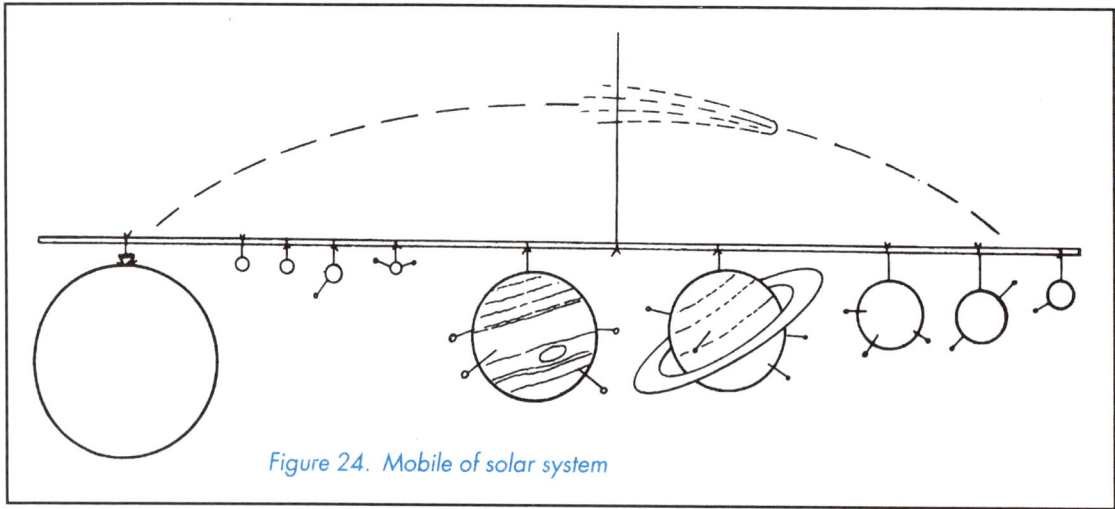

Figure 24. Mobile of solar system

What you need: large orange balloon; modeling clay; ping-pong balls; balloons of different sizes; papier-mâché; about two meters of light galvanized iron wire; art materials—paint, brushes, etc.; a two-meter length of iron reinforcing rod 5–6 mm in diameter, or a long stick; about two meters of string

1. Blow up the orange balloon, tie the neck, then tie to one end of the rod to serve as the sun. Why choose orange for the sun? Look at some pictures of the sun's surface. Can you decorate your "sun" to look the same?

2. For the inner, smaller planets, use modeling clay or ping-pong balls suitably painted. Can you show the rocky nature of these planets?

3. For the larger planets, use papier-mâché globes of various sizes. Build these around different-sized balloons. Which are the larger planets? Which planets have rings? Be sure to include these.

4. For moons, use small pieces of modeling clay on the ends of short pieces of wire. Earth has 1 moon, Mars 2, Jupiter 16, Saturn 18, Uranus 15, Neptune 2, Pluto 1. Show also the asteroids (minor planets) between Mars and Jupiter. As far as possible, try to observe some proportion in size and distance apart.

5. Support the sun, planets, moons, and asteroids from the iron rod and hang this high up in the classroom where it can swing freely.

6. You might also like to include shooting stars and comets in your mobile. Design your own way of doing this.

7. Some astronomers think there is a tenth planet in the solar system; it is sometimes referred to as Uncle Percy's planet. Find out what you can about it.

Chapter Four

Atmosphere

40. Atmospheric Gas Content and Pressure

> *The air moves like a river and carries the clouds with it.*
> —Leonardo da Vinci

For life processes to take place, we need oxygen. The amount needed is proportional to the energy being expended at any given moment. If the brain cells are without oxygen for three minutes, permanent damage is likely to result. Five minutes without oxygen spells death.

The human race lives at the foot of an ocean of air. Other gases in this ocean include nitrogen, carbon dioxide, and water vapor—all important in the planet's ecosystem. As we move out into space, the atmosphere becomes thinner, the pressure is less. The least pressure under which human beings can live and function comfortably is half an atmosphere (about 380 mm of mercury).

PLANET ATMOSPHERES

Planet	Atmosphere Main Components
Mercury	Virtually none
Venus	Carbon dioxide
Earth	Nitrogen; Oxygen
Mars	Carbon dioxide
Jupiter	Hydrogen; Helium
Saturn	Hydrogen; Helium
Uranus	Hydrogen; Helium; Methane
Neptune	Hydrogen; Helium; Methane
Pluto	None detected

Oxygen and Atmosphere

You can show that oxygen is necessary for life processes and that the atmosphere exerts pressure.

What you need: tall preserving jar; recently boiled water; peas suitable for planting; stick; two glasses; balloon; thread; kettle with boiling water, pins

1. Fill the preserving jar three-quarters full with water that has been recently boiled and hence contains no dissolved gases. Pin nine or ten peas onto a stick and place in the water so that some peas are near the surface. Keep the jar in a warm place for a few days. Note which peas germinate first. What do you find? Is it those peas near the water's surface or those near the bottom? How do you relate this to oxygen lack?

2. Blow up a large balloon and tie off the nozzle.

3. Steam the inside of a glass for a minute, then quickly place the glass firmly against the side of a balloon and keep it there until the steam condenses (Figure 1). What do you see? Can you explain what is happening? How is air pressure at work?

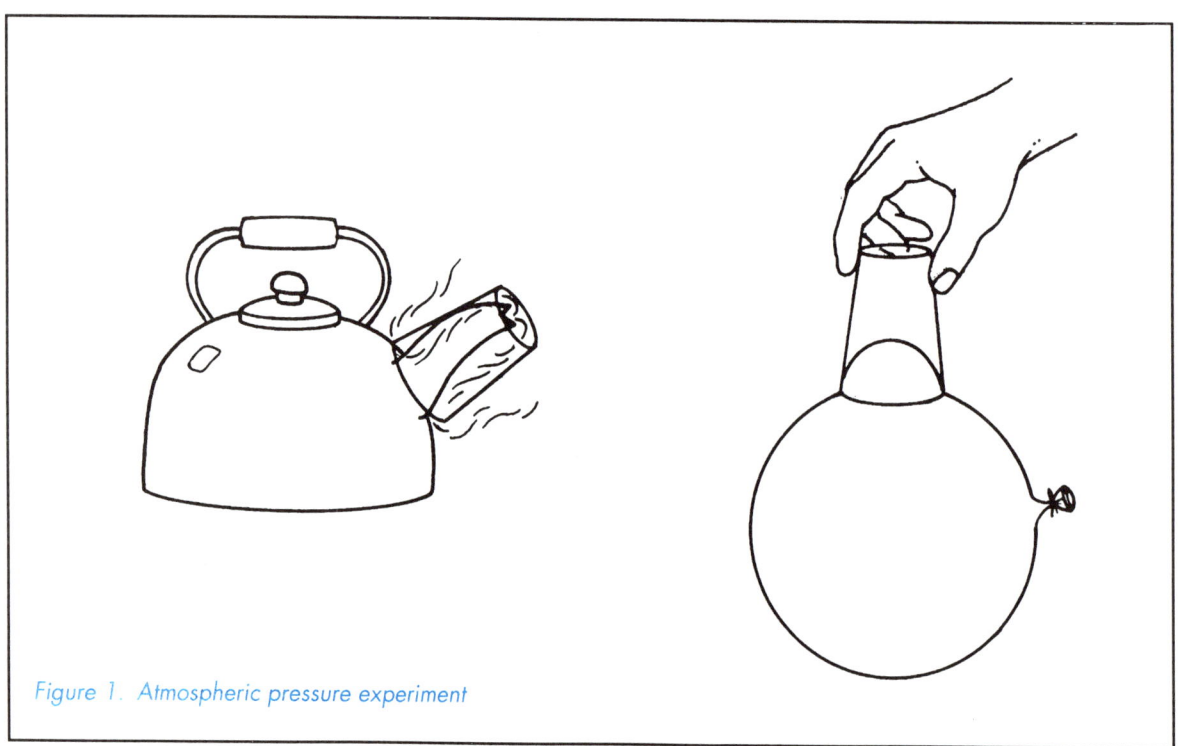

Figure 1. Atmospheric pressure experiment

4. Repeat with a second glass, holding it against the opposite side of the balloon. Describe what happens. What holds the glasses to the balloon? Is there a vacuum in the glasses?

5. Is space beyond our earth a vacuum? If not, make a list of the things it contains.

41. Space Environment

Astronauts have described fascinating and mysterious space phenomena. Traveling high above the atmosphere they may see the zodiacal light, a glowing band around the earth thought to be due to the scattering of sunlight by dust particles between the planets.

During orbital flights, astronauts may see the circle of light around the sun—the sun's corona—at sunset and sunrise, along with beautifully colored horizons.

Some other sights may be observed from the earth's surface—the beautiful auroras that play in the night sky over the polar areas. These occur when charged particles from the sun enter the earth's magnetic field and strike molecules of the atmosphere. The molecules then radiate light. Auroras are most visible from the poles because the lines of force of the earth's magnetic field guide the charged particles toward them.

Sights in Space

You can demonstrate some of these effects yourself.

What you need: 10 cm square of clear glass or plastic; talcum powder; starch; flour; light; black paper about 6 cm square; white paper about 6 cm square; pin

1. Place the square of glass or plastic in a refrigerator or some cold place for 10 minutes. When it is cold, remove and breathe onto it, then look through it at a distant light. What do you see formed on the glass (or plastic)? What do you see as you look at a distant light? Name the colors you see.

2. Dust the dry glass or plastic lightly with talcum powder. Hold it directly in front of your eyes in a dimly lit room and look at a bare electric lamp 5–6 meters away. Describe what you see around the lamp, and name the colors.

The colored rings are produced by diffraction—that is, the light rays bending a little around the tiny particles of powder, giving off the colored bands or coronas that you see.

3. Hold the piece of black paper 10–15 cm from one eye while looking toward a brightly-lit window (**NOT THE SUN**). Describe what you see. Now make a neat pinhole in the center of the white piece of paper and look through it at the same bright window (**NOT THE SUN**). Describe the pattern of bands you see.

These bands are known as Fresnel patterns after Augustin J. Fresnel, the French scientist who first studied them. They are caused by diffraction, the bending of light rays as they pass by an edge.

42. Inflatable Spacecraft

Echo 1 and Echo 2 were two giant aluminum-coated plastic balloons which NASA shot into a 1,500 kilometer orbit from Cape Kennedy, Florida. The balloons self-inflated in space and were used as passive communication satellites. Radio waves bounced off the satellites and reflected back to earth. The plastic skin of Echo 1 was only half the thickness of the cellophane wrapper around a loaf of bread. When rocketed into orbit it inflated to measure over 30 meters across and could readily be seen from the earth's surface with the naked eye.

A balloon will stay inflated if the pressure inside is greater than that outside. In the vacuum of space it requires very little pressure to inflate balloons like Echo 1 and Echo 2.

Self-Inflation

You can make a working model and demonstrate how self-inflation occurs due to a change in pressure.

What you need: small balloon; piece of balloon rubber; large glass jar; rubber bands

1. Partly inflate a small balloon, tie off the neck, and place the balloon inside a large jar.

2. Stretch a piece of balloon rubber over the top of the jar and fix it in position with rubber bands.

3. Lift up the balloon membrane at its center (Figure 2). How does this affect air pressure inside the jar? What happens to the balloon? Why?

4. Now push down on the balloon membrane. What do you see the balloon do? Explain why.

5. What difference would it make to this activity if there were a small hole in the balloon rubber over the top of the jar? What if the hole was in the balloon inside the jar?

6. When there is very low pressure on the outside, balloonlike spacecraft stay inflated with very little pressure from the inside. How does the activity you have just done show this?

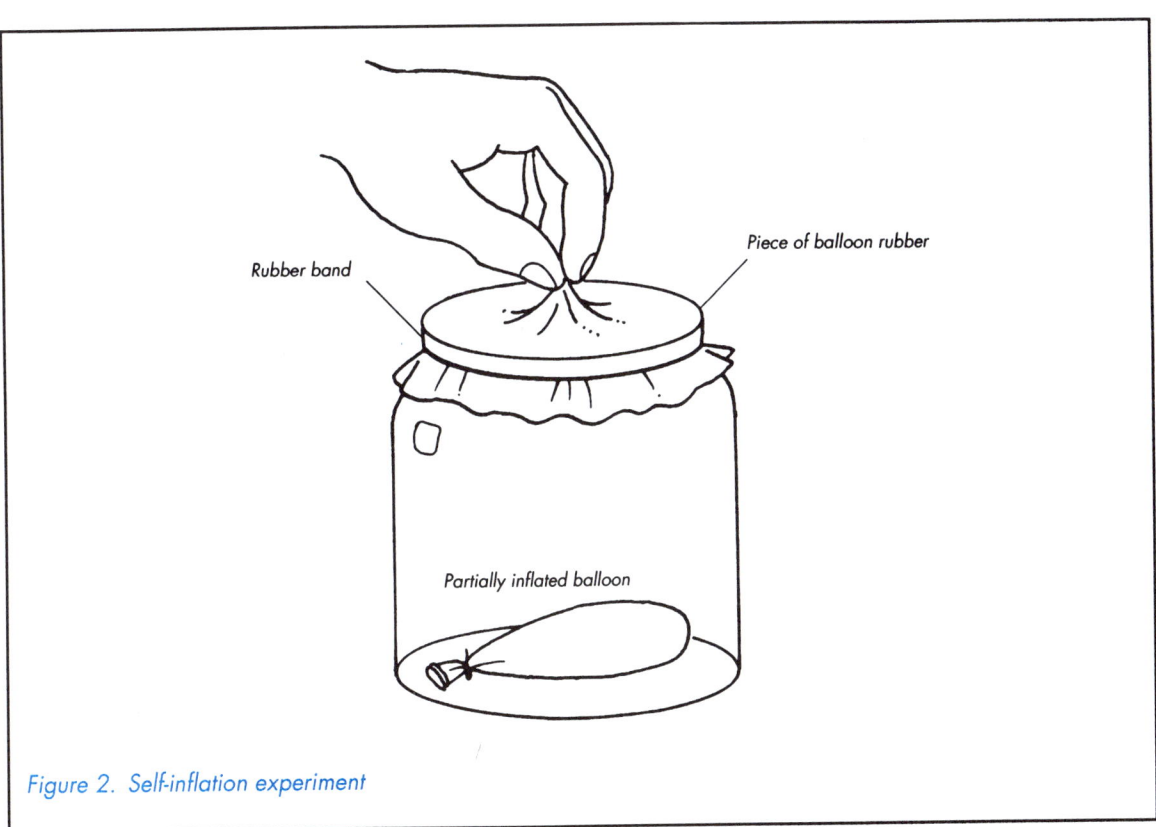

Figure 2. Self-inflation experiment

43. The Tyndall Effect

The light of the sky comes from the sun; when the sun is absent, the sky is dark. This much we know; but why is the sky blue when the sun is present?

John Tyndall, who lived during the last century, wanted to find out. He reasoned that to our eyes, something in the atmosphere scattered short blue waves of light but allowed the longer wavelength colors of sunlight to pass straight through. He proposed that countless fine particles form a suspension within the atmosphere around us.

It is these tiny particles of dust that influence color by scattering the short wavelength blue light much more than the longer wavelength red light. When the sun is low in the sky, the light must pass through a much longer layer of air. This removes the blue light, giving us the brilliant reds and oranges of sunrise and sunset.

Very fine particles, such as silt and starch in water or dust in air, form suspensions. These have the power to scatter or disperse light, and this property is called the Tyndall effect.

How Light Is Scattered by Particles

What you need: three glasses of water; soap; milk; flashlight; stirrer

1. Take the three glasses of water. Leave A as it is; move the soap around in B as you count to 10; add 9–10 drops of milk to C and stir in.

2. Now shine the flashlight down into each glass in turn (Figure 3). Describe what you see.

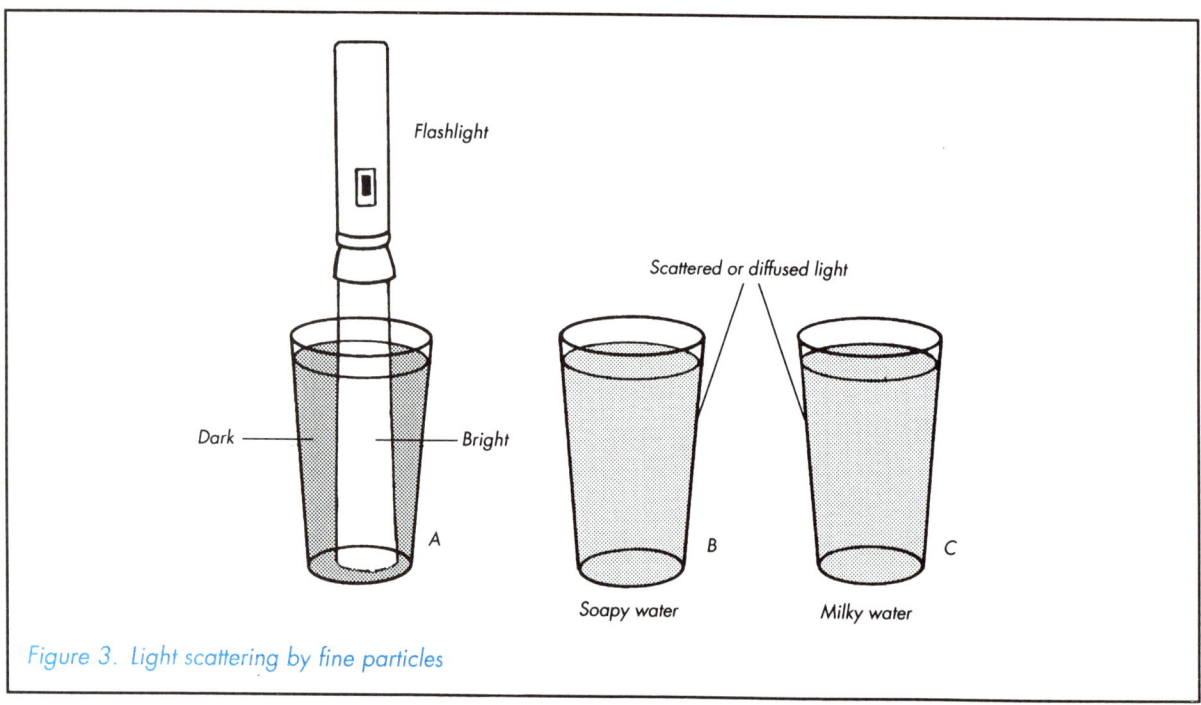

Figure 3. Light scattering by fine particles

3. Can you explain why glass A is bright inside but dark outside, while B and C are not so bright inside but much brighter outside?

4. What scatters the light? How is this like the scattering of light by tiny particles in the atmosphere?

44. Shock Waves

A shock wave is created when an aircraft approaches the speed of sound, 340 meters/second at sea level. Also, when a spacecraft slams back into the earth's atmosphere, the force and speed of its reentry create shock waves.

At these speeds the craft piles up molecules of air in front of it that form a wall of high pressure. As the craft increases its speed, it penetrates the wall. In doing this it is buffeted as though in a violent storm. A craft traveling faster than the speed of sound drags behind it a barrier of compressed air, rather like the wake of waves following a speed boat. Just as these waves strike other objects in the water or on shore, so also does the compressed air barrier following close on a supersonic craft hit the ground with a loud boom. This is often heard as the aircraft flashes across the sky overhead.

Frictional heat also builds up, high enough to disintegrate the returning spacecraft. But the design of the spacecraft with its blunt, forward area deflects the shock waves. Searing hot in themselves, the deflected shock waves form a protective cushion between the vehicle and the even higher temperatures of the adjacent atmosphere.

Producing a Shock Wave

You can produce a shock wave using a bucket fitted with a cloth or plastic membrane and observe its effects on paper strips and a burning candle.

What you need: large plastic bucket with base cut out; square of plastic or cloth large enough to cover the top of the bucket; string; candle; wood or cardboard stand for bucket; paper strips about 50 cm long taped to a meter rule; balloon; pin

1. Place the square of cloth or plastic over the larger end of the bucket and secure tightly in place with string. Tie off a handle at the center of the cloth.

2. Place the bucket in its stand with the open end facing the paper strips. Holding the bucket with one hand to steady it, take the handle in the other hand, draw it back fully, then plunge it sharply into the bucket (Figure 4a). Describe what you see the pieces of paper do. Is there a shock wave? Describe in your own words how it has been formed.

3. Repeat step 2 with a burning candle in place of the paper strips (Figure 4b). What happens to the candle? Explain why.

4. Repeat step 2 again with your hand in front of the bucket. Have a partner place one hand on the bucket to steady it. Can you feel the shock wave coming from the front of the bucket?

5. Blow up a balloon, close the neck, and hold it a little distance from the burning candle. Prick it with a pin so that it bursts. What happens? Are shock waves involved? Explain.

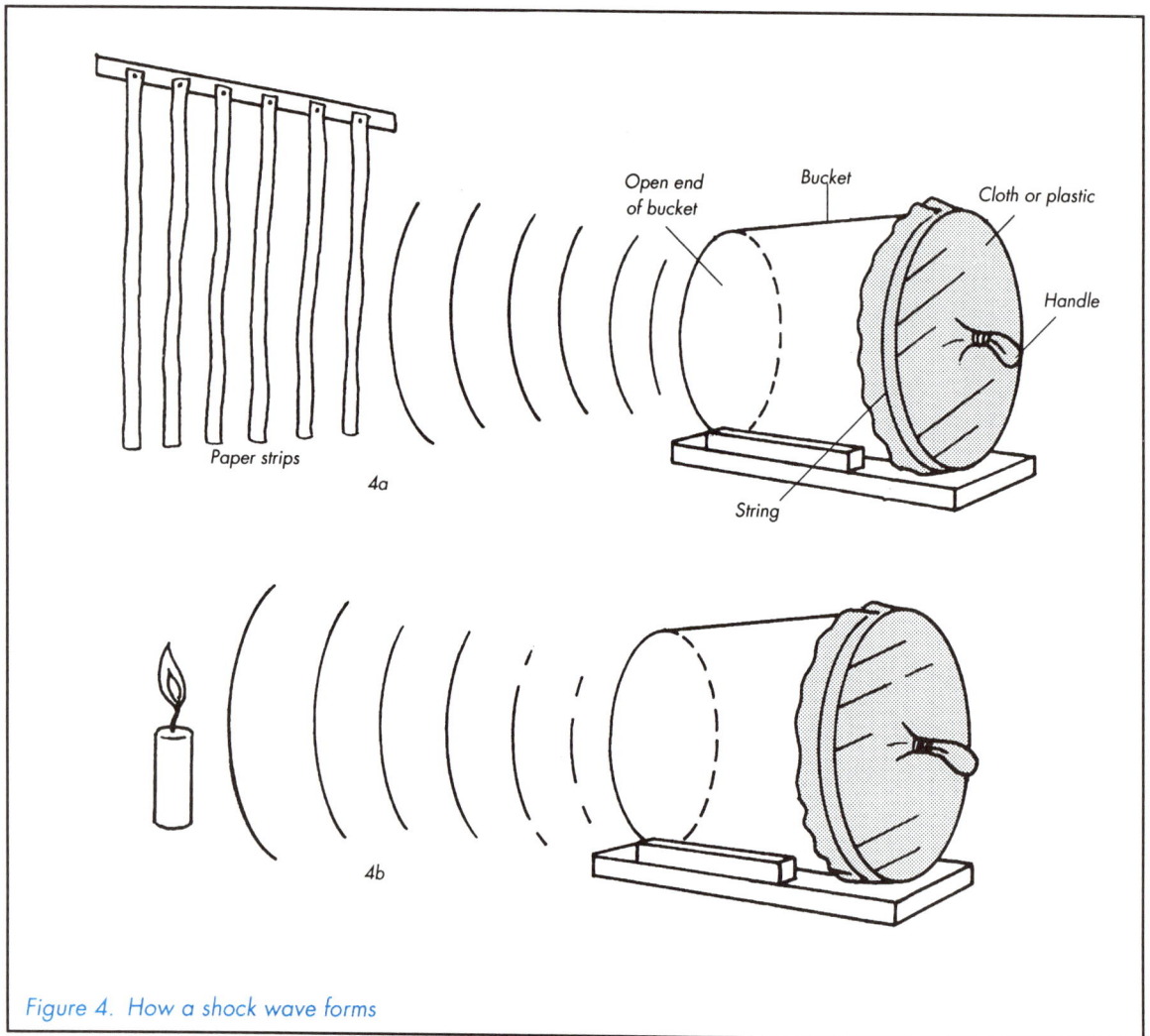

Figure 4. How a shock wave forms

45. Molecules in Motion

The air in which we live and which we breathe is made up of molecules, about four-fifths nitrogen, about one-fifth oxygen. Many of the effects we note in the atmosphere each day—winds, clouds, air pressure, and so on—are due to the continual movement of air molecules, traveling in straight lines, bouncing away from one another. In one cubic centimeter of air at sea level there are billions and billions of air molecules, hammering away at the earth and everything on it.

Without all the molecules that make up the earth's atmosphere, life as we know it would not be possible on earth. Held to the earth by gravity, the atmosphere not only supplies us with oxygen and moisture, it also acts as a giant mask to screen off deadly rays from the sun. The atmosphere absorbs heat from the sun and helps keep the earth's temperatures on an even keel.

Making Scents

What you need: strong scent; small dish; balloon; aquarium with cover or cardboard box with lid; screw-top jar; mint cookie; plain cookie

1. Put a few drops of strong scent in the small dish at the front of your classroom (Figure 5a). How soon do the students in the front row detect the smell? How long before those in the back row detect it?

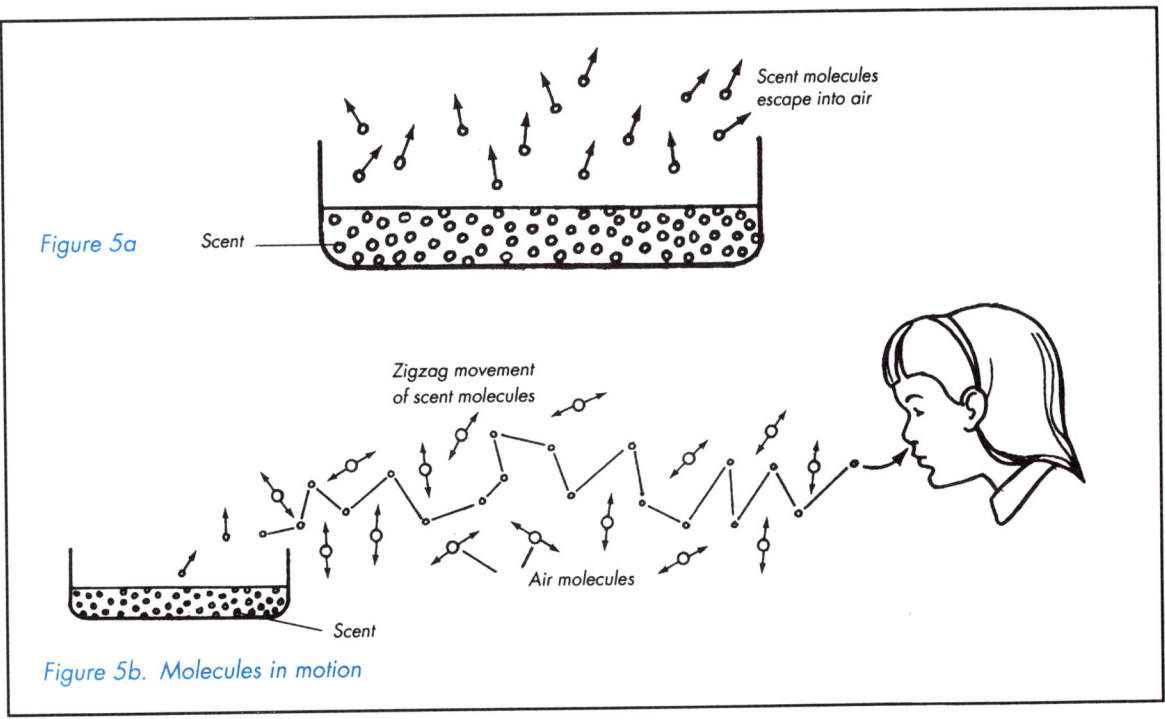

Figure 5a

Figure 5b. Molecules in motion

How do we smell things (Figure 5b)? How do the particles of scent reach our nose? How does the scent travel to the back of the room? Is the scent made up of particles also?

2. Put a drop of the strong scent inside a balloon (not on the neck), then partly inflate the balloon. Tie off the neck, then place it inside the aquarium or box and cover it (Figure 6). After about 15 minutes push back the cover from a

corner of the aquarium and smell the air. Can you detect the scent? How did the scent get from inside the balloon into the air of the aquarium? Could there be spaces in the balloon rubber which the constantly moving scent particles find their way through to the outside?

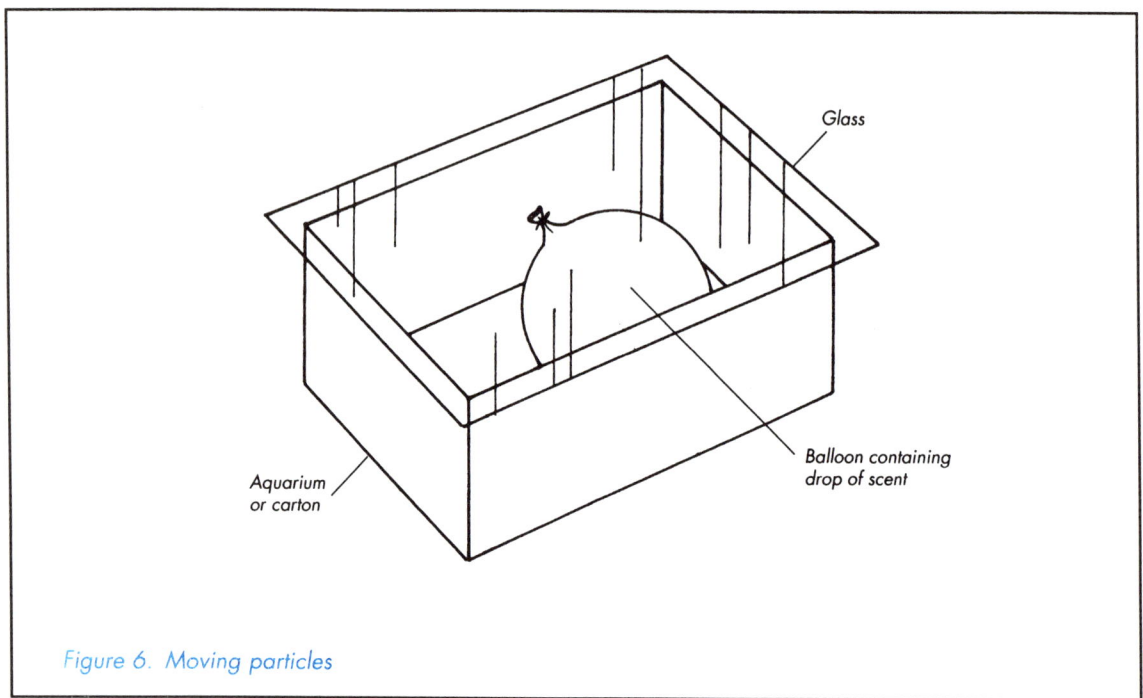

Figure 6. Moving particles

3. Place a plain cookie and a mint-flavored cookie in a screw-top jar and leave for two or three days. When you unscrew the jar, what do you notice about the smell of the air in the jar? Taste the plain cookie. How is it different? How do you explain this in terms of moving particles?

Index

A

Alcor, 13
Aldebaran, 6, 16, 17
Algol, 59–61
Altair, 6
Amalthea, 114
ammonium chloride, 67
Andromeda, 6
Aquila, 6
Arcturus, 6
atmosphere, 5, 31, 52, 131–133, 135, 138
Auriga, 6
auroras, 133

B

Baily's beads, 29
Bell, Jocelyn, 96
Bessel, Friedrich, 87
Betelgeuse, 6, 16, 17
big bang, 101
Big Dipper, 7, 12, 64
black hole, 87, 100–103
Boötes, 6

C

Callisto, 84, 114, 116, 118
Canis Major, 16
Canis Minor, 16
Canopus, 63
Capella, 6
carbon dioxide, 67
carbon dioxide (solid)
    See also dry ice.
Cassini, Gian Domenico, 114, 122

Cassini division, 122
Cassiopeia, 6, 12
Castor, 6, 16, 17
Celestial South Pole, 63
chromosphere, 81
Clark, Alvan, 87
Coal Sack, 53
comets, 65–72
constellations
    circumpolar, 12–13
convective zone, 81
Copernicus, lunar crater, 37
corona, 27, 81, 133
coronagraph, 26
Crab Nebula, 90, 97
Crab Pulsar, 100
Cygnus, 6
Cygnus X-1, 101

D

Deneb, 6
diamond ring effect, 29
dry ice, 67
    See carbon dioxide.
dust clouds, 53–56
    See also nebula.

E

Earth, 84, 105, 107, 129
    rotation, 74
    rotation and revolution, 109–110
    rotation of, 45–47
earth, 42, 109
Earth-moon, 41–44
Echo 1 and Echo 2, 134

eclipse(s)
    solar, 26–30, 35, 38
        total, 28, 38
eclipsograph, 27
Einstein, Albert, 47
Eta Carinae Nebula, 93
Europa, 84, 116, 118

F

focal length, 2
Foucault, Jean-Bernard-Léon, 45
Foucault pendulum, 45–46
Fresnel, Augustin J., 134
fusion, 67

G

Galileo, 1, 35, 47, 118
Ganymede, 84, 114, 116, 118
Gemini, 6, 16
Giotto spacecraft, 66
Goodricke, John, 59
Great Bear, 6, 7, 12, 64
    See also Ursa Major.
Great Dog. *See* Canis Major.
Great Magellanic Cloud, 97
Great Orion Nebula, 16, 77
greenhouse effect, 112

H

Halley's Comet, 65, 67, 71, 73
Hawking, Stephen, 101
Hercules, 6
Hewish, Antony, 96
Horse-Head Nebula, 53
Hyades, 6, 16

I

Iapetus, 123
inertia, 68
Io, 114, 116, 118–121
ionosphere, 26
IRAS (infrared astronomical satellites), 93

J

JCMT (James Clark-Maxwell Telescope), 77
Jupiter, 1, 4, 84, 114–117, 123, 129

L

Large Magellanic Cloud, 93
latitude, 62
lens, objective, 1
Leo, 6
Little Bear, 12
Little Dipper, 12
Little Dog. *See* Canis Minor.
longitude, 61
Lowell Observatory, 128
Lyra, 6

M

Mariner 9, 63
    space probe, 62
Mars, 63, 105, 111–113, 129
Mauna Kea Observatory, 77
Mercury, 51, 84, 105–107, 129
meteorites, 37
Milky Way galaxy, 53
Miranda
    moon of Saturn, 124
Mizar, 13
molecules, 138
moon, 38–41, 42
    craters, 1, 35–38

N

navigation in space, 61–63
nebula, 66, 77
    See also dust clouds.
Neptune, 127, 129
neutron star, 87, 90, 96, 100
Newton, Isaac, 4, 51
North Pole, 64
North Star, 7, 13
    See also Polaris.

O

Olbers, Wilhelm, 56
Olbers's paradox, 57
Oort, Jan, 66
Orion, 6, 16–17, 53, 77
outgassing, 71, 72

P

Pegasus, 6
Penrose, Roger, 102
photosphere, 81
photosynthesis, 33
Pioneer spacecraft, 115
Pleiades, 6, 16
Pluto, 127, 129
Pointers, 7, 12, 64
Polaris, 7, 45, 63, 64
    See also North Star.
Pole Star, 7, 12
    See Polaris, North Star.
Pollux, 6, 16
Procyon, 16, 17
pulsar, 90, 95–99

R

refraction, 1
    law of, 31
Regulus, 6
Rigel, 6, 16, 17
Rings of Saturn, 124
Royal Greenwich Observatory, 87

S

satellite, 62
Saturn, 4, 122–124, 129
Seven Sisters. *See* Pleiades.
sextant, 61
shock waves, 137
Sirius, 16, 17, 63, 87
solar flares, 82
solar paradox, 31–33
solar prominences, 28, 82
solar system, 42, 129
solstice, 75
Southern Cross, 53, 63
spacecraft
    inflatable, 134
space phenomena, 133
spectroscope, 81
Star Finder, 6–8, 12, 17
stars
    binary. *See* stars: variable.
    birth of, 77–80
    finding direction, 63–64
    red giant, 84–86
    twinkling of, 51
    variable, 60–61
    white dwarf, 87–89
sublimation, 67
subliming, 67
sun, 17–24, 80–83, 84
sun, Earth, and moon, 33–35
sunspots, 1, 82
supernova, 90–95, 96

T

Taurus, 6, 16
telescope
    Galilean, 1
    infrared, 77
    reflecting, 4–6
    refracting, 1–4
    solar, 82
Theta Orionis, 16
Trapezium, 16
Triton
    moon of Neptune, 128
Tunguska Event, 66
twinkling
    of stars, 51
Tyndall effect, the, 135

U

Uranus, 124–126, 127, 129
Ursa Major, 6, 7, 64
    See also the Great Bear.

V

Van Allen, James, 115
Van Allen belt, 115
Vanua Levu, 63
Vega, 6
    Triangle of, 6
Vela Nebula, 97
Venus, 12, 84, 105, 107–109, 129
    transit of, 108
Voyager spacecraft, 118
    Voyager 1, 114
    Voyager 2, 124, 128

Y

Yerkes Observatory, 1

Z

zodiacal light, 133